The Antebellum
of
SAVANNAH

GREGORY BONNER

#1-2488169571
ISBN: 978-1-48358-930-5

Antebellum ˌ *an'tē bel'əm*

adjective: occurring or existing before a particular war, especially the US Civil War.

PREFACE

The Antebellum of Savannah is the story of a prince and a pauper growing up in the Great South during one of the most splendid periods of our history, and one of the darkest parts of our American heritage, the antebellum; and a prince and a pauper of the mighty Congo in Africa, that were captured and sold by their own people to these "Fire Eaters" that lived under the vail of the beautiful princess Savannah, deep in the southern empire of Georgia.

The book takes you through the true and perilous journeys of the rivers in the African jungle across the Atlantic, to the rivers of Georgia's beautiful Savannah, as she dove through the antebellum and into a Civil War.

In most instances the events, people and places of this story are true. I have taken some exceptions to weave in characters and names to present the actual occurrences in a novel setting.

Gregory F. Bonner
The Author

TABLE OF CONTENTS

CHARLES AUGUSTUS LAFAYETTE LAMAR

June 14,. 1860, one year before the Civil War.

CAL LAMAR NOW THIRTY-SIX YEARS OLD IN 1860. HE stood in his office in front of a huge panoramic window at 44 Broughton Street that opened to his vast operations of Savannah, the capital city of Georgia. The air was thick and the morning's sun blazed through the blue skies that graced the city. The steam whistles of one of the boats at the shipping wharf ripped through the air of the Savannah River front and took Charlie back to the night the *Pulaski* was sinking in the dark ocean waters when he was just a boy. Charlie gazed into his pipe and stared at the embers the ashes made as he drifted back to that nightmare he'd had so many times before when he was aboard the doomed steam packet *Pulaski*.

* * *

Burning embers rained down from above; their ashes scattered and hissed onto the wet, wooden floor that gave way under young Charlie's feet as he made the last step onto the main deck, he remembered. The loud shriek of the steam whistle echoed through his entire body. "Abandon ship!" he heard from the far deck. The rush of water that engulfed the ship, which had split cleanly down the middle, immediately quieted the hallowed screams of the drowning and burnt souls behind him. The young boy was thrown across the deck as both the bow and the stern rose out of the water in the crash.

Charlie tumbled across the deck into the boiling epicenter of the torn ship and was slammed headlong into the bulkhead of the cargo bay that stood some two feet higher than the main deck. The ship's wooden floor was now covered in water, and the ocean waves easily found their way into the middle of the ship where Charlie lay.

Across the deck, Charlie could make out the horrified face of his sister, Rebecca, as the waves were beginning to overtake the starboard side of the ship where the gaping hole of the explosion took place. Charlie leapt from behind the hatchway and screamed out to his sister, "Rebecca!"

Gallantly Charlie slid down the decking and into the water. The cold night water felt like knives as he raced towards his screaming sister. Bound by his nightclothes, his movements felt like he was in quicksand as he trudged toward her. The thunder of cracking timbers was muffled under the sea as an eerie foam rose up from the water. Charlie made his way to her outstretched hands.

Just as their arms locked, Charlie felt a nudge on his shoulder of someone or something heavy that was trying to push him under the waves. He turned his head just in time to see the steel-clad piece of wood punch him above the eye. The scenery seemed to slow into the dark as his own blood overtook his vision and the shock seemed to drown out the explosions and steam whistle's blare.

The wooden ship's cargo hatch was being tossed about in the water. It made its way from the place on the deck to the now dark and open water of the Atlantic. The blurred scenery came into focus slowly. The noise and violence inflated Charlie from the semi-unconsciousness he was in. Instinctively, Charlie turned and grabbed hold of the makeshift raft that nudged at his shoulder again just slightly. He placed Rebecca on top of the floating door, and he himself scurried to the topside of the floating hatchway. Unable to speak, the two children now drifted away from the shipwreck and watched the *Pulaski* succumb to the dark ocean. Within a few hours, the two had drifted out to sea with some of the other wreckage and survivors of the shipwreck. A faint glimmer of light could be seen in the cool night air just a few hundred feet away from the floating band of survivors. "Is that our ship we've been looking for?" his sister asked as she tapped Charlie on the arm.

* * *

"Mr. Lamar? Mr. Lamar?" The young secretary spoke in a quiet tone as she approached Charles Lamar. The man now staring out of his office window seemed to be in another world overlooking the Bay Street operations below. His labored breathing gave the young lady the sense that he was in fact lost in a nightmarish daydream. "Is that our ship we've been looking for?" she said softly. Charlie quickly snapped from his terrifying recall and returned to the current day, 25 years from the horrible memory he was just having.

A scared look in his eyes was evidence that the lady's comment coincided with his sister's words while he was lost in a daydream. "Huh? What!" He turned to the young lady, grabbed her arm and squeezed the soft, pale skin of the young woman tightly.

Realizing he was no longer on a raft lost at sea with his sister, he panted and apologized to the young lady. "I...I'm sorry! Ms. Fay, I...uh, was just—" He was quickly interrupted.

"It's okay, Mr. Lamar. I didn't mean to startle you. Can I get you anything?"

"Yes, tea please," Cal replied.

Cal Lamar turned from his window overlooking the busy streets of the ship loading operations below. His leather soles made a scratching sound as he made his way across the long room and sat at the fine imported furniture he used for a desk. The springs in the chair's back made a raspy sound when Mr. Lamar leaned comfortably back and sat down in the fine leather surrounds. Immediately to his right, in the second of the two large picture windows, the towering mast of a grand ship slowly approached the Lamar pier below. The loud scream of a steam whistle echoed down the stony streets as the steamship *Lamar* towed the fine sailing ship to her destination. The long French cannons to stock his confederate arsenal had arrived. Behind his desk on a beautiful, silk-plastered wall, hung a large portrait of his father, Gazaway Bugg Lamar.

Born into money, and son of one of the richest men in the city of Savannah and New York, Cal, as they called him, for a shorter version of Charles Augustus Lafayette Lamar, was raised knowing he had it better than most. In fact, he carried himself as if he *was* better than all the people in Savannah; after all, his last name was written on the very Confederate money that his father was the treasurer of and that was in his father's pockets—and everyone else's in town.

Cal was raised on the docks of his father's piers along the Savannah River. The muddy, brown haze of the water and the smell of marsh and saltwater painted a splendid backdrop for such a boyhood in the Deep South. Southern royalty at its best, Cal walked along the docks of Lamar Pier as though he owned them; he knew, in fact, that one day he would. A tall and wiry tyke, with sandy-blonde hair and hazel-green eyes, he was in fact a cute boy. His clothes were not like those of the other kids of the day. More of a formal conversion to leisure, with a hint of dirt at the knees of his white pants and scuffs on his everyday black leather shoes. The blue-and-white cotton shirt flapped behind him un-tucked as he ran down the gangway to the docks along the river. The workers along the pier loved the only son of Gazaway; at least, they acted like they did. These dockworkers were a very helpful group of men who added a rich splendor to the colorfulness of Cal's personality. These dockworkers were a hardworking sort by day and a hard-drinking sort by night. The language was just short of the worst sailor tongue in all the seas, and the Southern sun and hot, muggy weather gave perfect opportunity for it to pour out of their mouths like the sweat out of their backs and into every description and conversation to be had. Every other word was filth and fowl.

As a young man growing up on the shipping docks of Savannah, Cal Lamar was always told of the pirates who stayed on the south docks of the city. Being that his father owned all of the piers and warehouses along the river, Cal was quite intrigued by the gallant tall ships and the stories that the dock men told him about the pirates. The things that were brought to port for young eyes to see were like watching a carnival of unexplained scenes from far-off worlds. As the ships were off-loaded, the people of the town would come and see as these treasures were unloaded from the belly of the ships that sat in the fast current of the Savannah River. Young Cal learned his way around these shipyards his daddy owned, along with the warehouses and docks that made up the port. But, he did stay clear of the docks to the south. The lifestyle of the dockworker and their drunken exploits were the primary influence that directed him into the fire-eater mentality, which he possessed. The stories of abduction and murder from these men on the South docks were received with wide eyes and open mouths as the dock men passed them down to the young men of the dock. Cal sat motionless through the stories and gawked at the ships that were just a few hundred yards away.

His father, having given safe harbor to the pirates of the day, explained to him the value of keeping the pirates on the family's good side. These "privateers," or protectors of merchant ships, would watch the shipments of Mr. Lamar in return for safe passage and port into the city of Savannah. All the other merchants who would hire these escorts were lucky if the very same men who were hired to protect its contents did not rob the ship they commissioned.

As Charlie grew up, he was introduced to the best of these privateers. A very rough group in every instance, it seemed. His father's frequent absences from Savannah to attend to business in his New York holdings helped fashion this growing boy amongst the pirates and into quite a unique soul.

* * *

"Mr. Lamar?" Ms. Fay quietly peeked her head into the office. "Your tea."

"Enter," Cal responded with a more refined and stern response.

Ms. Fay lightly stepped across the room and placed the fine blue Wedgewood cup and saucer on the desk for Mr. Lamar. "Is that the ship you've been looking for?" she asked, and very gracefully bowed and turned to exit the offices.

She was about halfway across the floor when Mr. Lamar said, "Ms. Fay."

"Yes?" the young lady responded. She stopped dead in her tracks and spun to face Mr. Lamar.

"Have someone sweep up this floor again. And have them do it right this time," he said as he stood, taking one sip from the teacup then placing it on the desk and walking past the mortified young secretary.

Tall, middle-aged, attractive in his own right, his personality and arrogance were probably his most prominent features. At six foot four and close to 250 pounds, Charlie Lamar was quite an outstanding feature in the genteel setting of Savannah. He had a slight gimp to his walk that caused him to hobble as he approached. Part of the rigid movement was caused by the Southern arrogance that had been bred into him over generations of opulence. Loud and animated, Charlie's presence was immediately known anytime he was near.

Charles Lamar walked out of his office building from the third floor and onto the oak-shaded steel bridge that landed perfectly in the city center. Bay Street was crawling with people, horses, and carriages that made their way through the thriving port city. Cal turned to the right and made his way along the red brick sidewalk that led along the wrought iron fences of the cobblestone embankments of River Street.

Just ahead were several wagons that were loaded over the side rails eight feet tall with bales of cotton and meticulously backed into spaces along the sidewalk where Mr. Lamar was headed. Each person along the way tipped their hat to the astute man as he strolled along his import and export operations. The stout man stopped and watched one of his workers throw a bale of cotton into a doorway that was cut into the cobblestones and through the ground, just behind one of the wagons. His suit crackled with starch as he reached into the inside of his jacket pocket and pulled out his pipe and leather tobacco pouch.

A cool breeze blew down River Street and up the stone embankment to the upper levels of Bay Street while Cal meticulously stuffed his ivory pipe with the finest of Cuban tobaccos. His sandy-white beard and mustache were slightly stained from the smoke of the fine Cuban blend he preferred and imported, his lips firmly holding the pipe's stem while he pulled in the aromatic tobacco from the pipe. He squinted his eye to avoid the smoke from the lit match and nodded to the man on the wagon who had just wished him a good day. Cal blew the pipe's smoke out and turned to the iron fencing along Bay Street's wall, overlooking River Street, to survey the stream of slaves that were carrying the cotton bales from the warehouse storage built into the ground just under his feet. The white bales formed a perfect dotted white line down the cobblestone streets below. A slight grin of satisfaction oozed from the stocky man's lips with the smoke of the exotic islands.

"Mr. Lamar!" The supervisor, or "factor," as they were known, called out to the man staring below at his operations. "Mr. Lamar! Mr. New in the receiving offices would like to have a word with you, sir!" With a simple nod, Cal Lamar turned from the iron fencing and walked along the sidewalk to the stone stairs that led their way down to the cobblestone streets of the river.

Cal descended the stone-gray stairs that wore just a hint of green algae down to River Street and smoked his pipe, blowing the fine Cuban smoke into the breeze that wafted up the stone wall. The wind blew through the streets and into Mr. Lamar's face, causing him to squint slightly to avoid any dust or sand blowing into his green eyes. Cal was baptized by a Revolutionary War hero and French magistrate, the Marquis De Lafayette, who gave Charles one of his two middle names. The other was from the Roman ruler Augustus Caesar. Cal was heralded as a hero during the fatal explosion of his father's ship, during which he was credited for saving his sister, and was heir to the throne of the Gazaway B. Lamar estate. He was the prince of Savannah, and the people there loved him.

The tiny pebbles from the cobblestone streets skittered under the fine leather soles of the handmade shoes Cal wore. He made his way down River Street to the receiving offices just above the docks of the Lamar piers.

"Mr. Lamar!" the young man said, sliding the chair back from his desk and returning the pen to the holder and into the fine brass desk piece that bore the young man's name. Mr. Christopher New stepped from around the desk.

Tall, slender, and just shy of his 30th birthday, Chris had a charismatic way about him that everyone enjoyed, especially the ladies of Savannah. "Mr. Lamar, may we speak?" he said, and stepped past the long front desk just inside the doorway of the receiving office.

A simple nod was all the stern-faced Lamar would muster to the request. "Uhhh...outside, if I may?" young Christopher offered, grabbing the door and opening it for Mr. Lamar. "Sir, with the new gin now processing cotton at such speed, it is hard to keep up with just the handling of the product in and out of the machine, and from warehouse to ship or train, what have you. We have ships docked for loading at over two days, and as many more weighing anchor off Tybee, sir." He motioned to the fifty or so ships that sat moored to the docks. The two men walked down the three wooden steps and onto the heavy wooden piers. The timbers were stained from dirt, mildew, and seagull droppings. "We are going to need more people, sir," Christopher said. They both heard the scurrying of what sounded like rats in the mud under the piers below their feet.

Charles walked to the edge of the pier and along the ropes at its end. He turned to look up the river's bank to notice a sea of men and horses transporting the goods throughout the many warehouses he owned. He lit a match and pulled the orange flame into the pipe to relight his passion. He paused and threw the burning match into the mud that silted along the water's edge, then stood staring as the orange flame was engulfed by the water, like that of the boiler on the ill-fated *Pulaski* off the coast of Cape Hatteras. Charles watched the small wisp of smoke that rose from the water as the match fell under the murky Savannah River. Just there in the corner of his trance he saw what he thought was a tiny footprint in the mud just at the water's edge.

Savannah

It was a beautiful day in Savannah that afternoon in October. The weather had not turned cold just yet, at least not in the South, and a perfect, cool breeze blew through the green grass of Forsyth Park. The locals of the beautiful Southern city sunbathed in the park and frolicked in the perfect weather before the chill of winter was to set in.

In a towering perimeter around the tranquil park sat the beautiful magnolias and palms, accented by the majestic oak trees adorned in Spanish moss that dripped from their limbs as they swayed slightly with the breeze that day. Their shadows, like giant ghosts, lay across the beautiful grass that exaggerated the slight movements of each tree limb.

The cool temperatures were starting to arrive, the annual leaves beginning to change in color and the confederate jasmine blooming in a splendid array, which added even more character to the lovely Southern city.

This park lay in quiet solitude now, nature's tribute to those veterans lost in the Revolutionary War who had died in this very space. Their honor and reverence accented this hallowed ground as statues stood to give credence to these heroes that had won our freedom just one generation before.

The Southern climates brought plenty of warm sunshine and even more ground-drenching rain, which, combined with the rich, red Georgia clay, would make for the most fertile soil the early settlers could grow crops in. Once it was discovered that cotton, rice, and tobacco would spring from the ground at twice and three times the size of that in other parts of the world, the tiny colony soon became the largest city in the South, and the capital of what would become the fourth US state of the union, Georgia. Her international trading and cash crops would outdo the production and the shipping anywhere in the other colonies, except, of course, for the original few in the North that still held the most advanced and well-constructed ports in all the land. Savannah was, however, the closest port to the lavish trading islands of Jamaica and Cuba that America could hold, and with this came all the beauty and riches from the tropical lands, which found their way to the docks of the Savannah River. She also hosted her share of pirates who frequented the Caribbean Seas, the trade winds blowing them into Savannah's reach.

The ladies, in their china doll fashions, wore beautiful flowing fabrics and lace draped over hoop skirts, while the men and their fine silk suits with top hats gave elegance that one could only find in the Deep South. The men of the day were aristocrats in nature and by appointment. As for the women, they were beautiful Southern belles, with all the elegance and grace one would find in royalty. This astute nature was what the South was known for; *royalty* was not a far-fetched word for the bluebloods they thought as they walked through the sweet Georgia sun that day.

Standing in his crimson-red brick office's plate glass bay window, C. A. L. Lamar stood looking over the beautiful and naive city below his feet. He watched as the city his father helped to create meandered through each day with the blissful enchantment that the southern winds carried through her.

Savannah was built to enjoy, and her simple beauty made it so easy to unwind from the hustle and bustle generally known in the Northern cities. Being that Savannah was the last colony to be built and the farthest south, she had the warmest temperatures in the country. So naturally, the wealthiest people in the world flocked to the newest land in the Americas so they could build huge homes that took up entire city blocks in the great Southern city. Towering over the city's streets and beautiful oaks, these grandiose homes rose to the sky, as their fine appointments and tall ceilings trimmed in plaster finishes set these homes apart from all that were built in the day in any of the other colonies. For the most part, they were statements of the opulence and extravagance that existed then.

The architecture in the new city of Savannah was not like the overcrowded Northern cities. Each house had its own courtyards and carriage houses that sat next to the three- and four-story homes along its main streets. All the streets were made of neatly placed red bricks and white granite curbs that ran around each square and along the edge of the streets in the thriving coastal city.

The beautiful redbrick streets, all laid in a herringbone pattern, trickled their way to the most prominent features of Savannah. The east ran to the beaches of Tybee Island, where the oaks and confederate jasmine gave way to the blowing sea grasses and palm trees that dotted the gray sands of her shore. The western streets turned to sculpted red-clay roads that complemented the green sprawling fields and St. Augustine grass that formed the horse racing tracks. The southern roads were sprinkled with the multi-story, multicolored row houses as they ran to Forsyth Park, and the northern roads ran to River Street and the port docks, where the salt air and sea grasses mixed pleasantly with the perfumes of the maidens and the confederate jasmine of Trustees Gardens.

Savannah was built on the river that slowly meandered through the gentle countryside from Tybee Island's beaches to deep into the state. The river was named after the great city that soon lined her edges with the bustling commerce that stretched from Tybee through Savannah to the ports of Augusta, deep into the lush foliage of Georgia.

You could almost smell the money in the air over the salt water and sea grass that the rich settlers of the beautiful port city had brought with them. Seagulls and slender palms with bushy fronds speckled the rich subterranean sea island foliage. Not only did America's most wealthy have homes here, but also the French and English patriots who had fought in the Revolutionary War on her very grounds. They owned mansions that spread for city blocks. New money was coming from the ground they fought on in the way of cash crops that would soon catapult Savannah into the wealthiest of the Southern colonies. Savannah was a spot on the earth that was set in a class by itself, and its now growing culture of pride and perseverance would prove to mold the city into a piece of art for the world to admire.

The shade of abundant trees and floor-to-ceiling windows helped provide a cool breeze that would blow through the twenty- to thirty-thousand-square-foot homes that lay in the middle of thousands of acres, where the city's famous cash crops grew.

The plantation homes held entire families, workers, staff, and hundreds if not thousands of slaves that were needed to pick the money that grew from the fields. The men and women who owned these sprawling estates were the wealthiest of all Southerners—and even some Northerners. Most all were born and raised in the North, and now they watched as their fortunes grew well past that of the typical Northern business in the lavish, moist conditions of the South. Their possessions of marble-inlaid accommodations and gracious, meticulously maintained landscapes proved it. The business mind-set they brought with them made the South a hidden cultural treasure trove.

The slow, winding railroads of Vanderbilt, with their steam engines wailing through the quiet pines, all seemed to head to the Lamar docks along the river as they provided the transit for millions of tons of cotton, tobacco, rice, and sugar to be shipped to the world. The air of aristocrats and businessmen was contrasted with bales of products being loaded on the shipping docks along the Savannah River. The money was so great that these new Southerners possessed, and the lay of the land was so different and developing, that the lower half of the Americas ultimately divided themselves off from the Northern states. The Confederate States of America was born, and they began to gradually secede from the Union.

The reason for this division was to hide the newfound riches being harvested from the taxing hands of the North, and to maintain slavery that was needed to help harvest the cotton and sugar—or white gold—from the ground. The greed of this new thriving land needed port and shipping development that would support the new money and business that was quadrupling with the invention of the cotton gin by Eli Whitney.

Thousands of slaves had been used in the North to form the roadways and buildings of the new Northern cities. But as soon as the work of the slaves was complete and the colonies of the North were built, there was no more need for the sheer number of slaves they had.

As the colonies advanced South, so did the hard-working slaves that built the great colonies' streets and buildings along the way. The further south the expansions of the colonies went, the further south the slaves were moved along to create it. Land was staked off for the taking in the South and these huge tracts of land, with thousands of acres, seemed to bring the opportunity to spread out the living conditions of homes. It was a completely new setting for the lavish lifestyles some of these Southerners would come to know.

The North was no place for sprawling plantations. The winter frost and the daunting, cold temperatures would not only kill the crops they would plant, but would also kill the slaves that were torn from their tropical surroundings and were not adapted to such harsh conditions. These slaves were shuffled from the North to expand the growing empire of the Queen, now expanding towards the South. The settlers of the Georgia lands found a climate more like that of the Congo, where most of the slaves were from, which would allow them to survive more easily.

As the climate got warmer, the farmlands got bigger and ultimately, the farther south they went into the great unknown, the settlers found that the lands there were bursting with opportunity, openness, and lush, lavish foliage. The settlers needed all the slaves they could get to prepare the vast acreage they had hastily staked off. The Northerners had finally found a place to spread out, and the ones who stayed in the North found a place for the ruffians and slaves to go—to the South. They had no idea that these outcasts had stumbled onto a utopia in the Southern Hemisphere.

The Southern belle of the colonies Savannah had just celebrated their centennial birthday in 1837 and she was about to explode with commerce and trading that would surpass any other port in the country. Transportation of these crops from the farmlands along the Savannah River to the rest of the states that could only be accessed by rail would be required, and Savannah, with her river that plunged deep into the southern regions and farmlands of Georgia, was the perfect spot. Ports along the muddy river dotted the shorelines and served traders and farmers alike, and helped transfer their products to the now bustling port city of Savannah and from there to the Deep South, and around the world.

With big trade and movement of products growing as they were, shipping docks and warehouses to store the cash crops in were needed, as were rail networks. Only a few men within the city had the enterprise within them to establish the required shipping rails and docks to service such a growing economy.

Gazaway Bugg Lamar was a not so gracefully aged man. He and his son directed the ideas of Southern expansion from high above their workers on the river streets below. His offices took up the top floors of the Cotton Exchange Building, near the center of the Lamar Pier, and provided beautiful rounded top-plate glass windows that looked over the Savannah

River and the dock operations four stories below. As a lawyer, Gazaway held several large homes in the North, and made most of his money on the plantations he owned in the South. His son, Charles Augustus Lafayette Lamar, almost forty now, added the youth and aggression that would complete the duo. The warehouses and docks they had constructed on the Savannah River were so profitable, in fact, that they eventually built and owned The Bank of Commerce in which to hold their riches.

The Bank of Commerce and Gazaway's signature adorned the bottom of every dollar that was printed in the great South. The Lamars not only owned the bank, they owned the docks, the warehouses, and several of the largest Southern plantations. They also owned the horse racing track where the Southerners could gamble away their dollars right back into the pockets of the Lamars.

Out of all the Southern aristocrats in Savannah, Gazaway was the one pulling the most money from the pockets of the people of the Confederacy. The South was alive with commerce and riches, and Gazaway Bugg Lamar and his son owned most of it.

Their railroads transported the goods to the Northern states, while their ships transported the precious cotton and tobacco to the farthest outreaches of the world. The goods would sit in the tranquil warehouses he had constructed while thousands of tall ships from all over the world came to Savannah to make port and take back with them the riches of the New World.

While the ships traveled across the vast Atlantic on their way to Savannah, they were designed to carry gross weights of cargo. Since they were to come over empty in most cases and return with the riches, these empty ships would be loaded with cobblestones from the point of origin to make ballast and hold the ship upright. As soon as they landed in beautiful Savannah, they threw the stones out as the precious cargo was being loaded into the ships' holds. The Lamars were smart enough to take this stone ballast and use it to build the warehouses and roadways that line Savannah's port riverbanks.

The warehouses rose to six stories high, made of stones stacked in mortar, with huge timbered floors and wooden hand-pulled elevators. These housed the cotton, tobacco, rice, and sugar that would be carried across Savannah's stone streets to the waiting ships of the world. The more ships that came to port, the more money and stones came to the Lamars. The ships were of course loaded with the Lamars' products when they left.

All the men of Lamar Pier worked for the men who ran Savannah. The people of Savannah loved Gazaway, an entrepreneur of industry and trading, for making her such a respected jewel of the South for the entire world to see. The finest boat timbers and masts used in the day were harvested from the Georgia pines to make room for the cotton plantations.

These beautiful wooden spires, some two hundred feet tall, with no knots, were then shipped to all the ports of the world. The steel that came mostly from the Northern states down the Savannah River was distributed through her ports to the likes of Jamaica and Cuba.

As the ships full of riches were coming and going through the new, thriving port, there also came with it people who would rob them. So the time of the privateer was ever becoming popular with the new colonies, providing escort and protection to the people traveling the seas and the expensive cargo they carried. The privateer's dock was erected in the south of town.

In this area, the gray cobblestones gave way to mud, and the astute people of Savannah did not venture there. These privateers had been at sea more than on land, and when the chance of making port for a few days arrived, they would frequent the local clubs and harass the locals with their intoxicated fights through the streets of the beautiful city.

* * *

Dusk settled slightly onto the beautiful city and the echo of gunfire carried through the streets of the newly founded port. The sneer of success radiated from the man who fired its fatal shot. Blowing the trickle of smoke from the revolver's barrel, with his eye still slightly squinted from the aim, Charles Lamar turned to his father and said, "I asked him to formally apologize! I mean, Daddy...All he had to do was admit that he was wrong." He pulled his handkerchief out of his pocket and polished the magazine of his French revolver.

Spinning on one foot and returning the revolver to the holster in one fluid movement, he walked towards the edge of the dueling grounds that lay along the edge of the cemetery.

"He should've known better, Daddy," Charles said to his father.

Gazaway Lamar was slightly on edge because of his son's nonchalant attitude as he walked away from the dying man who lay at the opposite end of the dueling field. His age, almost sixty-four, showed slightly, and his large build was shadowed by his son's approach.

Charles Lamar squeezed his dad's shoulder, and at almost six foot four, his presence caused the only onlookers to slightly step away from the expressionless killer who warmly smiled and caressed his father's shoulder.

"Dad, let's you and I walk down the street and look at the battery conversions to the wharf," Cal Lamar said in his scratchy, deep Southern accent.

Gazaway, shaken, now turned towards his son and headed with him down Abercorn Street towards the river. The sun was starting to set in the coastal empire and the stir of the night air was following the Lamars as they walked along the street that evening.

* * *

At night, Savannah was a different lady. She stood taller because the buildings seemed to disappear into the night sky. She seemed harder because the beautiful flowers gave way to the cobblestones and brick that were dimly lit with a few torches and streetlamps that were scattered throughout the city. She was a scary place to be with the drunken privateers roaming her streets at night.

On the hillside and up the river's bluff from the docks of the privateers stood a boardinghouse for the landed seamen. The pirate's boarding house was originally designed as a barn for the botanical gardens area that General Oglethorpe established in 1732 for the Monarch George II of England. During their glory days, these lands were home to the first pharmacy in the country. But as time would have it, the place on the south side of town simply became the outskirts. The desolate area made a perfect place to house the sailors who made port in Savannah. With a barn converted to a boarding house in 1754, its bar located on the first floor, it was the most prominent area used in the established pirate's quarter. The building was constructed of rough sawn logs for siding; there would be no pristine and ornate siding here. The rooms upstairs, with their unfinished wood floors and oak beams, creaked with movement when frequented by the women who would come to the privateer's house to provide other services that cannot be found at sea.

The smell of perfume, pipe tobacco, and rum hazed the night air in the place Savannah created for the sailors and privateers to carry on their business of being men at port, which for them was a well-deserved break. The merchandise they protected at sea made them a necessary evil that most had to endure to see to it that the people and products made it to their port safely. The business the privateers had at sea was that of a global armed escort service and it was quite dangerous indeed.

As soon as the morning's sun would rise, the drunken sailors would scurry like drunken rats down the cobblestones and mud as they returned to their ships to sleep off the drunkenness that the privateer's house had provided. With the sun slowly rising through the marsh grass, Savannah's beauty was once again coming into light.

The Wanderer

The early morning sun pierced through the thick, towering pines of the Georgia countryside as the expedition team deployed from Savannah to acquire the mast for building the largest and fastest sailing ship of the day. Even though it was first light and a bit cooler than what was to come that day; the humidity added a thickness to the air that made it hard to breathe. It seemed the early morning clouds had settled their way down to the earth, and the small group of men walking through them were already soaked in sweat as they chopped the vines that seemed to snarl and tangle these unsuspecting visitors.

Young Andrew grabbed the machete tighter as the sweat from his arm worked its way into the palm of his hand. He flicked the buzzing insect on his forearm to the ground before wiping the sweat from his brow with the soaked and tattered weed-covered sleeve of his shirt. "Where is this thing?" he asked as he turned to the expedition leader of the group just behind him.

Dylan Montgomery was there just behind the young black man when he paused from whacking at the vines to ask his question. A tall, young man with dark hair, a light-colored leather briar jacket and glasses, he looked up from his small notebook, peering over his glasses with frustration. His green eyes squinted into focus as he broke his concentration from trying to walk and write at the same time. It seemed to young Dylan that he had answered the same question several times that morning. "Andrew, I've brought us this far." He said reluctantly, "We should see it in the next clearing just up ahead there." He pointed with his pencil at the clearing that could be seen through the hanging limbs and vines just in front of the group. The answer brought a frustrated swing at the vines from Andrew, the leader of the group of slaves cutting their way through the thicket in the belly of the Georgia woods.

"Theys all look alike, Misa Dylan!" he said as he swung the machete again and again at the vines that were stitched together like a web, from one tree base to another. The ground here was thick and spongy with decayed leaves that had fallen in these woods for hundreds of years. The smell of the earth and composted soil below their feet, mixed with the smell of pines, overpowered the sweat that poured from their skin.

"Yes, they do; most of them, anyway. But, I think you'll see a difference in a moment."

"Get your black ass back to swinging that machete, boy!" a loud voice yelled from the rear of group, startling both men. William, the stern yard boss, as they were called, lurched through the small group as he removed his hat and wiped the sweat from his forehead with his coat sleeve. The whacking of the machetes seemed to increase with the order and the slight anticipation of finding the prize they were there to seek.

The sound of the machetes suddenly stopped, and the two men out in front of the group stepped from the edge of the thick forest and into the tall grass of an open field. The sun peered into the canopy's tunnel that had been created by the land-clearing crew out front.

Dylan squinted his eyes when he stepped out of the wood's darkness and into the clearing. The surrounding trees did not obstruct the morning's sun anymore, and the glare from the bright grass caused him to raise his hand to block the sun from his view.

Scanning the horizon, one hand over his eyes like a sailor, he saw it. "There!" He pointed almost directly at the low morning sun rising from the eastern tree line across the field. The fog of the early morning still sat in the shade of the towering trees just a few hundred yards in front of the men.

"Damn!" one of the men said from the back of the group.

Dylan turned and said, "Hey, Andrew...they all still look alike?" He chuckled.

Standing as a majestic green tower amongst the others was a pine tree that stood some two hundred fifty feet tall. It was at least seventy feet taller than all the trees around it. Its uppermost branches swayed softly in the air at such height, which seemed to ascend into the clouds. "That's got to be it!" Andrew said to Dylan.

"Yeah, that's her! Finding it was the easy part. Getting it to the docks from here is going to be the next challenge," he said as he slapped Andrew on the shoulder with a slight shove in the direction of the tree.

Old Man William grumbled to himself as if to mock the niceties coming from the front of the group and yelled at the slave following up the group with the pack horse carrying the provisions. "What you looking at, boy?"

Dylan stood back as the machete-wielding men cleared the way for the horses that were behind the tree line in the woods. The slaves quickly cut the path clear so the others in the group and the horses could enter the grassy opening buried in the woods near the border of South Carolina and Georgia.

"We'll make camp here," Dylan instructed Mr. William. "We can cut the tree, lay and strap it, and then drag it to this point before making camp for the night."

This particular area in the woods in Georgia was a designated quarry of pines that had been secured by Queen Victoria of England for the harvesting of tall timbers, used for masts in shipbuilding in Her Majesty's royal fleet. This tree, however, had a covert destination, and not one for the royal navy; this special tree was going to be secretly shipped from Augusta through the ports in Savannah to a shipyard in Setauket, New York.

The giant southern yellow pine swayed softly in the breeze and seemed to ache as the group neared. The breeze was not to be had for the poor souls who meticulously worked the two-man handsaw as they rocked it back and forth at the base of the monolith. "Could you just imagine a sail that tall?" Andrew exclaimed as he watched the men switch with two others to continue the sawing.

"Well," Dylan replied, "there would actually be two or three sails that would make up her height." He poked his glasses up onto the bridge of his nose with his index finger.

"Dey is gonna be two or three of dose masts there too, ain't they, sir?" Andrew asked.

"Most of the time yes, Andrew, but I'm not sure what the plan is for this ship. I do know we are not here right now and this is not happening," he said with a slight chuckle. Andrew shot him a perplexed look. "This whole mission is a secret," Dylan continued, leaning his head in closer. "All of these trees belong to the British."

"What's you say, masa Dylan? How's dey done bought up all da trees?" Andrew looked both ways as though some group of the Queen's army were now walking through the woods looking for them.

"Some kind of agreement for just these tall ones," Dylan said, now cleaning his glasses with his handkerchief. "Yep...Mr. Lamar owns all the others." He pointed with the small cloth and waved his hand over the horizon. "Yeah...all of these are Mr. Lamar's."

"Halfway through, Mr. Montgomery!" Mr. William yelled to Dylan.

"Good job, men! Let's tie her off," Dylan said in response as he turned from Andrew and walked towards several of the other men.

William's veins bulged in his head. "What he said, boy, was to keep a-sawing on that tree!" He wiped the sweat from his brow again as the water ran out of his skin and into his eyes.

"Wipe it off, boss?" one of the men on the saw asked without missing a stroke.

Irritated, William reluctantly replied, "Yeah...wipe it off."

Andrew looked up to see the thick rope dangling from the top of the tree being cut; its thick braids were being pulled across the woods as they hung to the ground. Their ends formed a pool of rope that piled up almost four feet high. They tied the rope to the next large tree behind it.

"All right, men, continue...now fast through the rest of the bottom so she don't split at falling," he said as he walked back over to the place in the field where he and Andrew were first talking.

"What they doing now?" Andrew asked Dylan as he approached.

"A tree that tall will fall with such a force on its own that sometimes they split or get a crack in the middle. It would be useless if that happened. Then we would have to cut our way through the woods to find another one," he said as he patted Andrew on the back with a slight grin. "Now go over there with the men on the block and tackle, and let's lay her down softly," he said as he pointed Andrew to the men on the rope.

Soon enough, the enormous tree was gently laid down and trimmed of all the branches and limbs. Carefully, after it was cinched and strapped to the horses, the team began to drag the beautiful spire out of the woods. "Good job today, men!" Dylan congratulated the group. "We have to rendezvous with the ship in the morning, so get a good night's sleep."

* * *

Colonel John Johnson, a rich sugar plantation baron from Louisiana and one of the wealthiest members of the New York Yacht Club, walked through the cool night air, through a light fog, to the warehouse door of the Joseph Rowland Shipyard in Setauket, New York. Rowland's shipyard sat on the tip of the longest island in New York that formed the busy harbor of ships.

The colonel—and only called this because of his deep military culture and heritage—was no more than a distraction to the process so that Cal Lamar could construct a ship that would outrun every blockade ship on the eastern seaboard. This design marvel would beat all of the ships of the world, only to win a race she could never covet in view.

"Where is she?" the colonel asked Thomas Hawkins' silhouette as the hinges on the hatch-style door creaked open. He entered the dark harbor ship house.

An incredible shipbuilder, Hawkins had aided in the design and fabrication just a few years earlier of the famed *America* sailing yacht, a ship that won the Royal Yacht Squadron's One Hundred Guinea Cup challenge held in England in front of the Queen, which now bore the name of the winner of that inaugural event, The America's Cup.

"Oh! You startled me, Colonel," Hawkins said with a jerk of his entire body. He had been working alone that night in a closed warehouse under the flicker of candlelight on his secretive new design of a ship that was to be built. The colonel waited for Hawkins to answer his question. "Sorry, she just arrived, Commander. She's right over here," Hawkins said as he got up from the drawing table and walked towards the far end of the warehouse near the wharf docks. He lit the brass lantern sitting next to the wood-smith's table. "We just finished debarking her," Hawkins said as he pulled the white cotton covers from part the long cloaked pine timber. The colonel removed his white military glove and lightly dragged his fingers along the smooth wooden shaft.

This wood was to be meticulously honed into the mast of Hawkins' newest commissioned ship, a vessel that would take the coveted America's Cup home with him to Louisiana. Everything about her had to be perfect; every line, straight as an arrow.

"It's the finishing touch," he said with a sense of excitement, shrouded by his military posture. "Usable length?" he inquired as he spun towards Mr. Hawkins.

"One hundred twenty-five feet tall, at twenty inches thin at the top, sir," Hawkins responded. "Come see the stern work," he added as he led the colonel to the one-hundred-six-foot newly constructed ship that was balanced carefully on the wood blocking in the middle of the warehouse floor. The ship was a giant compared to the space she was in; her height rose into the darkness of the warehouse upward and disappeared, as her dark oak matched the dimly lit berth.

Hawkins started at the bow and walked the length of the ship. He grabbed a lantern from the wood-turning table, blew the sawdust off of it, and carefully pointed a match into the brass contraption. It glowed brightly as Hawkins turned the squeaky wheel and advanced the wick into a large flame. "Look at these lines. The whole configuration only allows for a nine-foot draft at three hundred tons. None of the craftsmen here have ever seen the like," he said as he waved the lantern high into the air and walked with a gangly excitement towards the stern of the ship.

"She is gorgeous, and the work of your craftsmen is impeccable," the colonel said as he admired the racing yacht. "What class will she be placed in, Mr. Hawkins?"

"I, uhhh, I'm not sure, Colonel. She's so different than any other ship her size. One hundred six feet has her in with the tall ships. Her sails and height ratio come close to putting her in the schooner class; however, she is way too long for that one. Her lines and shallow draft would put her in a class of the much smaller boats, like a sloop. I'm just not sure there is another that can run with her at this size," Hawkins added with his animated arm gestures as he described his work of art.

"Will she outrun the *America*?" the colonel asked.

"If my calculations are correct, she should be almost twice as fast as she—or any other ship in the world."

The colonel smiled and started to put his glove back on his hand. "Very good then," he replied.

"Thank you, sir...thank you!" Hawkins said with the pride of an admired artist. "Oh, sir!" Hawkins said as the colonel was turning to leave. "You have to see the stern."

The two men walked along the ship to the rear of the beautiful yacht. "The men just finished this today, sir!" Hawkins added; he turned the corner to face the rear end of the ship. The colonel turned the corner shortly behind him to see his outstretched arm and slowly waving open hand. Carved in fine mahogany and inlaid with gold lettering, the name carried itself across more than half of the twenty-five-foot width of the ship. "I present to you, the *Wanderer*," Hawkins said excitedly.

The colonel crossed his arms over his chest and rubbed his chin with his right gloved hand as he admired the nameplate. "Very good, Hawkins, very good indeed!"

* * *

Once again the North was going to show that they regulated the commerce as well as the government that had been placed firmly in the motherland of the Americas by the North.

"Father," Cal Lamar wrote to his dad in his home up North. "Why is it that we must be forced to buy servants at a fixed price by the North? When and if we import men for work in the fields from Cuba and Jamaica they are deemed slaves, and that, of course, is illegal. Is it merely the title of a man that the North has issues with and not the servitude they perform? How can we sit and have this happen? The kings in the lands of Africa are now selling their people to a leased life in the Americas, and we cannot go there and purchase the same? I will not stand for this controlling North to regulate and dictate us any longer."

Cal Lamar set out to acquire his own servants straight from the source in Africa and bypass the loophole the North had put on the scene of slavery. By any name or document, the act was the same.

The eastern sea by this time was filled with ships. Most were commissioned, government-owned vessels that were placed along its coast strategically to keep the Spanish Empire at bay, so to speak. The only way past the fortress of ships, called a "blockade," was a fast boat that could outrun and outmaneuver the governing vessels. These boats were called "blockade runners." The ships were small, light, and had the ability to slip through the cracks of the floating fortresses that regulated the seas. Being small and light meant that the loads they carried were small and light as well, so this type of vessel would never pass the perilous voyage or test that the oceans would present should they try to make their way to Africa. They also would not make good slavers to bring in the hundreds of men who made these trips more lucrative on this perilous voyage reserved only for the North.

Lamar was in the market for a large boat, very fast, and that could be disguised away from the obvious slavers of the day. This brought the young Southerner to the docks of Charleston, South Carolina, where a new ship had just arrived in port. He found his prize ship that had been constructed for the commodore of the yacht club in New York harbor.

Originally built for the royalty of the yachting world, the *Wanderer* was on her maiden voyage to her owner in Louisiana; she was the latest production marvel of the waterways. Her lightweight, revolutionary hull design and an enormous amount of canvas in the wind did not fit her into a traditional class of ship. She was too long to be a sloop, and she had the sail height of a tall ship class. Her shallow draft made her too fast to be classed in any one category, which sadly ended her career by not being allowed to participate in the famed America's Cup race. Her fate was that she was the fastest of all the ships in the period with no one to race or hold title on. The tall racing ships in her length and height were capable of twelve knots; the *Wanderer* was capable of twenty.

* * *

Cal's father, Gazaway, being indigenous to both the North and the South, and having built an empire in Savannah's sprawling cotton industry, possessed the money to finance such a purchase. Having a Southern gentleman with a poor accent and big pockets was just as Cal would have it. Gazaway was quite capable of such an investment; however, he did not share his son's views on slavery.

* * *

The racing boat was bought by the Lamars' business partner, William Corrie, and was held up to the world as an entertainment vessel with a brilliant regalia of well-decorated sailors and marvelous crew. Her appointments set her far in front of the ships of her day. Her true colors and purpose as a slaver would soon be unveiled.

Under the cloak of such a splendid ship, capable of making twenty to twenty-two knots, depending on her tail wind—most ships in the rivers and ports she passed of this size could only make eight—she was to be fitted for an overseas adventure that few knew the truth about.

She needed the stealth of her beauty and crew to be a successful slaver. She had the capacity to hold 500 men, or the weight thereof, and still make these wind-known speeds in the cloak of secrecy. The *Wanderer* was fitted with two fifteen-thousand-gallon galvanized water tanks for this voyage. This water and onboard provisions were essential to the life to be enjoyed by royalty on the high seas—or that of the most capable slaver. She would prove to be the latter of the two.

Under her disguise, she made her way to the open water as a luxury cruise yacht and would soon shed the unnecessary weight of the glamour yacht she was. She would be turned into a slaver as soon as she made port in her new destination, the Congo.

Flying under the American flag and safe from the patrolling boats of the English because of the Act of 1807 the *Wanderer* made port and was quickly converted to a slaver. Additional decks were installed; cages, pens, and incarceration provisions were piled into the *Wanderer*'s hold. She was now ready to take on the anticipated living load of slaves that would make their way back to the southern shores of America.

The plan to have a ship that was fast was part of a twofold plot. She would easily outrun any ship that would try to stop her, but she would also allow the trip to be made in breakneck speed. This quick trip would allow for the most terrible part of the story to be played out.

Her new slave decks were designed to hold prisoners like spoons in a drawer, allowing for a space only sixteen inches wide by eighteen inches tall and five feet long. She was to carry five hundred men and women in these cramped quarters. The speed of her capacity would allow for the thousands of gallons of freshwater, if rationed properly, to provide hydration for the five hundred prisoners she would keep. By making the trip in half the time, the normal space of twenty square feet given to a slave in accordance with the Act of 1812 could be cut in half as well. Thus, a faster ship, in half the time, could carry twice the load and require less room.

The plan was well calculated except for the compassion of its captors. There would be no bathroom facilities, no movement in the cargo of men, women, and children held below her decks; and of course there would be death due to the deplorable and anticipated conditions of her doomed cargo. The plan was set, the boat was readied, and 500 ill-fated souls were soon to be branded with a hot iron and loaded below the decks of the death ship.

THE CONGO

THE HUMIDITY DRIPPED FROM THE LEAVES AS THE MOON gave way to the morning's sun. The rain forests of the Congo, located in the middle of Africa's vast and wild continent, are located almost directly under the equator. Her hot, humid air was perfect for the lush foliage that covered the savannas of the Congo River.

The mouth of the mighty Congo opens up into this Dark Continent and wends its way to the middle of an uncharted and enchanted botanical garden of life and land. This mighty river was a sprawling wonder, full of fish and lavish fruit trees that lined the river and provided shade to the water and banks below.

* * *

As in the early years, major cities were connected to the ports that the rivers would provide. After all, water was life, and life centered on the water. Much earlier than the people of the 1800s Congo could remember, the elders of the villages told wild stories of the old Congo life. They told of the great kings who ruled the beautiful empires of the region.

The Kiki were a proud people who told the young children and adult bystanders who were all listening to their enchantment: "The great jungle warriors were so highly adaptive to the land that they were raised to live off of the land, use the land, use the trees, and live from the death of animals that nourished their bodies. But, respect the land, respect the trees, and give thanks to the great beasts that kept the families of the region alive," the wise ones would say.

The clothes that were on the listeners were in fact made from these natural riches of hides and leaves. The appointments that adorned them were derived from Mother Nature, and they paid their respects to her diligently. Never kill more than they could eat, never take more than they needed. This world, to them, presented a paradise, and the climate and the serenity of the earth in this region truly resembled that very word, *paradise*. "Uncle," they would say, "Tell us of the brave warriors."

"Oh, these were real men! Men who walked into the wild jungle naked and made life happen. Men who, with their hands and minds, made clothes, weapons, and a living," the elders taught the younger ones.

Truly the words *make a living* rang loudly to the young, aspiring Congolese children. "You see, that's exactly what one had to do in this natural and wild world they were growing up in and had to manage on their own," the village wise men explained.

"It was make a living or die! Those who could not survive in this region simply didn't survive. A man who could not pull his weight under the sight of his peers was exterminated," the old man went on to tell the listeners. "It was a natural process of elimination to prevent possible spread of failure."

These people were very proud of who they were, expecting the unexpected around every corner and tree. They were trained by generations of forefathers to expect, adapt, improvise, and overcome the obstacles of this unforgiving world, and to pay respect to the same world. They worshiped the ground they walked on because quite simply, it provided life for them, their families, and the generations to come.

In the north of Africa, Egypt was a sophisticated way of life compared to the world they knew in the jungle. They wanted to have no part of the calamity and chaos of the cruel and "modernized" world. They saw how men treated one another, and how they enslaved one another and beat them to death. They wanted no part of this cruel, new world and retreated back into the jungle to tell the tales of the land to the north and the hardships that came with their miserable lives.

To wake up and know you had to survive every day from one to another off the land and to know that nothing would be provided for you as soon as you could defend yourself and walk, these young men of the Congo region, the "little warriors," were not at all intimidated by these thoughts; they embraced them. They took their education in these life skills very seriously, because a good grade in this class meant you would live; to fail these courses was certain death.

As soon as the European explorers from the north of Africa began to explore the southern regions, they found that they were not tough enough to survive. They were not strong enough to make it even for a day in this wretched place that these warriors called home. Being that slavery was common throughout every culture, throughout time, these modernized people of the north thought that if they could capture these peoples' spirit, then they would have the brains and might to rule the world.

So simple was the life in the deep Congo region that these highly life-trained people were mesmerized by the simple things of the modern world. Gunpowder, cloth, and jewelry were evil tricks used by these Northern Mongols to captivate the minds of the great Congo warrior chiefs. "Magic," they would say. These simple and unsuspecting people thought they were works from the gods above.

Once introduced to the trickery of the northerners, the villagers were eager to obtain this magic. Captivated by the splendor of these items, the desire of the chiefs of the villages grew stronger every day. Their will to part from these evils had died in the ancestors before them. They were weaker now, and desire and greed were soon to take their place amongst the Congolese ranks.

As the elders said, "The strong survive and the weak would not." But what if the weak, who almost certainly would die in the world ahead of them, were given another chance to live? What if instead of allowing the jungle to consume them, they would be given to the terrible people, who at least would not kill them? They actually would be kept safe from harm and the people would feed them. For this they should work for the people who would preserve their life. After all, the warriors were servants to the land and animals that provided life to them. These weak and considered nonproductive souls were to be traded to the northern visitors for mere beads or cloth. In exchange for these tools of deceit and false happiness, these poor souls reluctantly went with their new captors to an untold land and were never seen again.

The kings of the region appreciated their new gifts from the foreign visitors, and trading resources like copper and slaves was becoming an item that the king could enjoy. After all, they did not have to build prisons, keep the wrongdoers of the village alive, or provide for the weak people of the region; they could discard them. They were simply traded away to a life elsewhere. But life was not a requirement; being gone from the village was the benefit, and not being a detriment to the tribes of the day was good for all.

If a poor villager of the time could bring a piece of cloth or a string of beads, then obviously a good warrior could bring two. But where would they come from? After all, the warriors of the Congolese were responsible for the lives of the villagers and provided protection for families. "We can't use our best just to get two strings of beads; we must overtake another village far away that would not affect or harm our harmony or production," the kings would say to the people.

So the great warriors of the tribes would fight battles with rivaling villages and take the captors of war to the king of their Congolese empire. It was a win-win for the king of the Kiki village. He not only didn't diminish his village and warriors, he got rid of the bottom feeders of the village and sold off the spoils of war, the captive people from the surrounding village. He also claimed their land and expanded his own empire.

So the young men of the group were now listening intently. They knew wars amongst the villages would soon come, and they also knew that the polished skills of weapons and fighting would lead them through the valley of death that they faced, should they be caught and made a slave by an opponent. It was kill or be taken. Death would have probably been the easiest route for many, but the proud people of this great nation would not let that happen. The kings of the region were becoming wealthy for trading these items and people away, and yes, with wealth there is greed. Soon all of the seven deadly sins would come crawling into this once sprawling paradise.

CUFFIE

LIFE IN THE CONGO WAS A PRIMITIVE ELEGANCE KNOWN
only to the people who began their life there. Completely at home with
what most would consider a deplorable environment, the Congolese considered it being in the enchantment of the jungle. The ever-present dangers
of these conditions presented themselves in a quiet and stealthy way that
the normal, unsuspecting Americans would have easily fallen prey to.

Cuffie was a strong, young boy, about fifteen years old, and trained
well for his young years. Revered in his Congolese village, Cuffie was just
at the beginning of his independence and warrior perfection. He was physically stronger than most boys his age and more competent than some of
the adult warriors and tribesmen of his village. His youth prevented him
from gaining the respect of the older and more experienced Maliki.

Cuffie was left behind on the most daring of hunts and wars, which
were undertaken by the older more experienced huntsmen and warriors
of the tribe.

His day consisted of being reassured by his father, "While I'm away,
you are the man of the house," which led him with some dignity to hold
his head high as he walked throughout the village. After all, Cuffie was
the strongest of the young men left behind, and his friends, or "mini warriors," looked up to him. Not only were the smaller children left behind,
but also the king, queen, and a few warriors to protect them and the elders
of the tribe. The elders of the Maliki tribe, physically not what they once

were, held the storage of golden memories of the days long past in the Maliki village.

No one was allowed to approach the king or queen of Maliki; the warriors who guarded them stood silent and diligent as they guarded one of the most revered royal families.

The primitive place was highly regarded as a historical village, which was small in comparison to the huge TaTiki village to the north. The cozy village made close quarters for the friendly Maliki. Cuffie could often see the young Prince Cory, who was almost his age, behind the compound fence of the king. Cory's destiny was to become the king; his boyhood was filled with concentrated training from the best warriors. His head was filled with the most lucrative of secrets from the respected elders, and the blood that ran through his veins gave right to the soon-to-be king.

It was obvious to Cuffie while he looked through the makeshift fence of the royal compound that Cory was most likely a better warrior and smarter than he. Daily, Cuffie strolled freely through the village, and he noted that young Cory was jailed in the royal palace, even though the fence was made of the same sticks as around his own home.

Cuffie had the freedom to decide when he wanted to train for fighting and when the fighting and training turned to play.

Young Cory would look through the fence and yearn for the freedom the other children had. There would be no release from the prison of training he was born into, and he was snapped back to attention almost every time his mind wandered to the self-indulgences of childhood.

Quite often Cuffie would play-fight, but unlike the other children, he wanted to know the richness of knowledge that young Cory was hearing. After all, the knowledge that was obtained was from the aging people of the village would carry them well into adulthood.

Young Cuffie would often get lost in the adventuresome tales of the aging warriors who speckled the village. These were the same people who used to stand watch over the king when he was a boy; the same people who trained the king of the Maliki themselves. As soon as Cuffie figured out through his young wisdom that these great men were the professors of the king, he knew he had struck a gold mine and would receive the same training that young Cory was receiving.

Cuffie often saw young Cory looking intently at the other children playing in the village. Then one day their eyes met as Cuffie sat on a log listening to the great adventures that had been told to the king. Neither boy knew at the time that both wanted to play in the grass on the other side of the fence.

But at the same time, they were receiving the same training that was supposed to make them leaders of men.

Kia Longo was the retired advisor of the king. He lived in a modest shack near the royal living grounds and was revered throughout the Maliki village. You could clearly see his astute knowledge and his facial gestures in his stature as he somberly strolled about. As most elders do, they sit back and take it all in. They don't stray far from the confines of their comfortable lives and memories that represent it.

Kia Longo watched intently, as most elders do. He watched the young women farm and harvest the food that would complement the meat that was being hunted and most assuredly being brought back to nourish their bodies. He watched their mothers spend time teaching them the ways of the village and the respect they should have of the men of the village. They were also taught by their mothers that the young boys playing with sticks and spears would one day be putting food on the table for them and they were to be respected, too.

Kia Longo knew he was not put out to pasture. He knew that his job as an elder was to verbally train the young men of the village whilst their fathers were out cultivating and hunting. He also knew his training would be overshadowed by the children's fathers as soon as they returned. The basic seed of enlightening, remembered culture would grow inside them as their fathers pruned the knowledge now growing in their soul.

Cuffie stood out in the crowd compared to the other children; they would cling to him as if to follow him. Being so wise, Kia Longo saw this, and knew he would focus on the natural leader if that one would listen. However, as Kia Longo also knew, young boys, especially ones who are leaders, quite often don't listen to old men and lead by brawn. This was not the case with Cuffie. Kia Longo had for years observed Cuffie watching young Cory as he strained to hear the magical words that were being spoken to him.

However, Cuffie heard nothing and his mind wandered, thinking of all the marvelous stories that were being unfolded before the boy king and imagined their great detail of fights and battles. Cuffie wanted to know these things, and since he was apt for wanting this knowledge, he knew that, combined with his size and strength, he would be a mighty warrior if he had a sharp mind. The wants of both Cuffie and Kia Longo made them naturally attract. It was not long before the stories told would unfold into a friendship of the two men who were many years apart.

Cuffie sat contentedly on the wooden bench outside Kia Longo's hut. They could hear the other children playing and having fun in the background, and knew that part of him was there in the playing field with them. For the most part, Cuffie stared intently into Kia Longo's eyes; he studied the matured lines on the old man's face as he spoke the stories of past days of the wise man's life.

The scars on his body stuck out like signs from the past that added character to the stories that unfolded. Sometimes Kia Longo would point them out and tell of the battle or lesson that branded them into his mind and on his aging body.

Kia Longo was a tall man, of slender build and aching joints that visually reminded the listener he had been through a lot in his long life. The stories he harbored told of his advancements through the tribe and the tribulations of time.

As a young man, Kia Longo was a lot like Cuffie; he was an unofficial leader of the not so fortunate of the group, the ones who would be the backbone of society that lived in the Congo. Kia Longo was smart, trained by his father to be a gallant and very capable warrior, with the cunning of survival and fortitude that kept him alive. He was well respected in his younger years. Being a prominent warrior, combined with his diligence as a leader of the lower community, meant that Kia Longo was selected as one of the citizens for position amongst the royals. This acknowledgement would mature into a trust that the royal family would bequeath on very few as they selected him at an early age.

Kia Longo was appointed as one of the royal chamber guards who protected the king's grounds. The common word among the other guards was that Kia Longo was a great warrior, not only in size, but also in heart and head. It was not long before the biggest, brightest, and smartest would work their way to the top and be personally appointed to guard the king; he was well on his way to this position.

Kia Longo started out one day telling Cuffie a story. "On a day like any other, there was a ritual of the kings to go out into the lands and explore the kingdom which they ruled. So the king, his best guards, and several wise men went deep into the jungle to document the boundaries of the Maliki lands. In this region, with undocumented lines that changed quite often, true rulers would expand their kingdom and document their journeys across the savage lands that created the region."

Cuffie couldn't find a position to be comfortable in; he wanted the story out of the old man to come faster, but it was part of the presentation, and the delivery was carefully called for and applied.

Kia Longo went on, "At the reluctance of the wise men, King Ta Tiki Tia motioned for the group to go forward to the barriers that they had known to be the limits of their kingdom. The mere motion of his staff, the tilt of his chin upward, and the look of many kings past, put the group into motion immediately and without hesitation." Kia Longo watched Cuffie's wide eyes as he mentioned going out of the village to the uncharted lands. "For once, the group of men would soon find that the reluctance of the wise men should have been respected."

"Enchantment filled the faces of all but a few concerned souls who did not have the wherewithal to venture out into the great, wild country.

A few more turns and whacks of the steely knives that led the way, cutting into the unknown abyss, opened up to a new and beautiful region never before seen by any in this group of explorers."

"Where is this place?" Cuffie asked.

"Oh, my boy," Kia Longo said, "finish listening before you want to know this place." He continued. "There were some who were quite familiar with these grounds, and they were not the Maliki people that lived there. The group stumbled upon a marker carved from a tree and placed towering above the unknown land. The shadows of the carved winged and savage-toothed figures with open mouths insinuated that they were terrible mythical creatures." Kia Longo now raised his arms to add character to the story. "They were brightly adorned in God-like colors rarely seen by men and reserved for the sacred. The king and his men knew they had come to a holy ground of worship," he said to Cuffie, whose jaw was now open. "And it was not their own."

"Straight out of the shadows a spear pierced the heart of the mightiest warrior in front of the group." Cuffie's eyes widened as he gasped. "The men assembled a circle, guarding the king with their very bodies as shields from the attack. More arrows and spears, like bees from an angry nest, came from every direction, stinging and piercing the human shield. As the warriors fell one by one, the exposure of the king was imminent." Kia Longo, now standing, pointed in Cuffie's face. "It was not a time to retreat and run from the death sentence that had been bestowed upon them. It was time to turn and fight, king and men, to defend their lives and not to cower."

Grabbing Cuffie's shoulder Kia Longo said, "The king turned, grabbing the shoulder of the smallest and fastest squire as another spear flew just in front of the king's head. His swift reaction to the flying object caused the young squire to recoil his head as well, which allowed the tip of the spear to pierce the cheek of the terrified squire and rip through his smooth, brown skin. 'Go!' And immediately the young man ran for their life to seek help from the village of Maliki where the journey began.

"The young man ran through the jungle with all the might and speed that was left in his soul. The blood gushed from his face, partially blinding him as he ran. The fear of what was happening behind him and the desire for the help of others propelled him through the jungle at blinding speed. The vines and brush ripped through his skin as he carelessly sped through the jungle to seek help for the ambushed king he had so adamantly looked up to.

"He knew that he was probably one of the last to ever hear the king speak. The word *Go* was played out in the young man's mind as the jungle relentlessly tried to stop his dash for help. He knew that the command was not just to go; it was in fact a long speech that was to summon an army of men, raise them to battle, and tell of the desperation that the imperial leader was soon to succumb to. That word would echo in his mind forever."

Cuffie's eyes started to well with tears as he thought of the desperation of the young squire. Kia Longo said, "The word was never spoken from the young warrior as he ran into the village. The pain, anguish, and exhaustion of the young man spoke more loudly than any words he had concocted to tell the waiting warriors of the village. His wide eyes, despondent look and his bloodstained skin said all one needed to hear. The only words were, 'Where is he?' The dying messenger told the warriors where the doomed group could be found on the uncharted edge of the tranquil world they once knew.

"Within moments, the call to order was sounded by the jungle instruments that were only played in a time of war. The warriors assembled like a diligent army; the women helped ready them for the unknown and perilous journey into whatever compelled the messenger to run himself to death to deliver a message from the king.

"The warriors of the village left in the night, running as if there was a cleared road ahead. The powerful moon lit the way as the enraged men ran to help the king."

Cuffie cringed as Kia Longo continued. "The growls of these warriors were to cover the stinging of the whips the jungle presented them. Anguish or exhaustion was not a factor to the adrenaline that filled their veins.

"At sunlight they came to the area they were told by the dying messenger. The group of warriors slowed to that of a coiled panther stalking its prey. A quiet came over the group as they listened for any sounds of the doomed party of the king.

"A scuffle ahead; a snap of a twig was heard. All the men from the village in unison followed the noises intently, painting a picture in their minds of the mischief and dangers that were ahead. As a unified group and in motion with the jungle and air around them they moved towards the sounds with utter stealth.

"It would have been madness for the men to run into the unknown of such danger. They surrounded the noises in the cloak of the dim morning light, and like the silent rising of the sun behind them, the noises fell silent ahead. The group eased towards the location and the eerie silence. There were hundreds of footprints and bloodstains on the ground, which were all that was presented by the sun's early light.

"The king and his entire group of explorers were dead. Their corpses were decapitated and their heads hung from poles that cast shadows on the ground that would never be traveled again. Their mouths were open and their eyes rolled back into their skulls. The men stood silent as the sun now illuminated their mutilated souls." Kia Longo sat down next to Cuffie. The boy was paralyzed with fear as he listened to the old man.

"As the warriors returned with the bodies of the dead, the village knew from the somberness that preceded them that the news of the king was grim."

Kia Longo told the story with such dismay that at some points Cuffie couldn't bear to listen. The thought of remembrance of his horrible story made the old man's voice scratchy, only adding an exclamation point to its credibility. Cuffie looked at the scar on Kia Longo's cheek that ran across his now aged and wrinkled skin.

"You...you were the boy that carried the message?" Cuffie stood wide-eyed, with mouth agape.

Kia Longo went on in the days to come as he told the boy his stories of his once great king and the deaths of the warriors that provided, by default, the position he was soon to take. Kia Longo was appointed Chief and Council, and served as counselor to the young prince who was to be the king

Training an heir to the throne was not in any way what Kia Longo imagined his life to be. Within days the boy, around the same age as the wide-eyed Cuffie, would be made king of the land of the Maliki. Soon the boy-king would grow into that man that his father had envisioned him to be as he died that day, spear in hand, and one step in front of the men who were trying to protect him. The last thing to pass through the king's mind as the spear took his life were the thoughts of his son becoming a man and king of this region.

Kia Longo had quite the job as he and the young boy grew older together. Kia Longo shielded the young prince with his heart and knowledge, delivering him to the steps of the throne he was soon to sit upon. As he aged, Kia Longo retired to that of the wise man he was, and lived in the shadows of the palace of the king he had led there.

Cuffie couldn't believe he was the one who got to share these memories with the king's great mentor. He knew the same training had led another like him to be a king.

Jekyll Island

SITTING IN THE STILL COASTAL WATERS OF THE SOUTH IN America lies a chain of islands that dot the coastal region's mainland. Named after Sir Joseph Jekyll, the islands originally were home to the Creek Indian nation. The great Indian nation soon fell victim to the advancements of the explorer Juan Ponce De Leon. After several years under Spanish rule as the Northern outpost in the Spanish-settled territory of Florida, the islands were soon relinquished because of the difficulty of defending their position from the Northern settlers who established the colonies just upriver in Savannah, Georgia, and neighboring Charleston, South Carolina.

The islands made a perfect harbor, being just south of the heavily patrolled and fortified Savannah River ports, for the blockade runners to unload their small cargoes brought in from the southern islands of the Bahamas and Jamaica.

Often the goods were brought into these less patrolled islands, which reached far south and dangerously close to the Spanish colonies in Florida. The waters of this region were heavily scoured by pirates and the like, so they made a perfect safe haven for the goods that were to be smuggled in by these lawless groups.

* * *

The light waves crashed against the wooden hull of the *Wanderer* as she sat perched off of the Congo River's mouth. The plan was beginning to unfold that would make history, and the horrible memory for two countries that barely knew of each other's existence. The only word of the Congo in the Americas was that it was a wild and untamed jungle world. In turn, the only word of the New World that would have been told to the people of the Congo was of its horrible inhabitants and the bad intentions of the white men who roamed this bleak, new world and would come looking for slaves.

As the *Wanderer* made port in the mouth of the Congo, the elegant sailing yacht was stripped of her appointments and brought into the light of the simple characteristics that were devised upon her purchase. Her beauty and speed would set her apart from the other slave ships that had made port before. Gone were her suites that filled the large areas below her decks; removed were the appointments of the staterooms that were put in place for the comfort of the passengers who were to sail her, and gone were the good intentions of this once majestic sailing vessel. Outside, the hull of this great sailing ship was left bright and shiny, portraying the beautiful grandeur that would cloak the horror of the cargo that would soon be loaded out of sight. She was a slaver in disguise.

It took several months for the transition from sailing vessel to spirited slaver to take place. The word was out to the slave merchants of the Congo that five hundred slaves would soon be needed to fill her cargo hold. These merchants of death had plenty of time to spread the word that another ship full of slaves was needed at the mouth of the Congo River.

* * *

Cuffie sat in the tranquil village of Maliki, where he would sit and listen to the stories that were soon to make him a mighty warrior, one like the king of the community, and like the prince who would rule this land when his father passed. The Maliki village sat quietly in the shadows of the mighty TaTiki Empire that was to the west of the peaceful village. Often visitors from the ever-powerful TaTiki would pass through the serene Malikian village and visit the boy turned king, TooTaKia.

The colors the TaTiki adorned gave them the respect one would give a ruler of the lands, being the imperial warriors they were. Their iron faces and dark eyes gave no question as to the superiority of the TaTiki Empire they protected. They were the elite fighters of the jungle.

It came as quietly as the unopened mouths of the steel TaTiki warriors, the murderous plot that was soon to be unveiled. The TaTiki king entered through the perimeter of the Maliki village with a close entourage of warriors who carried him in on a throne. The Maliki guards respected his unannounced visit, and the king was summoned to meet the royal visitors. The small party of men and king waited patiently as the guards placed the visiting king's royal throne to the ground. The TaTiki king stood and was surrounded by his guards in perfect profile, the men patiently waiting for the Maliki king to come forward and receive his unannounced guest. The maidens of the Maliki palace led the way, as always, distributing flower petals for the king to walk on. To follow was the king and then the royal family, a respectful ten steps behind him.

As usual, the kings would meet and hug each other as brothers, kissing each side of their face, as this had been passed down from generations of kings before them.

The greeting went as usual, except for the knife that immediately plunged into the Maliki king's heart. As the TaTiki king kissed the dying face of the man he once called brother, the Maliki king collapsed, falling dead in his arms.

At once the royal TaTiki flags were waved in the air and the entourage of TaTiki guards stabbed the surrounding Maliki warriors with swift and deadly blows. The waving of the flags was the signal for the hundreds of waiting TaTiki warriors to come from the jungle's cloak and spring an attack on the unsuspecting village.

The murderous plot continued at knifepoint; the TaTiki had led an attack similar to this on many other villages that were peaceful allies in the Congo jungle.

As the Maliki warriors later returned to the village with their spoils of the day, they were met in ambush and captured immediately. Hardly any resistance was made; the certainty of death filled the air and within hours, the Maliki village was under silent siege and its people were swiftly taken hostage as captives in an un-fought war. Before the night could fall the entire village was bound, tied by the neck to poles and led away at the point of deadly spears. The faces of their captors never flinched as they followed out their leader's murderous plot.

The Maliki tribesmen, along with women and children, walked in dismay towards the west. They saw the sun setting on the last day of the rest of their life, thinking of this horror and unbeknownst horrors to come.

* * *

The wooden fortress in the evening's sunset cast shadows on the band of captive souls that would be sold in short order to the waiting vessel just outside the mouth of the Congo. As they entered the gates of the once revered fortress of the TaTiki kingdom, they were taken aback by the faces similar to theirs that were going about life in the village, just as the Maliki had done a few short hours ago. The anguish of disenchantment took over as these fellow brothers and sisters of the Congo watched themselves be herded like cattle to the waiting human corrals.

There were hundreds of people there, crying and sobbing as the hatred spewed from their eyes. These prison camps built by the TaTiki housed the Maliki captives as they looked in awe at the people who killed their brothers, kings, and anyone who resisted the march of death. The crying children from different villages all sounded the same as the sun set on the first night of their new living hell.

These were probably the first dreams of freedom as they lay on the ground in the deplorable conditions. No bathroom, nor any cover from sheer disgrace of the noblemen and women of royalty who had been crowded together with those who were soon to be their shipmates. They were all about to be loaded below the decks of the waiting *Wanderer*.

* * *

Once the slave hold modifications were constructed, the ship sailed from the docks deep within the Congo to the mouth of the river to wait for the human load. The plan was to build at port, doing nothing wrong, and load the captives below on the newly constructed decks while the boat was at sea. The *Wanderer* did not want to get caught at the docks, where her speed could not be used. She waited at anchor just outside the Congo River; her men perched to receive the small boats of prisoners that were coming to her during the night. Signal fires and smoke let the transfer boats know the coast was clear. Everyone aboard had a sneaky demeanor about them as the savagery commenced.

Cuffie could hear the others from his village as they were loaded into the small vessels that would take them away. To entice the scared people, some of the resistant warriors were beaten to within inches of death, right in front of their wives, children, fellow villagers, and people they never even knew. Lying in their own blood, the mighty men of respect whispered one word: "Go."

That word again; so mighty, meaning so much, in such a simple phrase. It meant in this instance that if you don't do as you are told, your fate is soon sealed. Most took the harrowing advice of the dying men as they lay on the docks and watched their crying families loaded aboard the waiting ship in chains.

Cory's eyes met that of Cuffie's once again as the monotony was played out. This time there was not the want of freedom from their teachers; it was terror in each other's eyes.

They were loaded down into the bowels of their floating hell. As the daylight disappeared above them through the cargo hold doors, so did the fresh salt air they breathed. The environment changed in seconds as the musty air from the ship's holds overpowered them. Candlelit lanterns dimly illuminated the way as they walked along the wooden decks that had just been constructed below their feet. The new decks had not been sanded smooth; on the contrary, they were rough planks of split wood and comfort was not in the mind of the constructor. The hollow sounds of the chains that bound them dragged across the odorous decks they walked on. The sobs of so many, briefly broken by the crack of the whip and the scream of its recipient, were all that gave way to the chains dragging on the wood as they lumbered in the direction they were led. Above them, and below, they could see thin shadows through the cracks in the planking as the Congo families were being chained down.

Finally, at the end of the march, each person was instructed to lie like spoons, face to back, on the rough wooden decks, each of them chained to one another and to the steel shackles placed along the deck at their feet. They would lie in this position for forty-five days as the *Wanderer* set sail for the so-called free world.

The waves made a hollow thump on the wooden hull of the ship. Weighted with such a heavy load, the hull sank low into the water. The sounds of splashing waves were saved for those on the upper decks of the wooden prison. Small portholes were opened during calm seas to allow for the ventilation of the urine and vomit that dripped through the cracks to the poor souls below. The circulation of air did not exist on the lower decks, and the stench of five hundred souls stuck to the wooden deck that they lay on became overpowering.

After a week of this, dehydration started to set in. All of the Congolese who lay there would push and encourage each other in whispers to not give up. The words of the whispers were for comfort; the push was to see if they were still alive.

Screams echoed throughout the wooden cave. A scream of one, not like that of a beaten person at the hand of a whip. A torrid scream; like that of a push that came with no reply. A noise one would make in the dark as they rolled their loved one over to see the death stare in their face looking back at them. Mouth open, eyes back, and the skeletal look of a person in death.

The white man knew the screams well, as did all the others from the decks above and below. Those around would barely look, as they knew the crack of the whip was soon to be given to any onlooker. The people below could see small slivers of light from the decks above and shadows as the lantern lights approached. The ones above the horror peered through the one-inch cracks of the decking boards to the panorama of the disenchantment below.

As the screams rang out through the hold of the boat, the self-test of pushing for a life check became more frequent. There weren't as many in the early days aboard the ship, but as the *Wanderer* sailed on, they became more and more frequent in the weeks to come.

Cuffie and Cory were on the upper deck of the ship's slave hold. The stench of death and humans below was thick, and sought its way to the portholes they could see near them. There was a trickle of more light on this deck than below, and the boys could see the actions of the sailors as they walked along the decks, inspecting the chains that bound them. After a month lying there, not a soul could move. The deplorable conditions made it hard for life to go on; truly, only the strong would survive this perilous voyage.

"Cuffie ..." A muted whisper rose between the cracks of the deck just below Cuffie's head.

"Cuffie..." The weakened voice again beckoned to the boy. Kia Longo's once strong voice was now muted in whisper.

Cuffie scurriedover to face the wooden deck beneath him. "Master!" the boy breathed through the crack of the deck below him. He could see a small movement just to his left on the deck below. His view was limited by the crack; the view would be better if he could shift over slightly and look through the next crack in the deck. Cuffie slowly gathered the chains that bound his wrist and tried to stretch his body over the deck to peer through the adjacent crack. It was an inch too far away. The steel shackle stretched and began to reopen the cuts in the skin that the rusted steel had caused.

"Cuffie..." came through the searing pain the boy had inflicted on himself to see his longtime master. Cuffie pulled against the steel in agonizing pain as the infected skin on his wrist tore against the metal restraint. He craned his neck as far as possible, pressing his face hard into the wooden deck. He could barely see the glisten of Kia Longo's eyes.

"Boy...I will not leave you on your journey." The old man spoke softly to the young boy just a few feet above him. "But you will not see me in the light of the day. No...my son..." The old man winced and closed his crackly brown eyes. "You will see me in the light of the fire that burns in you." His eyes opened and he peered directly into Cuffie's eyes. "Your light is the brightest of the Maliki, and you will live to be free again, my son."

Cuffie pressed his face further into the stench of the damp wooden deck. He could taste the smell of weeks of human waste emanating from the wood as he pushed his eye into the crack of the wood. His restraints, merciless and firm, continued to cut their way into new flesh as he squirmed. Kia Longo's eyes opened wider as if to make his point, and then they seemed to retract back down into silence.

From the deck below Cory and Cuffie there was another scream. Unlike the other death screams before, this one scream sounded very close and loud. Towards the end of the trip there were about five screams a day. But this one was different; much like the ones when a mother lost a child or if the child lost the mother. Lower, and from deep within, as an expression of one sound that a soul close to you had just escaped through the cracks of the deck and ascended to meet their maker.

Cory, Cuffie, and most of the people on the upper deck slowly rolled over to peer through the cracks at the horror that lay just a few feet below them. Four or five feet separated the scream from the ears above. Cuffie could see the white men squatting through the hold below as they made their way towards the area of the frightened mate that lay next to the dead man.

Then came the jingle of the steel skeleton keys, the unlocking of the chain, and the chain's sound as it was pulled through the rings mounted to the post supporting the shackle. Without regard to the once great warrior and teacher of kings that he was, the white men hastily snatched him from the wooden deathbed. The unshackled remains of the Kia Longo were pulled from sight of the audience that watched in horror above through the cracks. A deathly silence fell over the boat, as it did anytime the captors were near, and it made every sound seem louder as the captives sat silent. The sounds of lifeless heels hitting the wooden steps echoed across the floor as the sailors pulled the man up the stairs from the deck below. The sound of leather from the boots did not cover the sound of dragging flesh over the wooden deck. Out of reverence, the boys lay silenced as the men dragged the wise man right by their heads to the top deck of the ship. Cuffie's eyes met Kia Longo's one last time.

The portholes gave light to the dust that was stirred from the deck by the march above, the waves making a crisp noise while they hit the hull just inches below the small ray of light coming through the porthole. Not often, but every once in a while, the light was broken by the water that leapt from the top of the biggest waves as the *Wanderer* parted the seas. A small commotion above, a few men in the same general area and their footsteps being heard painted a picture in the minds of the captives below. Again, after the small break of light, the sound was heard of the water's splash as Kia Longo's lifeless body was cast into the abyss of the ocean. The crash in the water interrupted the waves that rhythmically hit the ship, and a splash of the water again interrupted the ray of light that Cuffie stared at. There were ninety-two splashes like this one in all over the forty-five-day voyage while the boat made its way through the entangling sea.

* * *

A roar like no other rang out in the darkness. The sound of an incredible splash and the rip of chains speeding across the wooden deck above indicated the anchor had been dropped off the waiting coast of Southern Georgia. The air stopped, and the large cargo bays above were opened. A rush of fresh air came in with God's light as it pierced through the opening of the hold's door, letting the survivors know their voyage had come to an end.

It seemed like forever, but eventually came the ringing of keys, the moving of chains, and the groans of movement of men and muscle that were stiff and lethargic. The whip's crack did no good, as the poor souls were not afraid of those noises after the screams of horror and the journey they had just endured.

Immediately the morning's sunlight above was blinding. Everyone began breathing in the fresh air of the land that was a few hundred yards in the distance. The boys on deck could see the people who had made landfall from the small boats that carried them ashore. In almost every instance they watched as the survivors fell to their knees and kissed the sands of Jekyll Island.

JUSTICE OF THE SOUTH

May 12, 1861, one month before the Civil War.

THE TALL MARSH GRASS THAT LINED SAVANNAH'S BANKS quieted the waters of the river, and the docks and streets above it presented themselves with the noise of production as the men worked in the hot Georgia sun. Lamar Pier was the busiest of all the docks in the region. The piers in the docks were formed from the strongest timbers, firmly joined with steel nails and screws. Gazaway Bugg Lamar not only owned the finely made docks and the warehouse buildings, he owned many of the sprawling plantations that sent the products there to be shipped around the world. Gazaway and his son, Cal Lamar, paid for all the many hands that picked, baled, and loaded the ships with these products. Gazaway was such a superstructure to the South that his heirs were considered pillars of Southern society.

From a young age Cal was a scrapper, a courageous boy who tried in vain to save his five drowning brothers and sisters who all died one day as the steam-powered *Pulaski* exploded just off the North Carolina coast on a family trip up North.

Cal and Gazaway were left all alone in their Southern empire, and both father and son ran the now bustling Southern jewel. Many of the dollars spent in the city were banknotes issued for credits from the Bank of the Confederacy. The Lamar name was handwritten across the bottom of every denomination of bills presented for payment.

When you own the products, people, transport, and the money, you have the entitled feeling you own it all, bestowing the term *Southern aristocrat*. Charles Augustus Lafayette Lamar was a born aristocrat. Christened as a baby by the Marquis De Lafayette of France and given the surname of the leaders of an ancient Roman Empire, and having his last name on the dollar bill in the pockets of the Southern people; one could say he was justifiably arrogant.

At a mere insult of Cal's character, some met their fate on the dueling grounds at the hands of the young Lamar. Those who were friends of his were invited to the lavish balls and parties the Southern gentleman was well known for; Cal Lamar was the aristocratic, charming Southerner of the day. To know him was to appreciate the lineage he possessed, and he carried himself through the cobblestone streets of Savannah with a dignity that very few people could imitate, much less command.

Cal was voted in as the railroad's chief financial officer. He was president of the bank; police chief, and even owned the horseracing track in Savannah. He was financier of many business endeavors that ultimately would rule the South. He owned a copy of the cotton gin designed by Eli Whitney early in the 1800s, and housed the machine that was made for separating cotton in his warehouses along the Lamar pier during their peak operations in 1855. This building, the Cotton Exchange, was also the first established Masonic Temple in the Americas; and Savannah was the thirteenth and last colony.

Lamar was also the primary silent partner and owner of the slave ship the *Wanderer*. News of the *Wanderer*'s plans circulated the cigar rooms of Savannah. The gentlemen's clubs of the elite were abuzz with the stealthy plan of the Southern aristocrat and his intention to import slaves from Africa; even though the men knew it was a crime.

As rumor would have it, these slaves were coming into the homeport of the *Wanderer* and right up the heavily fortified and blockaded Savannah River. The rumors speculated that this ship of slaves would be unloaded right into the Savannah warehouses that Lamar himself owned.

All the gossip included stories of outrage that the law was so to be broken, and it included Lamar's certain arrest for piracy, the charge for the flagrant violation. The law strictly forbade the import of African slaves; the penalty was hanging and the North, hearing rumors of Lamar's game, watched from afar to see this obvious violation of the law, and just how far these Southerners were going to take it.

The message was clear as his secretly devised plans were relayed a success to Cal in a few words, "The *Wanderer* has arrived." Not in Savannah, no, that would not be Lamar's style. The *Wanderer*, as planned, had landed far south of the Southern port, on the deserted island of Jekyll, and almost in Spanish territory waters.

Those simple words, which were given to only Lamar, were transferred to the others in on the grand scheme; the finale of the plan was about to be carried out. The well-appointed vigilantes who would benefit from this landing sat poised for instruction; it was here, the *Wanderer*, and the hundreds of thousands of dollars in slave cargo was here. The time was now. A wave of the jewel-encrusted rings, the nod of his head, and the quiet response in one word that meant so much, "Go," came from his lips.

Go, as spoken, accounted for so much in that small phrase. It meant the final developments and instigation of the cruel plan to disburse the slaves of the *Wanderer* throughout the waiting Southern nation. This word was the start to the cleaning of the ship and the installation of the appointments of luxury that it once had. Before the ship was to sail into Savannah's port it was to lose the slave decks, the chains, and the smell of death that painted her a slaver.

The artful and master plan was carried out with great diligence. Only a few loyal souls would decommission the *Wanderer* from slaver before she made her fake return from the land she never went to. New paint was applied and new logbooks for the voyage of her travels were carefully tucked away inside the lie she now was.

The deceitful entrance to the beautiful city was well scripted. She once again bore the skin of a fine yachtsman's ship. Her soul, however, was hollow, and meant for hell. As she made port and docked as scheduled at the Lamar piers, the crowds flocked and the reporters came. All were amazed at her majestic qualities that withheld her guilt. The crew said all the things they were instructed to say. The reporters wrote what they could see and dared not mention any gossip, for the certain doom of a duel that they would find by writing such a thing. The people watched on as the fake plunders of a foreign world were unloaded for all to see; not one slave was aboard.

The ghosts of the ninety-two men, women, and children who lost their lives at the hand of the ill-fated voyage watched on as the pseudo-cargo was laid on the docks for the onlookers to see. Not one person could hear the ghostly screams of warning that this charade was all a lie. Many people felt the whispers of them in the wind that blew over the docks that day on the Savannah River.

Denial, deceit, and guilt were not a part of the face that Cal wore as he watched his fleet's pride unload the cargo of lies. He knew his real money was on a beach far from the sight of all those fooled on the docks that day. So many knew this man was behind a much greater, devious plan. Most knew also that the smart man and cunning plan would be played well by such a Southern mogul.

The word was out; the *Wanderer* was unloading a lie. The Northern reports flourished with accusations of piracy and treason laws that were to protect the souls he'd brought here. The slaves, though, could not be found. As always, acquisition reached the source, and Lamar was ready to defend his position as he revealed the facts he had placed in the plan.

The magistrates of the North were adamant that justice was to be served. Abraham Lincoln had just been elected into office, and the South knew that the country's temperature was starting to boil between the progressively dividing North and South.

Systematically, the crew and captain were put on trial. They were questioned and as always, one would give to the better good. They told of the illicit plan and unfolded the authors of its scripts to the court. Cal

Lamar was to stand trial for piracy and slavery import, which would carry a penalty of hanging by the neck until dead.

It was the words of these crewmen that would put the entire nation on the edge of their seat. The North wasn't sure that justice would be served, and the South could not believe, at least out loud, the truth. The truth, though, had yet to be proven in court. The trial date was set.

It was late in the year of 1860 as the aristocrat Cal Lamar sat in his house arrest quarters. A gentleman such as Lamar would not be put in a common jail until he was proven guilty; on the contrary, he was allowed to stay above his offices that overlooked the beautiful squares of Savannah.

There was no evidence of crime; the words of these seamen and the foraged thought of guilt from the North could not convict a man of this stature. Not even the denied thoughts of guilt from his fellow Southerner. There was no proof, no evidence, no record of wrongdoing and worst of all, no slaves were found to make it all true. Supreme Court Justice James Moore Wayne had to swing the gavel in favor of Cal Lamar's captain and crew.

Words of corruption ran through the streets of the small town and they sped to the North to the waiting ears of many. The "Captain not guilty" verdict echoed loudly in March 1861. It was clear; the South was knowingly on the brink of war. It knew that a guilty verdict would only crush one of the pillars that supported the Southern cause. To cut one's nose off to spite its face, regardless of "truth in knowing," was played.

The North, in outrage, and the South's humbled supporters drew tension already growing to the threat of war between them. The nation appeared to be waiting to unleash the coiled carnage of war that seemed to hinge on this one verdict in the Cal Lamar piracy trial.

A New Home in Chains

THE NEW SLAVES OF THE GREAT SOUTH WERE ALLOWED to bathe in the estuaries of the islands that seemed to still rock like the ocean under their feet as their bodies acclimated from sea to land. Their garments, heavily soiled and having the stench of five hundred fellow captives, reeked from their bodies with the smell of death.

Like bathing in the Congo, the men, women, and children washed themselves in the clear waters of the small, rain-filled estuaries of Jekyll. The mud from the small ponds provided the cleaning solution for them to scour the soiling deep within their brown skin. They wanted to wash away not only the smell that was enduring, but also the memories of the horror they had just lived. With every splash of water on their face their eyes closed, taking them back to the Congo and being free in the waters there. The memories of childhood play quickly ran away as the water fell from their faces to their bodies below and their eyes once again opened, revealing the pond in Georgia.

Being led to the water in small groups was strategic and controlled. The white men held steely spears that puffed of gray smoke and roared louder than any animal in the land from which the captives had come. As the group was unharnessed and unchained, the weight of their chains fell to the ground. The bleeding and infected reminder of their position would forever be scarred onto their body. The water stung these wounds as the wounded moved towards the pool's center to clean themselves.

There was a chance that once these chains were dropped to the sand, one might be able to escape. Some, if not all of the warriors held this thought, looking for a way out from this torment.

The woods provided a sanctuary of this thought, for these few had concluded that one simple step into them, and they knew the run of their life would be set in motion. It would be a run that could not fail them, giving them a second chance to run free through the woods.

As the chains hit the sand in one instance, the Congolese warrior moved towards the water as the others did from the motioning butt of the steel spear the white men held. His mind was racing now; he would make a run for freedom. Just then his training came over him. He would study his attacker, study the method and plan, strategizing his move like when he hunted the beasts in the wild. This time, though, he did not have to kill an animal, he simply had to slip into the tree coverage and elude his captor as many an animal had done to him. His eyes wider than most, he entered the water and began to bathe as the others did before him, but there was something different.

The young white guard watched the small group closely as the chains were dropped. These bound men were obviously warriors; their strengths talked to the white men with every move the warriors' bodies made. He gripped his gun higher as his scared finger made its way to the trigger. Palms sweating now and amplified by the hot sun above, the man stared intently at the bathers' every move. One slap on the back from a friend would have caused the discharge of his weapon. His eyes were as scared as the people he had to watch; their eyes met often, the captives' and his.

As cunning a hunter as the Congolese warrior was, reading the scared look on the young man's face was easy. Through the water he could smell the fear as it came to him over the strange odor that most of the white men gave off. Different than that of his people, the white man smelled to him. They reeked above the waste he washed away from his body. The thick woods were not like that of his Congolese home; he studied them well as he washed, looking for a portal through the thickness and a passage to freedom.

The warrior made his plan. He would attack the man with the look of no fear in his eyes, then run into the woods just beside the large tree; he would then use the tree for cover to his back as he sped into the woods. He didn't have to worry as much about the man with the fear in his eyes. He continued to wash his body with the nourishment Mother Earth provided. His skin soaked up the water, as well as his parched mouth; he secretly stretched his muscles as the time drew near for the group to leave the water. He knew once the chains were back on, he had no chance of freedom; being on a small island, the white men knew he had no chance at all.

The small group was motioned out of the water and the warrior walked with precision behind several others, to close his attack on the bigger man to his left. He knew he had but one chance, and he would only get to temporarily immobilize one of his captors. He simply had to outrun the scared one.

The group came towards the waiting chains on the beach; without hesitation, the warrior executed his plan. A well-placed punch to the throat struck the large guard with such a force, his reaction to the jab discharged his weapon. The gun fired aimlessly into the air, signaling all on the island to look in the direction that the warrior was seeking freedom from. The noise did cause all to watch the plan fall apart in slow motion as the warrior was trying to run through the unfamiliar Jekyll Island sand.

Feet slipping in the white mixture of granulated earth, the warrior's weak legs made his final steps toward his salvation. The unchained people of the group fell to the ground as the skirmish erupted. The loud gunshot left only two men standing in the small party there on the edge of water and freedom. The scared one turned and focused on the brown skin that stuck out from the white sand as he brought his armament down to bear. Another loud roar ripped out of the silence that lay on all who watched. It was only a few steps of freedom the warrior would feel before the musket ball ripped through his back. The man fell, to the screams of the women and children, and to the dismay of all the warriors who had thought the same plan through.

The steel ball of almost an inch of cast metal met its mark with such force it knocked him forward, contortedly facedown in the sand that seemed to bind his feet just seconds before. His eyes, open in death, gave those survivors the sign that life was no more for the man. His spirit continued to run through the woods, unseen by all.

"You killed him!" The gun butt flew from the choking sailor who had been knocked down by the warrior's last blow. The scared man looked in horror as the force of the blow barely moved his stiff and shaking body. "Now he's worth nothing!" the man said. "You'll owe the captain for this. It will come out of your pay, not mine!" He took his weapon and thrust it into the back of the dead man. No movement from the warrior indicated the truth of the worst fears of the others. There was no escaping this hell.

The groups of people were from then on forced to wash in the chains of their torture. The jingle of the steel broke the brief memories of the Congo they saw as they washed away the tears of old and new. The sailors left the dead warrior lying in the hot Georgia sun for all to see their fate should they try for freedom as he did. The only movement from the warrior was in his blood as it cascaded down the footprints in the sand. Those were the last steps of freedom the man would ever feel.

The makeshift rags were re-adorned on them, and then the captors pushed the slaves in the direction of the northern shores of the beach. No one spoke a word as the group marched into the dark, away from the bath place now guarded by the dead warrior. No one knew what words were spoken from the white man, and moved in a group in the direction they were shoved.

The morning light would come all too soon for the distraught new visitors. The rattle of chains interrupted the night as the merciless mosquitoes began to eat the blood of the unsuspecting Congolese. How could this hell be any worse? they thought as the mosquitoes relentlessly buzzed in the ears of the captive group as they tried to sleep.

The DuBignon estate was the first plantation where the group was assembled. Secluded in the southernmost part of Georgia, on an island, the DuBignon plantation provided a great cloak to the starting point for which the Congolese slaves would be readied for their long journey into the Southern lands and plantations owned by Lamar.

Several of the guardsmen were appointed to ferry the captain and first crew of the *Wanderer* to fresh quarters. The men were assembled onto carriages that were bound for Savannah, which was a day's trip away by horse-drawn carriage.

The logbooks and ship's manifest records were clutched in the hands of the man that would take the news to Lamar while he waited in the jeweled city of Savannah. The coach master cracked the whip and the horses flew to order as the carriage sped the news to the awaiting man. Lamar had drawn a successful plan for what would be one of the last slave ships to ever come to America.

Fires were started at several locations throughout the slave encampment, while several of the captives were returned to the *Wanderer* to make ready her appearance to the waiting eyes of the Lamar pier. The wood of the disassembled slave decks had an unruly odor as it burned in several piles throughout the plantation that held the captives. The big cast iron pot glowed in the early morning light. Meals of slop that were barely worthy for the farm animals were readied, and the water boiled wild rice that had been harvested from the area by the slaves that lived on DuBignon. The unsatisfying nutrition was temporary support, and ordered to be given to the slaves for the trek they were about to make. As the skies darkened on the day, the groups held close to the fire so the smoke would ward off the mosquitoes and gnats that came to prey on the tormented people once again.

The next day came and the slaves could see the *Wanderer* afloat; her sails lowered, her towering mast slightly moving in the sea. The cleaning of her bowels was complete, and the dismantlement of the cargo hold floors was piled along the beaches of DuBignon.

The morning's sun that day seemed to be carried in on the backs of the white army that approached the marooned group. Torches lit the way as the dim morning fog turned gray with smoke at their arrival. The dew had collected on the partially sleeping Congolese people who slowly awoke to the footsteps of many.

Cold, lethargic, and hungry, the group woke to see the torches and the flame-lit faces of the white men who held them. Jumping to their feet, they could feel the chains settle into the positions of many days, the infection of which ached as the black group rose to meet the lights.

More white men obviously meant more torment and more trouble. The sparse fires of the four hundred and eight cowering people were embers now; the dew and fog had dampened their brilliance. The new white men's small fires introduced them to the group as they made their way around the now standing people. The slaves watched as the torches the white men held now encircled the field.

Some of the men's eyes were not open wide, from either side, white or black; these men were not scared, and both sides knew by this sign alone that they needed to be aware. Diligent as they were, the warriors of the Congolese studied the white men's approach, not realizing that their studied stare gave way to the fact that they weren't to be reckoned with.

"Get that look off your face, boy," one of the captors said as the torch came from above and was lunged toward the steely eyed Congolese.

The fire came at the warrior swiftly and directly at his face. His hands in defense were raised but fell short of their required position when the chains stopped their movement.

The gasp of the scared added to the whoosh of the fire when it pressed into the brown skin of the warrior. His scream rang out to the others, as did the musket blast that killed his brother just two days before. Hell was here again, it seemed; it appeared every time they had their eyes open. With the calamity of the early morning taunt, the people were all wide-eyed, even the whites.

This was not the norm for any, the unpracticed herding and changes in direction were confusing to both groups. The yelling was at the black group, and some between the whites as the chaos began with the sun slowly lighting the field of the DuBignon plantation. The torches now were not a necessity for light, however, they still held torment in their flame, and every time the crackling sticks of fire were thrust at the terrified group, they would move. They were split into smaller groups and separated across the big, open field.

Several of the men who were not holding torches stood staring out over the group, holding muskets and long rifles. To the Congolese view, none of them had wide eyes of fright. The glare they held caused just the opposite as the scared eyes widened of the captors.

Divide and conquer is a simple rule. The captors had used the rule for years as they began separating the groups. The warriors watched the black advantage of outnumbered men went to the smaller white group. Their heads fell in despair as they saw the chains that bound them. Looking at the steel and rusted shackles as they weighed their hands, the men lost some of their desperation and will. The others of the group, the weaker ones, lost all of their hope. The bravest of warriors stared at the same chains issued to all.

The small groups were led off down the dirt road of the DuBignon plantation and the pace was kept from pushing of the chained ones in the rear as they moved away from the torches at their backs. The groups moved on, lumbering in the chains that made an overwhelming sound that broke the silence of the morning.

The animals along the path stared down while the group looked upon them. Constant gunshots could be heard as the group pressed forward, their shoulders on each instance trying to cover their ears as the white men killed the animals that stared in at the group. The animals were all collected and were to be prepared for meals throughout the journey into the Southern unknown. The huge cast iron pot was loaded onto a wagon at the group's rear.

Swing Low, Sweet Chariot

As the slaves were marched like a delirious bri-
gade of broken soldiers, the noises diminished slowly. The groups of slaves
were led from the main road of the DuBignon plantation. At the plantation's entrance, there were several roads that came from different directions and all converged at the big black iron gate that guarded the entrance.
Oddly, there was a sense of home here for them, as this place was their first
vision of land. All of them were at least at one point glad to see the sands of
her beach and feel it beneath their feet. It was to no one's disregard to leave
the gnats, mosquitoes, and sand spurs that nature provided to intensify
their already suffering bodies.

The day wore on, the groups divided now as they were headed down
a pine tree-laced path on Georgia's back roads. They headed into the hot
day's sun, and the chains wore deep into their already aching feet.

Half of the original group walked on into the day; the other half of
the slaves were headed off in a different direction.

There were 20 men in charge of the weary group. The man in front
set a strong pace, and the ones at the rear held guns that the group knew
outnumbered their ideas of any rebellion. They were too weak to run away.
The strongest of them knew that in their best condition, without cover
of the jungle, the guns of the men would make their mark, as they had
seen before.

The poor child who was in the group could no longer carry himself
and the chains that had been shackled to him. He also had ropes around

his tiny arms to keep the chains in place. The leg shackles wore his feet tops bare while the little boy walked; his mother spoke words of encouragement to him as the day wore on. After several miles, the tiny boy fell and could go no further. Not more than twelve years old, the small, motionless body stopped the group. The lead man of the captors turned to see the clatter as the boy's mother tried to pick him up. The break in the informal platoon formation caused two of the men at the rear to stand back from the group and raise their weapons. Their eyes were not wide with fear; on the contrary, they were squinted down the barrels of the guns pointed straight at the submissive group.

The leader of the men turned in anger and pushed his way through the crowd. He stopped at the boy, looked at the struggling mother, and grabbed her by the shoulder. With a swift jerk he stood her up, and the two men at the rear pointed their weapons wildly at all in the group. All eyes left the boy and focused swiftly at the black holes in the ends of the men's barrels.

The white man removed the chains, picked the boy up, and with some care, handed him abruptly to the large warrior standing closest to the child. No words were spoken, and none would have been understood. The look between the two men was cold yet wavering; the white man's look was that of a father with a boy the same age. To disguise this moment the two men shared, the white man turned quickly, heading back to the front, shoving his way out of the small pack. Cuffie looked forward and took in the scene of brief mercy; he had just been playing games with the boy in their Maliki village what seemed like days ago.

The group walked on. As the day was beginning to end, surely the Congolese were thinking the darkness would help as they plotted their escape from the few guards, who would easily be overpowered. The glancing looks gave much information, using eye language as they all entertained the thoughts within.

* * *

Having been split from the others at the beginning of the journey, the second group marched forward down the path of their brothers until it divided down the darkened road. All heard the gunshots from the first group killing animals for food, and they thought that the others were being slaughtered in the group ahead as before when they had heard the shots of the white man on the beach.

The open eyes and draining blood on the beach while the Congo warrior lay dying played over and over through their minds. They could only imagine that the others planned and instigated a revolt that was met with the gunfire they heard. The tension amongst the Congolese was high; the time was now, some thought, as most cowered at the noise of the gun blast ahead.

"*Kum bay yala.* (The time is upon us.) *Tiki man a!* (Run, my brothers!)" the Congolese warrior yelled. Most in the group were terrified by the certain calls of disruption.

"*Dia!* (No!)" Cory shouted as two of the Congolese men ran in chains to the road's edge, another to the left running as well.

"*Do Lamaba!* (Not now!)" the young African prince shouted, just before he was silenced by the blast of gunshots.

The crowd froze at the calamity, covering their eyes and ears from the loud noise that most had never been that close to. Most of them were sure not to look, as the escape plan on the beach, just days before, had resulted in death.

The group had all been chained together to prevent such a dash. The freedom seekers would have made movement, had all been brave as they. But the small ones, scared as they were, made a human anchor to prevent such an escape. The few men fell in place not more than a couple of feet from their beginning as the shots were fired just inches away from them.

The onlookers, not knowing that the white man would not shoot them for fear of having to bear the cost of a slave, stared down at the three would-be escapees, all still awkwardly trying to run as they lay on the ground tied to their brothers of the Congo. Their eyes were wide with fear now as the miserable plan unfolded quickly and they fell to the ground as well, the white men quickly descending upon them.

They lay there for all to see as the first signs of a whip were falling on the weak men lying there. Time after time the men were struck as the leather from the whips whelped and marked their skin. The men being beaten screamed, as did the women and children onlookers. The men and women watched again as another faint dream escaped their minds of freedom.

After the merciless beating under the protective eyes of the others with weapons, the men were reassembled and forced to walk next to their brothers; not a word was spoken. All had the thought now that this would surely never end.

Cory spoke out, head facing down and said, "*Dim bu la*, (I will tell you,)" with his face to the earth disguising the direction of the boy-king's order. The Maliki Congolese knew the voice of the informally appointed boy-king but the white men did not. The group settled; the white men supposed the unseen voice had directed them to silence.

The lead man from the white captors saw fear in the eyes of the crowd. He knew from watching the man with the whip beat the men lying there that the whip only brought hatred that could be seen in the eyes of those who watched. Pulling his revolver out and firing it three times over the heads of the group gave fear this time and not a panic. The waving of the smoking barrel brought the crowd to movement as the white men shoved them back to a walk down the road. The walk, slightly downhill, gave indication to the brilliantly trained hunters that the low land ahead would bring water, a sign that had terrible memories of before.

As the familiar smell of the salt water came to the terrified group, it brought back memories of their terrible journey across the sea. The group of travelers walked slowly as the trees opened to reveal Saint Andrew

Sound, a vast body of water that opened to the ocean just off Jekyll Island. Out in the channel sat an all-too-familiar sight; the *Wanderer*.

Her masts high and sails drawn to the top of them, the now gallant sea conqueror sailed toward the ocean. The Congolese could hear the faint sounds of the ropes and sails of the slave ship as the stern of the ship presented itself to view; the ship from hell had sailed off. No one saw the souls of the ninety-two men, women, and children who died looking back at them when the empty *Wanderer* made to sea and off to the waiting docks in Savannah just up the coast.

Louder than the guns and seeming to last so long, a steam whistle roared up ahead of the terrified group. The long brass face of the whistle spewed steam from its mouth as the captain pulled on the chain. A second long roar silenced the crowd as they stared at the whistle's face, its mouth still open like that of a totem pole and the mythical beings of the Congo, warning of danger.

Down the banks and onto the wooden docks, tied to its moors was another ship. Unlike the *Wanderer*, there was a deep, thunderous roar that came from within the floating beast. Black smoke bellowed from the tall, black tubes at her sides and huge wheels like that of the wagon sat on either side of the *Lamar*. Her waiting crew stood on the decks to receive its cargo.

These men on board the roaring ship stood at attention; they were there dressed beautifully as kings of the floating mass. Perfected appointments gave way to the steely glare that they gave back to the scared and amazed group. The whistle wailed again and the chained group was led to a holding area below the decks of the waiting steamship.

It, too, was lit like the *Wanderer*'s holds, but the floors and the walls were not the same; they were smooth, well-worn, and clean. The crowd was packed into the cargo hold. In contrast to the four-foot ceiling of the slave decks in the *Wanderer*, the ten-foot ceilings seemed to tower as the crowd, now all standing, looked upward at the lights in their place high above them in the large, dark wooden room.

Once the loading was complete the whistle wailed, followed with three short blasts, giving signal to the brightly dressed crew above to cast the lines that held her to the dock. The scurry of footsteps was heard from above the terrified group.

Whoosh! came from the rear of the vessel as the steam engines came to life. *Whoosh! Whoosh! Whoosh!* The engine noise was almost deafening to the terrified cargo. The ship lunged forward, causing the frightened crowd to all take a step back at the same time. The wheels outside the portholes came to life and the ship moved through the water as the deafening sound of the steam engine propelled her.

Mr. Lamar lay down in his elegant private quarters aboard the *Lamar*. The air that blew through the portholes of the suite was like the night air that had blown cold over the black seas of the Atlantic that ill-fated night as the pride of the Lamar shipping fleet pushed through the restless winds and waters that fought her progress North. Weary from the journey from Savannah, Lamar drifted off to sleep from the throbbing steam engines and into the reoccurring nightmare of his mother and sisters who had died that night aboard the *Pulaski*.

The dream was as clear as it had been since he was a child; he lay in the bed slightly twitching from nightmarish dream that was once again haunting his sleep.

* * *

Having just a few hours earlier departed the bustling docks of Charleston Harbor, the steam packet *Pulaski* trudged through the June night air and the restless seas. On board was the Gazaway Bugg Lamar family, owners of the shipping line, along with one hundred fifty passengers and thirty-nine crewmembers. They had all just bedded down for the evening around ten o'clock that night.

Having rested his eyes briefly during the beginning of the second leg of this voyage, the first mate sat in his stateroom staring at the wooden ceiling of his cabin. He was a young man, around twenty years old, with blonde hair and very white skin for a first mate at sea quite a bit. The quiet, practiced commands he would shout out to the crew ran through his head silently as he played out his imaginary role of being a steam packet captain.

The dank, wooden confines of the cabin and the musty salt air that had soaked into the old oaken hull made it easy for the ship's movement to maintain the young sailor's trance. His stare, past the knot in the ceiling's wood, was broken by the rhythmic jerk of the ship as she crashed through the waves and the quiet aches and moans of the wooden hulk. A steady muffled roar from the twin steam engines provided a tranquil vibration as he drifted in and out of his sleepy state.

"Mr. Hibbert!" followed a sharp knock on Samuel's door that caused him to sit up straight from his trance at the knot in the ceiling. Another loud and repetitive knock came. "Mr. Hibbert!"

Samuel sprang from his quarter's bed, boots still on and the covers neatly folded down to the foot of the cot. "Coming!" Samuel said as he grabbed to secure the last few buttons at the top of his shirt.

The door to the stateroom opened briskly and the ship's night watchman burst into Samuel's quarters. The startled look from Samuel to the newcomer let him know that "coming" didn't mean "come in." Samuel took a few groggy steps toward the small cabin door.

"Sorry, sir!" the young messenger said as he stood in a full and finely pressed uniform holding a stern salute with a non-wavering hand just above his brow. "The captain has requested your command to the main deck, sir!" With one swift move, the look on Samuel's face changed. He grabbed his sailing hat and jacket and barged past the messenger's arm to exit the room. "Night shift on the boilers has been appointed, sir!" the messenger informed Samuel as he led the two down the dark, poorly lantern-lit wooden hall to the stairs up to the main deck. "Captain Dubois is at the main steerage, sir!" the young man said, and saluted Samuel as he took his first steps onto the dark wooden floor of the ship's main deck.

"Very good! Check the engine rooms and secure the decks and guests. Report to me at the completion of your rounds," Samuel said as he saluted back and spun sharply on the leather soles of his perfectly shined boots that seemed to crackle as they turned on top of the damp wooden planks below him.

"Aye, sir!" the young man replied, now turning for the aft of the ship towards the engine rooms as directed.

Samuel walked towards the raised steerage deck near the ship's center. He adjusted the stiff collar on his woolen naval jacket to soften its irritation to his neck. He accustomed his eyes in a calm stare at a slowly swinging lantern near the steerage door that creaked slightly as it ground against the steel hook protruding from the wall of the wheelhouse.

The door to the wheelhouse room flung open suddenly, startling him from his gaze. He stood in the dark shadows of the lantern while the chief engineer stepped from the steerage room and onto the deck where Samuel was standing.

"He'll be just fine, sir!" The engineer spoke with a disrespectful tone back towards the open room from which he'd just stepped. The lantern flickered as the door swung just inches away from its perch and was caught at the last second before it slammed into the wall of the wheelhouse. A very abbreviated salute came from the engineer as he turned to shut the door.

Samuel quickly stiffened his posture and saluted the engineer as he stood there wide-eyed at the higher-ranking officer, which had caught Samuel's paled face in the lantern's light. The engineer grumbled past Samuel with yet another sarcastic jerk of his hand, in even less of a salute than he had just given the captain. The engineer's coarse hands, blackened by coal, swung down from his galvanized face as he barged his way past the scared young man towards the engine room at the ship's stern.

"Sir! Reporting for duty, sir!" Samuel said sharply as he entered the wheelhouse.

Capt. Davis Dubois stood staring at the front window overlooking the promenade deck and into the black, misty air that seemed to cover the ocean that night.

Average height, with a slim French build, he stood motionless, his dark eyes seeming to glare into his own reflection from the glass that he stood in front of. The tassel on his French sailing hat moved with the ocean as he stared into the abyss.

"You know, Mr. Hibbert, there are 143 souls aboard this ship right now!" he announced with a slight French tone that made its way through his otherwise perfect English accent. Samuel stood silent. He knew the captain, and he also knew he wasn't to interject, since it was not a question. "They have put their lives in my hands, just as you have, as they all lay down to sleep tonight," the captain said, leaning down slightly to the left and picking up the fine blue Wedgewood cup and saucer that sat quietly on the map table. "Do you know why, Mr. Hibbert?" the captain asked as he glared up from his survey of the tea.

Samuel knew better than to answer this either, because as many times before, the captain was about to answer it for himself. "They trust me...they trust my crew, and they trust in this ship," he said as he stood staring out the night-blackened window that mirrored his every move. He took a sip from the finely printed blue and white Wedgewood cup and placed it back down on the map table. The captain turned to Samuel, who was still standing at attention. "And I...I place my trust in you now!" he said as he turned and put his hand on the young man's shoulder. He flipped the golden tassels of the first mate's jacket with his thumb. With a slight squeeze of the thick cotton fabric, he said, "Hold her at 210°. Keep the engines at 95 percent until the winds from the north settle."

Samuel snapped his right hand to his forehead. "Aye, Captain!" he attentively said. The captain smiled and with a very subtle salute, walked out of the wheelhouse, closing the door behind him.

Samuel turned to the helmsman, whose diligent forward stare was unbroken until the door shut fully. Samuel gave a short salute to the helmsman he had grown up with in the Lamar shipyards. "Jamison," he muttered as he walked to the table where the maps were laid out in the corner of the steerage. "What was that about?" Samuel asked as he leaned on the table with both hands flat down. Across the table he rested on what was a neatly detailed map of the eastern seaboard of the Americas. Its curled edges were weighted by small leather bags of sand.

"You mean the coordinates, sir?" Jamison respectfully responded, both hands still placed firmly at ten o'clock and two o'clock on the wheel of the ship.

"No, the engineer. Is there a problem there?" Samuel asked, turning his head from the table.

"No, sir." Jamison seemed to exhale and dropped his guard just slightly. "The engineer is training someone new on the engines and the captain was ensuring that there was to be no issue."

"I see. As well as he should. Very good then...ship's position?" Samuel said as he leaned up from the table and stared out the window into the night air.

Jamison craned his head slightly and said, "The lighthouse is just there, sir. We are just past the breakwaters of Cape Hatteras."

Hibbert looked up from the map and stared at his reflection in the glass as the faint glimpse of the whitewater crashed onto the rocks in the distance.

Below deck young Charles Lamar sat in his stateroom aboard the *Pulaski* with his father on one of the lower decks of the ship. His father, Gazaway, had just blown the flickering light out in the lantern that sat next to the bed. In the darkness Charles could hear the mechanism shut on the lantern's door.

"Father?" young Charles said to the dark. "Why do Mother and the girls stay in a room so far away?" the 14-year-old asked his father as the red glow of the wick's end was all that he could see.

"The women and children stay on the upper decks so they can have the portholes and the breeze that will keep them from being sick while we are at sea," Gazaway said in a quiet voice as he pulled the covers up and shifted into a comfortable position in his stateroom bed. "We men have to stay below them, because we are stronger than they are." Charlie smiled as he pulled the fine linen sheet up close to his chin and took in a deep breath of the new fabrics he was swaddled in.

"Men," he said quietly to himself as he smiled and closed his eyes to sleep. The quiet rumble of the steam engines drifted in the background.

Charlie Lamar was falling off to sleep just five minutes later with the gentle movement of the ocean and the sound of rushing water just on the other side of the wooden hull that his bed was up against. With the sound of a lightning strike that was just a few feet away, a shimmer from an explosion ran through the wooden ship. Eyes wide with fear, Charlie sat up straight in bed. The sound was like a cannon being fired, followed by a mechanical shuddering and the sounds of screams that echoed down the once quiet wooden halls of the ship. "Father!" Charlie screamed as he could hear the clamor and rustling coming from the other side of the room while his father tried to light the lantern. He could see the match strike and the little door of the lantern swinging as the small match burst into flames, interrupting the dark. His father lit the lantern with one shaking hand and motioned for Charlie to stay put with the other as he got up and made his way toward the cabin door.

* * *

Samuel Hibbert had just shut the door to the wheelhouse and stepped outside for some fresh air. He walked to the port side of the ship to get a better look at the lighthouse that shimmered in the distance. A familiar shadow approached from the bow as he stood next to the railing staring out over the ocean to the moonlit, white shores of the Carolina coast. A light splash of water drifted up from the side of the ship as one of the larger waves crashed against the hull. Samuel looked up from the impact with a cumbersome smile and seawater dripping from his face. "Now that'll wake you up!" he said to the shadow as Cooper walked out of the darkness and into the faint light of the lantern's hanging from the steerage house. Just then the rear of the ship exploded in the night. Samuel was slammed against the rail and onto the ship's deck as orange fire and splintered wood from the explosion flew through the air. He stared at the dark wooden planking of the deck just inches from his eye and watched it blur into his unconsciousness.

* * *

Charlie sat uncomfortably in the dark room as his father walked into the hallway of the ship; he knew something was terribly wrong. He spun out of the bed; putting his feet down, he could feel water on the floor that had not been there just moments before. Charlie shot across the room to the doorway and into the faint light of the lanterns that lit the corridor. The rumbling of the engines now was quiet, and the screams and footsteps above caused a sense of urgency in the young man. He felt the water rise higher on to his bare feet. The wood began to splinter in the walls next to the bed where he had just been lying. His own intuition led him into the corridor and to follow the others who were urgently walking down the dark hall towards the stairs that led to the upper deck. The screams of the women and children were much clearer now as Charlie entered the stair-well that led to the promenade deck. He turned to see a glimmer of water starting to form on the floor behind him as he ascended the stairs.

"Sir! Sir!" Cooper yelled at Samuel as he lay on the deck of the ship. "Sir!" he said, rolling Samuel over and slapping his face.

"What happened?" Samuel managed after Cooper pulled him upward from the deck.

"The starboard boiler exploded, sir! The ship...she is awash!"

A just panic set into Samuel. His thoughts were reeling as he rose to his feet. He felt a sharp pain from his forehead as the blood rushed to his head. He instinctively reached up and could feel the opening in his skin just at the hairline, and the matted hair that was now soaked in what he imagined was blood. He pulled his hand down to reveal the moonlit crimson that stained his hand. The sound of wood cracking under his feet brought the dizzying reality into focus to the young first mate. "Man the lifeboats!" he screamed at Cooper, and he pushed him towards one of the tiny boats, then ran across the deck towards the steam whistle chain. With all his might he tugged on the swinging chain's wooden handle to release the steam and alert the passengers. The whistle's steel mouth opened and poured out a long belch of steam that gurgled with water as the screech ripped through the night air. "Abandon ship!" Hibbert gasped with what seemed his last breath.

* * *

The whistle's blast drew Cal Lamar from his nap. He awoke, like a thousand times before, sweating and panting as though he was still on the exploding wreck.

The cargo holds were packed with Lamar's weary travelers and they lightly tossed side to side while briefly at sea as the ship made its way into the Atlantic Ocean just outside of Calibogue Sound. The group inside would have fallen at the waves' movement, had they not been packed so tightly as human cargo. The dark remembrance of the ship's motion gave the people on board her a grave concern as the engine and wheels roared on.

It was not long that *the Lamar* was at sea; the captain sailed her a very short distance up the coast and past the gray banks of Savannah Beach, then turned the vessel into the mouth of the Savannah River. The few slaves in the light of the portholes that beamed inside could hear the sounds of waves crashing on the beach and seagull screams from afar. The brilliantly dressed people standing freely on the shores of the beach waved at the passing ship.

The people inside the boat's hold, on the far side of the boat that could see only water, murmured amongst themselves and asked where the noises were coming from.

"We are at a beach; many people are waving clothes at us and smiling," one of the viewing Congolese replied.

A short ride now up the river for the group as the captain of the *Lamar* made her way past the many sandbars that were lurking just feet under the water's surface. The marsh grass and cattails were seen on both sides of the ship now as she made her way down the river Savannah.

Within minutes, the cargo portals provided a view to the port side of the steamboat of a great wall. The stone walls of Fort Pulaski rose up high above the green marsh and filled the small scene. Her walls seemed to go on forever and filled all of the portholes in view to the left of the group. Fort Pulaski's walls were topped with well-appointed men like those on the deck above them. Spaced in point were her cannons that were eerily pointed at the gazers within the *Lamar* as they stared at the holes in the cannon's ends. These holes looked like the ones from the guns used to herd the poor souls aboard the ship but much, much bigger. Only one cloth waved above the men on a high flagpole, a red and blue cloth with bright-white stars.

Soon the scenery changed back to the riverbanks and marsh grass as each in the group tried for a glimpse of what was outside. Occasionally yelling and screams of exuberance from the people who lived along the river's shore could be heard. A passing ship going the other way led the crowd inside to think that there was another group of Congolese passing by them. The pumping sound of the steam engine slowed, as did the giant wheels that spun outside the back portholes.

More buildings began to come into sight; a tall grain tower, and docks like the ones they walked to the ship on and then, the start of a beautiful row of buildings began to line the banks of the river. The city of Savannah was being presented in slow motion to the port side portholes and all on board were now taking it in. Even the men on top of her decks, with the shuffle of footsteps, gave the diligent stamp of the boots on the wood. All eyes were looking west to the beautiful and differently colored city on the river. Several boats of various sizes were lying along her walls; men were like ants walking and working on the docks that lined the entrance to the city. On one of the buildings the huge words "Lamar Pier," came into view; those inside did not know what it was a sign of.

It seemed like the city began to pour with people of all colors, shapes, and sizes. All were dressed differently. There were women with parasols and men with top hats. They were all waving, with white gloves and hats in the air. Cheers could be heard from River Street as they gravitated towards the big wooden docks in front of the Lamar Building. It made the Congolese inside the boat feel warm and somewhat welcome, as it seemed they were now cheering louder and in unison. Whistles and bells from the other ships rang; the eyes of the group inside the boat's hold widened. These wide eyes looked on as the boat they were on almost chugged to a stop. The loud whistle from the deck above blew one long blast, and the crowd seemed to cheer louder. A slight wisp of excitement came over the captive souls.

The people inside took in portholes full of the events as the light started to dim in the shadows of a mighty ship that was coming into view and was slowly making her way to the docks in the foreground. The crowd inside the *Lamar* gasped as they realized it was the vessel from hell that had brought them to this wretched place. The whistle's screech startled the mortified people as the *Wanderer* and her crew came into view.

The Savannah crowd was now at full roar at the arrival of the ship, and not the one the slaves were on. The steam engines once again roared to life as the chug and compression could be felt of the ship's motors. The mighty wheels outside began to spin as the captives looked on in dismay. The beautiful city was disgraced in their eyes by the ship that tried to kill them for forty-five days. Her captain waved back at the waiting people of Savannah, then he turned to look one last time at the *Lamar*. He knew his plan had worked as he watched the steamship carry the cloaked cargo past the unsuspecting city.

No one was ever the wiser; not one of the townsmen of Savannah would know the suspected slave cargo was in the *Lamar* as it made its way up the Savannah River.

The ship and the city faded away, and it seemed that the green marsh grass went on for miles. No more buildings, no more cheers, and no more of the *Wanderer*. An occasional passing ship or small fishing boat would be seen, and the people on board them waved, not ever seeing the cargo of souls below the *Lamar*'s decks. They waved in respect to the Lamar name brandished on the side of the vessel and the majesty of the steam engine's thick, black smoke. The *Lamar* pressed on, up the Savannah River to its destination; Augusta, Georgia.

Just a few hours north of the excitement, the docks of Augusta came into view of the portholes. So close, in fact, that the wood of them seemed to hit the ship as they made port in the northern town. The shadow of the ropes flying to the waiting hands of men on the docks drew the boat near and rested it on the docks. The docks above the portholes blocked out all of the light from coming inside. Once again for the Congolese, it was dark.

"Move out!" came bellowing down the hatch as it was cracked open, bringing in the light from above.

"Come on, get!" was heard as the men from above descended into the dark hold.

All these men bore guns and all had the steely eyes of deceit. The scared group moved opposite of each one of them, while the white men made their way to the back of the crowd, pushing and shoving the scared, and avoiding the larger ones. The most done to these large warriors was a simple, "What you looking at, boy?" and there was no testament behind their words. The group was herded out of the ship's hold to the docks and land above. The ride this time on water was much shorter, and the stay on land would be much longer.

The soft Georgia winds blew through the South Carolina fields that they would be coming to know for just a day. The lumber mill there was full of freshly cut trees and the smell of the beautiful richness of pine oil. This was the first machinery like this any of them had ever seen. The once towering pine trees were stacked high and then handed over to a huge spinning wheel of teeth. The steam engine of the saw roared as the wheel spun at such great speed. They could not believe their eyes as it ripped smoothly through the tree. The loud noise was not so much from the engine; they felt it was from the trees weeping as they were ripped in half. These peoples' culture led them to know the kindness of Mother Nature, and she provided all living things from animal to tree. But these white men seemed impressed with the cruelty that came from such enormity as they heard the tree scream from the teeth of the beast. These men had no respect for life; not that of the Congolese, and not that of the world around them.

The lumberyard was quite active, mostly filled with black men much like themselves, and just a few white men. They were a lot like the Congolese, but these black men had no chains, and were wearing clothes like the white men. Most of the whites had guns on their side, and several white men were perched in high towers, thirty feet tall, made from pine logs and split wood with a small, fashioned roof above them. From this height they could see over the crowd well, and they pointed their rifles downward at the wondering group of men below.

A heavyset white man and a very skinny black man who followed closely behind him approached from the cabin at the end of the yard. The black man smiled the entire time. They walked up to the group and spoke to the one white man who had been on the boat and yelled the loudest. After a brief talk, the one white man turned and yelled to the other whites who were at the rear and on the sides of the group: "Gather them around so they can hear, now!"

The gun-toting white men pushed the Congolese into a half-circle around the three men at the front. The portly white man said, "You all listen to him," as he pointed to the black man in between the two whites. "He is going to translate what I am saying."

"Tell them!" Loudly he spoke, as if it mattered.

Clearing his throat he said, "Tell them that if they try to run off, the men in the towers will shoot and kill them."

The little black man stepped a half-step forward and yelled in broken Congolese: "These men are evil! They will kill you for even looking at them wrong! The men above you in the perch will not miss if you try to escape!" The wide-eyed group looked up to the towers that were around the lumberyard.

The white men looked at each other as though the translator's direction was heard and understood by the group. The Congolese smiled, as this was the first time since Africa there was any communication between them and any other.

"Tell them that they will only be here for a little while, and then they will go to the Butler Plantation, just the other side of the river there," the portly man said.

The translator spoke loudly: "I am so sorry for you; I know what you have been through. I, too, wore those chains. These terrible people will move you from here, across the river," he said as he pointed across the river. The group again followed his gestures with their heads. The whites acknowledged with a look at the translation.

The white man spoke again. "Tell them that someone will bring them some water in a little bit and feed them before we make the trip."

The translator cleared his throat. "Oh, brothers, please don't look at these men wrong. When they bring you food and drink, eat it and smile. When they say something to you, smile, or they will hit you. Start smiling now." The whole group looked up and smiled on queue.

The white man dumbly thought the translator was doing as told and thought the Congolese appreciated the food and water about to come.

"Now, sit down and shut up, and don't say a word to anyone or I will personally put my boot up your ass," the other white man from the boat said. "Now tell them that, boy!" The two white men laughed.

"You, strong warriors; I know you could kill these men dead with your hands. Don't try to; they will shoot you dead in front of your family and leave you to rot in the sun as a sign." He motioned his hands downward for all to sit. "Now sit on the ground and do not try to speak. Smile the whole time or the wrath of these men will come to you." The group sat and smiled as the two white man looked at each other, knowing he had said more than they had wanted translated.

"Come on, boy," the portly man said as they retreated back to the cabin they came from.

About ten minutes later, several women came with buckets of water and began to feed the crowd of waiting Congolese. Not a word was spoken, not a smile was broken. Those words were the first they'd heard aloud in two months. The words of the man burned into their heads now as the women walked amongst them with smiling faces. They all knew that the smile was fake, and many days of horror were suppressed behind it. The new Congolese faintly smiled back, not yet perfecting the best advice they would ever hear, and the hardest to practice as they sat there in the sun.

The break from travel did not seem to last very long. The white man came out from the shaded area and walked towards the group. The little portly man and his translator came out to speak to them again. They approached the sitting group of people. "Now get up!" the fat man said. No one moved.

The little interpreter yelled loudly in Congolese: "Get up now! Please hurry!"

His words were followed by two gunshots into the ground from the lead white man's pistol. The group sprang up quickly, looking straightaway at the little black man.

"Now I'm going to let Tom here go down to the Butler farm with you," he said. "And, Tom"—the little black man turned—"if you let them get out of hand I'll beat you good, boy, ya hear?" His words came with a swift slap on the back. Tom turned and smiled.

"Benjamin," the portly man added, "Old Tom here is going with you down to Butler; he is going to help you get this lazy-ass group of slaves cleaned up. Tom, now, you do whatever Benjamin says, you hear?"

"Yes, sa!" replied Tom obediently, almost bowing this time, hat in hands over his chest.

"Now get in the back of that wagon and tell those niggers to follow you," the portly white man said with force.

Tom sprang into action. "Thank you, massa. Thank you, massa," he said, then he climbed into the back of the wagon.

"Tell them they're gonna take a little walk and follow you, and listen hard," the fat man said.

Old Tom spoke to the crowd and rallied them to a group ready to travel.

The fat man turned to Benjamin and said, "You should unshackle their feet, or all this walking is going to make them lame from their leg irons. And," he added, "if you lay a hand on ma boy Tom here, he will tell me. You don't want him to tell me you hurt him. Got it, son?" he said to the white leader of the group.

Looking up at the smiling Tom, who could not hear the direction, "Got it," Benjamin said, looking at Tom in disgust, as he had to ride with a black man and be somewhat nice to him. "Men, you and you. Come here!" Benjamin roared. "Now!" With rage the man said, "We gonna unchain they feet...you two"—pointing at two other men—"put your weapons right at their heads. Anyone moves and you take their head off." He looked up at Tom. "Now you tell them that, boy! And tell them to line up so we can take off their leg irons. Be real clear, boy, that if they so much as try to run, they will be shot dead where they stand. Tell 'em now, boy!" he shouted at the wide-eyed Tom in the back of the wagon.

Tom, perched higher than all in the back of the wagon, and in plain view like that of a prophet, spoke diligently to the Congolese prisoners.

"Dear brothers, I want you to form a line. The white man is going to unchain your feet. Do not try to run at all; they will kill you, or cut half of your foot off. Don't do anything to make these terrible people hurt you. Trust me, brothers they will, they will!"

The Congolese formed a line and the white men began to remove the leg irons that had been put on them in Africa. The irons had cut into their skin, and the blood now covered the black iron. One by one the Congolese moved by the wagon. They could hear the people in front wince as the men grabbed the leg chains that cut into the open wounds again as they were released. The chains, one by one, made their sound one last time as they were dropped into the back of the wagon.

Tom looked down at the bloody pile of chains that was growing and looked over to the disparaged crowd. In a beautiful voice the man began singing to the crowd, "Swing low, sweet chariot. Coming for to carry me home..." The whole crowd eased some as the black men moving logs in the distance joined Tom in song.

The whole camp was singing now as the angelic voices of the camp's enslaved women carried the notes to make a beautiful song. The chains gone now, the Congolese heard the music and listened.

End of the Antebellum

THE BUSTLING STREETS THAT MADE UP THE CITY MARKET of Savannah created a beautiful backdrop to the dirt beneath its ambience. The market itself was different than most in the South as the smell of the confederate jasmine that climbed the walls and fresh fruit emanated through the market place. The Savannah City Market was tied to the Lamar pier on River Street and was an outlet that shipped out the precious cotton and sugar throughout the world. The world reciprocated by bringing fruits and flowers from its far reaches, all gladly traded for cotton on the piers of Lamar.

Amongst these colorfully dressed people stood James Bryan. Bryan was a curator of these marketplaces and one of Savannah's most prominent businessmen. Snide and somewhat villainous, he sneered as he smoked a pipe, which was filled with the finest tobacco grown in Cuba as he watched the women look upon the products to be had. They would motion for the servants with them to pick up the items of their instruction.

"Mattlind! I do declare, whilst I am trying to buy good fruit you're dropping it like it don't matter!" the lady turned and yelled at the servant girl.

"I iz so sorry, Mrs. Cowart." The small black girl picked up the apples that fell from her overladen basket. The merchant jumped to the ground as well and grabbed up some of the rolling fruit.

"Mrs. Cowart, don't you worry none about these apples. I'm going to give you fresh ones for you and yours." The street market merchant spoke sharp and loud as in higher respect to this woman than those around and he wanted them to hear it. He sat the few apples behind him on the wooden table and began to polish their replacements. "I'll get the wife to peel 'em and make me a pie," he laughed.

The young black slave looked with sorrow to the ground as Mrs. Cowart watched the merchant and slave give respected way to her presence.

Mrs. Cowart was the widow of a respected and highly decorated war hero. The people of Savannah loved her so much, showing her the respect they would have given her late husband. She welcomed it with a beautiful Southern smile. "Well thank you, kind, sir," came the soft words from her porcelain face.

James Bryan watched the grandeur of the Savannah-scape laid out in front of him. It was by far the prettiest part of the city as the women at the market spent the riches of their husbands, and the merchants, dressed in charade, were bound to their commanded respect.

At the end of the street was where the men of the day shopped. They browsed in astute attire, top hats and all the appointments of a civilian general. Their pipes smoked of tobacco raised in the fields of Georgia as they kept to the South as much as possible. They strolled along the stone street and looked upon the horses and mules that were in the stables at the end of Johnson Square. With their white-gloved hands behind them, a simple gesture would set his entourage to task to purchase his bidding.

This particular group were following one man and marching in order, and kept to the order without direction. First came the sons of the man, dressed one step down from their father, but still the informal stripes of respect flew from them as their God-given right would have it. Following behind the sons would be the white slave masters, in wait of direction from the high command to be passed down the lineage ranks and then to them. Once the slave master received these orders, they were to be dispatched out to several slaves who followed the group. The well-appointed aristocratic assembly made their way along the market square.

The brilliant smell of Bryan's Cuban tobacco gave way to the men circling the square. Its aroma carried itself amongst them and gave proof of the riches that came with the rich tobacco. This merchant was different than all the others of the day. His product was the most valuable of them all along the market there, and his rich smoke gave proof of it. He slowly drew from his pipe again and gave out another puff of Cuban smoke to the grand marshals of each parade. His products stood behind him in cages; they were the slaves to be had.

The slaves were in cages behind the rich aristocrat, Mr. Bryan. The fine, steel black bars were better than most, like his tobacco the man puffed into the air. Their eyes were white and wide, and skin dark and rich, which gave proof that the most precious of items to be had at the market were here, behind the bars.

"I say, sir, may I see your best slave?" the father of the aristocratic group said. "I am in need of a strong slave who can handle the plowing of my fields. I had a boy get hurt the other day."

Without a word, Bryan turned. His long, dark cloak spun like a prima donna's dress as he made his way towards the cage at his rear. A large white man rose from his position behind Bryan and grabbed his pistol, pointing it at the slave in the cage. His gun came from the right hand first, before his left hand ever grabbed for the keys that hung heavy and still on his waist. The look in his eyes gave scare to all but the steely eyed employer who watched the man begin his job.

"You and you, get out here!" the man said, almost with a growl. He then waved the pistol in the direction of the two slaves' heads.

The crowd parted like the sea, as did the parading squires, who moved back from their positions. The fresh group of wild men were being released from the cages as only the cocking of pistols added to the silence for all who watched.

Slowly walking forward, the African men stood there in the Southern sun as it shined through the majestic oaks and reflected off the Africans' skin. The men, strong and tall, stood in handcuffs, and tightened their muscles as had been instructed to them before they were caged. The process that preceded this show was similar to the stable of horses down the way. The men were bathed and cleaned with fragrant soaps, their hair combed with a brush, and their skin wiped with lard to give shine and a healthy appearance to the torso.

"These are the finest niggers that can be had, sir!" Bryan spoke, his pipe now waving like a king's scepter. "Take a look; I assure you, they won't bite! Actually, that pistol there assures you that they won't bite." His slight chuckle set the now growing crowd to laughing along with him.

The men in the circle of bystanders stood looking downward as the buyer motioned his glove for the slave master behind him to inspect the potential of purchase.

Without hesitation, the slave master started the process. "Open your mouth, boy!" He shoved his thumb beside the slave's teeth.

The slaves had been instructed beforehand, and knew to open their mouth as wide as possible as the man ran his fingers around the inside of the slave's mouth. He then removed his one hand and shut the man's mouth with the other, which began his inspection of the head. Grabbing the ears, he pulled the man's head down to see his hair and inspect for lice.

He then ran his hand simultaneously down the side of the man's jaw and neck, listening intently for a whimpered sound of lameness. Grabbing his arms, he raised them high by the chain above the man's head and jetted his ear toward the black man's mouth, again listening for any sign of pain or fatigue. All that was heard was the blinking of his eyes and his now heavier snort as the wide-eyed slave gave way to the bidding of the slave master.

"How much?" came from the top-hatted leader of the aristocrats. "What's your asking price?"

The merchant turned and came straight to the man; their faces were close, and the smoke from the Cuban tobacco spilled the words, "Three thousand dollars."

The top hat was leaned back on the man's head as the smoke and the presence made him step backwards.

"Three thousand dollars!" came straightaway and sharply with no respect in the voice of the inspecting slave master.

The top hat and sons looked on as their dog "the slave master" had entered the ring for negotiations. The two men who stood behind Bryan pulled their weapons and crossed their arms, facing the negotiations.

The now stammering voice of the top hat replied, "Is that the best one can do?"

Bryan quickly remarked, "Unless you want both; then I can do better."

"Pay him, son!" the top hat said as he spun in retreat with his dignity squarely placed in his hands now by the character of the man Bryan.

The boy pulled from his coat a large leather pouch with a small leather tie and proceeded to pay out the three thousand that Bryan had asked for. Quickly the other slave was re-caged and the little parade of aristocrats led their new purchase away. The two pistoleers sat back in position and un-cocked their intimidating weapons.

Bryan looked at the bank notes he had been given by the young man; "the Bank of Commerce" in bold print across the top of each. A beautiful picture of the ship *Wanderer* was set on one of the bills' denomination and the *Rawlins* on the other. Both had pictures of slaves in the fields holding up their overflowing baskets of cotton and the same man, G. B. Lamar's signature, on both.

The City Market Square regained its luster after the wild men were re-caged and the sounds of leather on stone and marketers' broadcasting the likes of their wares took over from the brief slave sale. The parasols and massive oaks gave shade from the hot sun as Bryan slowly leaned back against the post and observed his money now over the pleasant and color-ful crowd that did not look his way often. The man puffed his fine tobacco again, laying bait to the nose as he counted his money for a third time. The reflection of the Confederate bills twinkled in his eyes as the smoke slipped from the grin on his steely face.

In the distance, something started the displacement of the crowd, like that of a wagon team coming through the people. The small parades of civilians parted as the calamity drew near the Bryan cages. It was not a horse team at all that had created this parting of the sea of people, it was the single top hat; a foot taller than most, leaned sharply forward as though it was holding onto the man's head. The up-and-down motion of the hat gave signal that the man parting the sea of people was coming at an abrupt pace.

The blonde beard came down from the hat like a strap, while the sun-lightened mustache and eyebrows of its wearer accented it. The silk suit in light China blue gave a glimmer to the afternoon sun as the burly man approached in silence. The top of the glossy black cane matched to every other step of the black shoes that clattered loudly across the stones of the roadway. The right hand laden with gold rings pulled the ivory pipe from the man's mouth as the sweet smell of Cuban tobacco matched that of Bryan's. The crowd now hushed as the well-appointed man stopped in front of Bryan's slave trading post.

He stopped and whispered a few short words to Bryan and then made off through the more glamorous parts of the market. His smile and brief bows gave part to the sea of ladies in Savannah as he walked slowly through the City Market. The crowd knew if they had any money in their pockets it had his last name on it; they also knew that the beautiful items before them had either come into port on a Lamar boat or the trains that Lamar owned that lined the Southern states.

* * *

The evening sunset and the market gave way to the night, which erased the color from the glamorous streets below. The words spoken by Lamar earlier in the day to Bryan were a call to rally the rich men in the city. The meeting place was the Cotton Exchange, which was a common place of the night, with the ever-present aroma of Cuban tobacco's sweet smell and that of whiskey. The clandestine group barged around the room with boast and long pipe as the curator of the event was expected shortly.

A patterned knock came sharply to the heavy wooden doors at the rear of the room, which hid the small group of aristocrats behind them. The coded rap on the door gave signal to the armed guards who governed the event. There was a special knock code given throughout the day to the merchants and men inside the building, as this meeting would be like none other before it. The leader of this group had arrived; the shiny gold lion's head handle on his cane roared when it struck the oak doors.

Cal Lamar barged into the room that he owned. The crowd was silenced by the slam of the doors behind him; they parted in reverence when the tall man made his way to the front of the room. The clamor of men started softly again as the sea of people assembled to hear the man who had just entered the room to talk.

"Gentlemen, gentlemen! Please let me have your undivided attention. As you know, the ship *Wanderer* made port today." The sea of men cheered at the comment. "The very people who wish to break the South of our God-given right to own slaves quickly examined her contents, and these capitalists from the Union found not one clue for which they searched." The crowd erupted again and started to chuckle as Cal Lamar spoke.

"No! They found only one thing about the supposed slave ship...they found simply that she is the finest vessel in the waters of man and country!" he proclaimed.

"Hip! Hip! Hooray!" came from one man, and then the crowd repeated the call to honor with him. "Hip! Hip! Hooray!"

"Nor will they ever find what they search for, as long as I have any say in the matter. But...there do happen to be four hundred new slaves who are soon to hit the market." The room of men crashed with a roar above that of the first.

"We knew you could do it!" a voice from the group said.

"Will Bryan be the man to sell these new souls to the waiting South?" another asked as the crowded room hushed awaiting the answer.

"Being the most prestigious human trader of the day, my answer is yes!" Cal let out as the men cheered and Bryan basked in his moment, a small puff of smoke slithering from his grin.

"Did you say four hundred in all?" a voice came.

"Yes, you heard correct; 408, to be exact." Such a large number hushed the crowd.

"How long, may we ask, will it take for Bryan to distribute so many from the small corner marketplace he holds?" another exclaimed.

"You may not ask. You can read about it in the paper to come within the next few days. There will be a post of sale for all to read," Cal said as he waved his cane's head over the smoky room. "This is what I want from you men here."

The room, now silent, received their directions from the man for the sale of the slaves to come. The men were all instructed to be on the lookout and to label anyone who was from the North or would be a threat to the underhanded task of human sale that was to come. In fact, it would be the largest sale of human beings ever in the history of a county. This was a plan of biblical proportions and straight from one of the pillars of the South, Charles Augustus Lafayette Lamar.

Cal's father, Gazaway Bugg Lamar, would have no interest in the underhanded misdeeds of his son. Gazaway wrote in his memoirs that his son "would be better to plan a trip to the moon, than try such an event."

His cousins, however, would stand behind the man who had just landed what would be the last ship of slaves. Thomas and John Lamar owned a sprawling plantation to the north in Augusta. Their plantation empire was not titled in the Lamar name; however, a gentleman named Butler, who supposedly ran it from his offices in Pennsylvania, over-signed this possession. Running the operations would be left to the charge of the two real owners, the Lamar brothers. Butler would soon buy ownership of the title and would be listed as one of the largest slaveholders and distributors of slaves in the South. All the while the Lamar brothers collected the profits of the slaves.

The plan was simple. The Lamar brothers would receive the slaves upriver from Savannah at their lumberyard. The slaves would then be integrated into the faux Butler plantation that currently housed in excess of nine hundred fifty documented slaves. The plan was that four hundred sixty documented slaves would be sold to the public at auction in Savannah while the new Congolese cargo was integrated into the fields in Augusta, and back into the workforce needed to maintain the vast cotton fields and timber yards of the Lamar brothers.

Butler was set in Pennsylvania to act as if the sale was to satisfy an insurmountable gambling debt where he supposedly used his plantation and slaves as collateral for a bet. The debt would be paid through the bank, to his creditors, and release Butler from the tyranny of the gambling collector's knife. No such bet existed, and Lamar owned the bank that the money would be distributed through. As the money would pass through the accounts of Lamar it would've then been used to pay the man who was supposedly owed the money from Butler, Cal Lamar. The plan was again another ingenious design by Lamar to close the evil misdoings of his first phase, the shipment.

Cal Lamar supposed that the auctioning off of the property of Butler would be carried out at no other place than that of where the supposed debt occurred, the Savannah Ten Broeck Race Course, which also was owned by Lamar.

The plan was spinning into action as the accounting for the slaves to be sold was brought to order. The documentation and records of four hundred sixty established slaves was set to order. Bryan posted the bills that would let the people of the South know of the largest human sale in the country. Lamar, as always, did nothing in small affair. The sign's headline read:

FOR SALE.
LONG COTTON AND RICE
NEGROES.

A GANG OF 460 NEGROES, accustomed to the culture of Rice and Provisions: among whom are a number of good mechanics and house servants. Will be sold on the 2d and 3d of March next, at Savannah,

by JOSEPH BRYAN

* * *

Cal Lamar sat watching the jurors from the chair he was in at the Supreme Court of Savannah. He watched with great pleasure as the Union lawyers tried to place blame for the import of slaves against the *Wanderer* and crew in the tiny Savannah courtroom. The smile he wore was one of content as the man watched the pre-orchestrated charade begin.

First the charges of piracy were brought down for sentencing against the captain of the *Wanderer*. The captain confessed under pressure, to Cal's dismay, that he did in fact go to the Congo and retrieve five hundred slaves, make a forty-five day trip past two blockades and land four hundred eight souls on the Georgia banks of Jekyll Island. His words came with truth, and the Northerners wanted nothing more, except for proof.

As the counterarguments were heard in front of the well-compensated Southern jury, Cal's smirk grew larger. There was no proof; the jury had not been given one piece of evidence that the *Wanderer* had done anything wrong. The logbooks of the journey were all long gone by now, as well as the slaves she brought here. Cal knew the captain and crew could not be convicted without any proof, especially from a bribed jury of Southern patriots.

"Not guilty!" The gavel slammed in the Southern courtroom not less than an hour later. Cal Lamar was halfway out the door as the hammer of the judge hit the stone striking pad of justice. A long path and exuberant relief, with fine Cuban tobacco surrounding his head as he walked from the chambers of the Savannah Supreme Court.

The crowd outside in wait of the decision did not need to hear the bailiff's call of the orders passed down. The arrogant nature of descent from the courthouse steps of Lamar said it all. The Northern reporters and journalists silently protested except for one.

John Whittingly loudly objected to the obvious trickery of justice that Lamar had just devised. His loud taunt did briefly stop the swagger of the descending Lamar, just long enough to lay eyes on the face of the

Northern man who was not welcome by Cal or any other Confederate brother in his surroundings. His black attire stuck out from the brightly dressed Southerners, as did his Yankee accent. The brief hindrance to Cal's descending was quickly waved off by another puff from the fine ivory pipe that Cal pursed his lips on. Blowing the smoke in Whittingly's direction, Cal raised his eyes to meet the lawyer's glare. Their eyes met. Cal's eyes squinted and he mouthed the words, "I will see you later, boy!"

Soon after the trial, and in elaborate detail, a story came from the Northern man who sought justice. It was the story of how the South did not give up one of its own, a story of a miscarriage of justice and a corrupt Southerner who ruled over the cowering Southerners as he did. Whittingly mailed his article in and sat back in reverence of the truth in the tale he had just told the waiting Northerners. The *New York Times* quickly ran the article of the injustice of the South.

It humiliated his father in the North. Cal took great offense to the self-appointed justice the reporter held in his pen. "To come to Savannah, mock our Supreme Court, and to write of convictional thoughts that only he held, was surely the output of a cowardly Northern reporter," Cal remarked to his friends. "I'll see to his undoing now!" Cal said days later when the words of the story trickled back down to the Southern city.

With a copy of the article in hand, Cal marched forward through the tranquil streets of the city to the place where the Northern reporter was still staying. Cal entered the building and pushed open the dining room door where Whittingly sat amongst several other men. The only thing in Cal's hand was the article of dismay that the Northerner had let out. The people of the room moved back as the chair legs slid across the hardwood floor. Cal's eyes were fixed on the wilted eyes of Whittingly as he approached the sitting man.

Behind Cal stood a room full of people who had followed the hot-headed Southerner to the place where the reporter sat. Cal's walk alone, with just the article showing in his left hand, let all know that this man was out to seek revenge on the insulting, yet truthful, reporter. Many people turned and followed the son of the South as he made his way towards the Northerner.

Whittingly stood as Cal approached the man who was almost his same size and height, but not in stature; the man rose to face the blonde-haired Lamar, whose temperament had reddened his face.

No words...just a swift slap across the face of the Northern man; this total lack of respect for one meant only one thing in the South; a duel.

Cal turned to the door that he came from and walked swiftly through the crowd to the yard across Abercorn Street to the dueling grounds. The dueling grounds lay next to the cemetery of the great Southern city. The gasp of the barmaid was the first sound heard after the slap to the face. The next sounds were from the people who had made friends with Whittingly as he sat back down. His eyes were wide as the cowardly man's spirit ran through his soul and out of the room. Whittingly's short-term friends now acted as coaches for the scared and trembling man. They told him that Cal Lamar was no stranger to the dueling grounds outside.

"He's killed several men, starting with the same slap as he gave you," a young confidant said.

Whittingly's eyes sank; he was not a marksman, nor had he ever handled a gun, and would surely die today should he choose to rise to the dignity that he should. Being a journalist, he quickly devised a story he hoped would talk his way out of the short death sentence that was presented to him. He would lie...what would it hurt? This whole town was the most corrupt thing in the States.

"What on earth is he accusing me of?" he said to his table after he got his voice back.

They all stared at the article Cal had thrust onto the table before the invitational slap was heard. He quickly picked up the article and read to himself the words he had written about Cal and how he managed the jury and courts to relinquish their "not guilty" verdict. "I did not write this... these are not how I penned the notes to the editor!" He ran outside to the street where Lamar was removing his coat.

"Wait, sir! I did not write the story...I mean...I wrote it, but this is not how I worded it at all! I would not have written in this style whatsoever. You must believe me!" the man said as the pitch of his voice rose with despair to save his life.

Cal just looked at the man; he put his jacket back on and said one word, "Go." That was the last the Savannahians would see of their Northern friend. This one word carried with it the direction to get out of the South and take your acquaintances with you. The south was becoming a very dangerous place for people who held northern ideas of human rights and displayed them to the rebel souls that were living there.

The next day, Cal made straight for the courthouse to reclaim his yacht, the *Wanderer*, which was being auctioned in front of the Savannah courthouse on the steps. He spoke out over the crowd to the auctioneer: "What is your starting bid, sir?"

"Four thousand dollars, sir!" the auctioneer replied.

A gentleman there in the front said, "Four thousand!"

"Okay then, four thousand and one!" Cal said as he looked over the crowd. "You all know me; don't any of you bid against me or you will see my wrath."

The auctioneer said, "Four thousand and one, going once, going twice, sold for four thousand and one to Mr. Cal Lamar!"

Cal turned and walked towards the bidder who had placed the four-thousand-dollar bid and knocked him out cold down in front of the onlookers. Later that day, Cal found the same man he'd knocked down earlier and apologized to him, then left. This man was one of the only people Cal Lamar would ever apologize to; he was the police chief.

After the *Wanderer* was neatly re-secured on the docks of Lamar Pier in Savannah, the time of the largest American slave auction drew near. All that could be talked about was overshadowed by the buzz of the giant slave sale to be held at the horse track. Workers would prepare the horse racing grounds for the hundreds of slaves who would be there to be purchased.

The stables were to be converted to human pens, and more corrals were added in which to house the large quantity of slaves who would be auctioned off. Word was sent upstate to the Butler plantation as the time of the sale was set and the facility for the event was being secured and re-configured to hold its human occupants. There were hundreds of people involved in the logistics associated with such a large group of people. Almost 500 slaves had to be fed each day, along with hundreds of contractors and herdsmen used for the event. The sale had to take place quickly, as the soaring cost of the corralled people would escalate into the thousands of dollars rather quickly.

* * *

The Butler plantation was in full swing with the arrival of the *Wanderer* slaves. Two hundred came by boat on the Savannah River and two hundred traveled by train from Jekyll Island to the largest plantation and slave trading post in the South. With four hundred people added to the some nine hundred or more slaves at Butler already, the sheer numbers in cost of the event were staggering. Through all the mayhem of new arrivals, the several plantations in the Butler regime worked together to train and feed the newcomers to the Southern hell they would soon call home.

Cory, once a Congolese prince, now worked diligently as a new arrival to the Butler plantation. His first job was to peel potatoes for the hundreds of people who were there to be fed. As the days passed by, he would sit in the shade with several other slaves, peeling what was a mountain of potatoes with a knife. He thought back on his days being trained with the knife in the art of killing the wild Congo animals that were lurking in the woods near his home village. He looked up at the white man with the gun, and knew he would have no problem cutting his throat; he wanted to peel the skin off of that man instead of the potato. He smiled at the white man, as instructed long ago by Old Tom. Through his closed white teeth

Cory cussed the man, singing the words of his hatred like an old Congolese song. His low tune sat well with the others; they chuckled at the melody coming from the boy's smiling face.

His mother, the queen, was inside, cooking away for the masses. She worked tirelessly all day, as did the others around her. Cory knew that the kitchen was one of the worst places to work on the plantations because of the heat from the cooking fires and the steam from the boiling water, which made the Southern climate even more unbearable. The huge, black pots glowed red at the bottom as the potatoes boiled.

Around eleven o'clock on a regular day, Cory sat peeling his potatoes. He heard the wheels of the wagon that came around the same time every day. He noticed today that only one man sat atop the wagon, and the boy who normally accompanied him was missing. The young prince smiled larger today in hopes of getting off of the log he had been perched on, and maybe getting to ride on the wagon.

The queen, just inside the door, walked out on schedule with the large pan to greet the food carrier. She knew Cory was eager to do something else and said in a shroud of angry words. "Get up, boy! Carry this pan." These words were not in Congolese.

The white man on the wagon smiled as the young boy jumped from the log and ran into the kitchen. "Y'all speak English?" The man said to the queen of the Congolese people.

"So little," she exclaimed. "Him a smart boy." She spoke in a slow, reverent tone, not looking at the white man.

Cory came from the kitchen grin-first as he lit up the pan of potatoes with his beautiful smile. "You speak English, boy?" the man said to Cory, now with a harsh tone in his voice to show authority.

"Very little...but I am learning." The boy looked straight at him, talking through his big smile.

The man looked over the small crowd of people to size up another who could help. Cory saw that his opportunity was slipping as he spoke up.

"I is a good, strong man," he said as the white man stopped his survey and glared back down at the boy.

"Go get the food then, boy, and quit looking at me," he said to Cory.

Cory now, without a smile, ran into the kitchen as though he would load all of the pans himself. He came back out of the screened shack smiling, despite the amount of weight his little arms were now carrying. His mother smiled as the boy looked at her for acknowledgment as he loaded the pans into the wagon. She thought how much the young man looked like the king she had been married to, when he was the same age. Her boy, trying to be a man, and doing the job required of him, no matter what the circumstances were.

With the pans loaded, the two men set off with the meal of the day. Cory was instructed to stay in the rear of the wagon and mind the pans, which made him so happy not to have to peel potatoes for a while that his smile was more genuine than ever.

The wagon made its way down the oak-lined drive that led to the master's quarters. One pan of potatoes was delivered to the detached kitchen in back of the house first. Cory did as instructed and handed one of the pans of potatoes to the smiling lady who came out. With a crack of the whip, they were off to feed the rest of the people on the surrounding plantations one part of the meals they would eat.

Cory watched, eyes wider today as he looked at the surroundings of the fields and the sheer number of men working there. As it was in the kitchen, there was a man with a gun overseeing the operations of each group of slaves. They passed the other slaves and their eyes waved at each other while the wagon of food rode on. He saw them picking the potatoes in the fields around the plantation they lived on, and as they rode along he saw some men picking corn, sugarcane, tobacco, rice, and miles and miles of fields of cotton.

They came to a smaller plantation where the cows and livestock were held. The barn out back was teeming with animals waiting for slaughter; the stack of bones behind the kitchen gave the sign of which. This place smelled worse than the others as Cory dismounted the wagon back. He was instructed to offload three pans of potatoes, and followed the man's instructions exactly.

Cory walked towards the kitchen. He saw another boy his age walking out of the kitchen. The boy, dressed as he, wore rags fashioned into pants that hung just below the knee and a shirt that was made to fit a much larger person. The boy looked downward as he approached Cory and was not smiling. Excited at seeing all the new faces, Cory began with a grin, and as the unfamiliar boy looked up, he managed a smile when he noticed Cory's radiating excitement. The encounter was brief, and Cory finished loading his pans and jumped back into the wagon. The whip cracked again, and the strange new pair were off to finish their rounds.

As soon as the food was disbursed throughout the different plantations, Cory's world opened up in one day. He got to go pick up a load of corn, meet new people, and ride in the back of a wagon. The slight breeze felt good as he looked forward to every mile he traveled. He found that the man's name who was leading his new adventure was Chris, and that the horse's name was Dot. He said their names over and over in his head as the trio bumbled along the backwoods of Georgia. His childhood innocence allowed him to forget that he was a slave and that Dot was more revered than he, a prince.

At the day's end, Chris brought the wagon back around to the potato kitchen to drop off his grinning accomplice. The wagon came to a stop near the kitchen that sat idle in the now dark field of the Butler plantation. "Boy, Imma gonna come back by here in the morning and let you help me some more. You be right here ready and early now, ya hear?"

"Yes, sa!" Cory said, springing from the wagon back.

The young man tore out across the fields to the shack where he lived; he had so much to tell his mama. She heard him come from way down the dirt lane. "Mama, Mama!" His voice was accented by his breath from running all the way from the kitchen.

"Calm down, boy, now calm down," she said to Cory, who could barely get the words out.

Cory went on to relay the stories of the day with much more splendid color than actually existed. His mother smiled at the boy's excitement and patted his head, as if to calm him down. It was the happiest she had seen the boy since his father was murdered and they began their horrible journey to the place where they sat in the shack.

She said, "Don't worry, my prince. The sun will surely rise tomorrow and you can take off on another adventure."

* * *

Cory was the first one up in the shack; he paced and paced, waiting for the sun to rise and the strike of the bell at the main house that signaled the start of a new day. *Clang!* the bell rang out, and Cory was off like a racehorse to the kitchen. He sat there alone, just him and the flies as the group of women came up the same path he had just run down fifteen minutes before. He was discouraged that the group was not Chris and Dot coming to take him on another tale.

The women walked past one by one, and several men came from the field area and sat down on logs to begin peeling the potatoes again for the day. He couldn't believe his mom had suggested he take his place on the log and peel potatoes till his new friends arrived, but reluctantly he did as he was told. The disgruntled look got stronger and stronger as the boy waited for the two to show up.

It was not long before he heard the lovely sound of Dot's clopping feet and the gentle crack of the whip. His mama, just inside, looking through the kitchen, motioned for the boy to sit back down. The wagon pulled up to the kitchen backyard and Chris, with just a nod, motioned for Cory to come on and go with him. Cory flew from the log and ran towards the wagon. Using the wooden spokes of the wheel now as a ladder, he was in position in a second. "We got to go get some corn down by the barn and take the horses some hay. You ready?" Chris said, with all the mundane of a typical day's work.

Cory nodded his head up and down with all the excitement in the world. Cory's mom looked out the window and smiled as the boy hung on when Chris cracked the whip for Dot to go. The boy's head jerked back as the wagon took off, but his eyes never came off of Chris. His mama laughed at the boy's concentration as his head bobbed and the wagon rocked down the dirt path to the barn.

The two came back with a wagon full of big ears of corn. Cory and his mother had not seen such wholesome growth as this in the South. The corn was off-loaded onto low wooden tables to keep the produce from lying on the ground. Cory and two other men placed the corn on the tables as Chris watched over the laborers. Cory's mom watched from the kitchen while the men unloaded the wagon.

It was eleven o'clock and the potatoes, having been cooked, were loaded in pans and placed in the wagon. Cory's mom brought out several pans, and Chris watched the people around him buzz into action. It was not long before the two were headed off with the load to feed lunch to the men in the fields and at the other plantations as they had the day before.

As nighttime came, Cory and Chris returned. Cory ran to the shack to tell the stories of the wide world that the adventurer saw in his day. His mom listened to every word as she kept pointing at his bowl of food for him to eat. She was making a piece of pottery from an old jug while she listened, with what seemed to be an African warrior's face fashioned onto it made out of the red Georgia clay.

The next day barely came fast enough for the young boy. Again, up before the sun and out the door running as soon as the bell sounded in the main yard. The women and men came up to find young Cory shucking the corn with much zeal. They all sort of chuckled as they watched the boy shuck away the time till his new friends arrived. As expected, Chris and Dot showed up around thirty minutes later and the trio was off to perform the morning's duties before distributing the meal the women would be cooking.

The sun was staring straight down now on the kitchen; the smell of boiling corn made for a wonderful aroma. Chris and Cory both smiled at the trio of themselves and Dot as they clopped up and the wagon full of potatoes stopped in front of the logs behind the kitchen. The potatoes were thrown on the ground in a pile in the middle of the log seats. No sooner did Cory finish unloading the potatoes than the women emerged with the pans of corn that were to go out as the meal of the day. The smell gave a little mood to the group as the pans were loaded on the wagon.

With the last pan loaded, Cory's mom came from the kitchen with a small skillet-sized loaf of cornbread. It was hot and aromatic. The queen handed the small gift to the now wide-eyed Chris. She spoke softly and said, "Thank you," as she presented the bread to the man. Her eyes closed gracefully as she bowed at the man who was being kind to her son.

Chris noticed that she had a different way about her. With grace, he accepted the gift and nodded in appreciation. The whip cracked, and the three were off for another day in the young man's adventure. Chris stopped not a quarter of mile away from the kitchen and turned to the boy, who was confused as to why the adventure was not continuing.

"Here you go." He handed the young man a huge slice of cornbread.

The queen knew that the man could not take such a gift and show it about. She watched as the two in the distance ate away at the wonderful, rich cracklin' corn bread. As she'd hoped, her son would be the benefactor of it too.

* * *

The men in the lumberyard on the Savannah River were just finishing their meal and the steam whistle blew from the sawmill's steam engine, signaling the end of the lunch break. The tin dishes were set in a pile, as always, and the misery of the day would once again resume.

The saw came to life and the Georgia pines cried out as they were cut into shapes of wood that were to be run that day. "What's all this thin wood for?" one of the white guards asked the conductor of the mill.

"Fencing and corrals!" the man yelled over the bustle of the steam engine. He talked much louder than necessary, as the pines being cut had deafened his ears. With a shrug of carelessness the man walked away, rifle in hand as he watched the wood stack start to grow.

"I'll have you loaded soon enough," the portly man said to the riverboat captain.

The two sat in the small house by the lumberyard. The smoke of the steamboat's stacks matched that of the sawmill's engine. "Your boys loading out my coal?" he finished as he drew off his pipe full of Georgia tobacco.

"The last of it is being brought up now," the captain's raspy voice answered. They both looked out the wide window that overlooked the lumberyard.

"That coal is as black as them slaves you brought here a while back." The fat man let out another breath of smoke.

"So, what all do you know about those that I brung?" the captain inquired.

"Oh, I know plenty. I know you only brought about half of 'em," the portly man replied.

"Oh yeah? Who brought the other half? I had about two hundred aboard the *Lamar*!" the captain shot back.

"Well, you brought all that was to be brung up the river. A separate load that big was brought up the roads, the back way, by foot," he said as he leaned toward the captain. "In case you got caught." The fat man leaned back in his chair, basking in the rare moment of knowing more than the captain.

"You see, Lamar didn't want to risk his whole shipment in one mode of transport." The match struck as the man lit his pipe again. "Lamar is no fool; he had you bring in half the slaves, the train done brought some of the others, and most of the other half walked their way up here. They is all holed up on his cousin's plantation down the way. They all passed through this yard, some four hundred of them," the portly man went on.

The captain said, "I couldn't believe how many he had stuffed on that ship. A couple of the other captains laughed at my waterline being below the surface as I brought them up here." He recovered some of his captain's posture.

"Well, sounds like you know much about half of 'em," the portly man acquiesced.

The captain stood and walked to the window. "Do you know where that wood you're cutting is headed to?" he asked.

"Yeah, Lamar ordered it for the horse track. He is going to add some stables or something," the yard keeper said as he rose and walked over to the window.

"Seems like you don't know much about the wood," the captain now said. "Of course, you wouldn't know, being stuck up here in the woods, would you?" The captain reached to his side and pulled the leather tube that held his charts and maps of the river. He unzipped the top of the document tube and slid its contents out into his hand. The thick stack of rolled papers twenty-four inches long came slowly out of the tube. With his left hand the captain stuck the tube of papers towards the man's expressionless face. "This is what I know, old man." He released the rolled papers onto the table and they uncoiled immediately; the big, bold print said it all.

FOR SALE.
LONG COTTON AND RICE
NEGROES.

A GANG OF **460** NEGROES, accustomed to the culture of Rice and Provisions; among whom are a number of good mechanics, and house servants. Will be sold on the 2d and 3d of March next, at Savannah, by **JOSEPH BRYAN**.

TERMS OF SALE.—One-third cash; remainder by bond, bearing interest from day of sale, payable in two equal annual instalments, to be secured by mortgage on the negroes, and approved personal security, or for approved city acceptance on Savannah or Charleston. Purchasers paying for papers.

The Negroes will be sold in families, and can be seen on the premises of JOSEPH BRYAN, in Savannah, three days prior to the day of sale, when catalogues will be furnished.

* The Charleston Courier, (daily and tri-weekly;) Christian Index, Macon, Ga.; Albany Patriot, Augusta Constitutionalist, Mobile Register, New Orleans Picayune, Memphis Appeal, and Vicksburg Southron, will publish till day of sale and send bills to this office.

feb 8   td

The portly man leaned over the stack of documents, his mouth open as he took in the news. He missed his mouth with the end of his pipe several times.

The captain watched, his eyes gazing over the post. "Now get that wood on my ship so we can finish off these 'horse stables,'" he said laughingly as he walked to the door. "And post those bills around! Mr. Lamar's orders." He turned and walked out the door without slamming it.

The fat man closed his open mouth around the pipe. The Georgia tobacco had long since burned out and the taste of ash was pulled into the man's mouth instead of the rich Georgia tobacco taste. He turned back to the window to see the captain motion to his yard workers to finish loading the wood as if he were director of the yard.

* * *

Savannah was buzzing with the news of the big sale of slaves at the racetrack. The posting of the bills for the sale took some of the headlines away from the Cal Lamar trial and the other ghost owners of the ship *Wanderer*. Even though the captain was found not guilty, now the big to-do was for the North to have their day in court. With Cal's uncle the president of Texas, Mirabeau Bonaparte Lamar, and his father, Gazaway Lamar, two of the most influential figures in the South and the North, it was now a fully rigged show. Abraham Lincoln was just elected into office, and the division between the North and South was reaching a boil.

Cal sat in his offices pondering the visitors who were in town to see justice done. He also knew that these people would be watching the sale of the slaves that was supposedly unattached to the affluent Southerner. He peered down over River Street, his mood a little off because of the trial's untold futures, the new president, and the sale of a few more slaves than anyone would have supposed could have fit on his ship.

His assistant entered the room. "Mr. Lamar, word is in from the track, sir, and the accommodations as ordered are complete."

Lamar, not breaking his stare of the people on the river, replied, "You know, those ungrateful bastards down there couldn't care less what I do for this state. As long as they have their beautiful little city and pretty little houses, they couldn't care less. If I let the Yankees have the run of it, there would be no slaves! No one to pick the precious cotton that keeps this and all the cities of the South alive. They would have to take their lazy asses out into the fields and do it themselves!" He paused as if to hear a comment. "You think they would? Hell no! They would let the city and all the rest of the South fall apart. They would probably walk right up and kiss Lincoln right on his ass! Damn the president and his stupid laws. The Northerners are mad because they can't use slaves to pick the laws, because they can't vote, nor to write their idiotic articles in the paper because they can't write. I hope we get the opportunity to show those bastards in Washington that slavery is our God-given right. I do hope we get the chance." He declared this all as if he were on a soapbox, waving his pipe at the unsuspecting people walking under him along the river, his face now red. "Goddamn Yankees."

His assistant provided the single audience during his rant. "You're very right, sir, very right indeed."

Lamar motioned without a word to the young man to leave as an inaudible grumble came with his hand gesture.

* * *

The wagons came to the Butler plantation under the cover of darkness. The drivers of each of the seventy-five horse teams gathered at the main plantation fields of the Butler house. The drivers and sidemen gathered around several fires that burned in the field, giving signal to the rendezvous point. Like clockwork they had arrived to make the haul of human cargo for the big sale that was about to take place.

"Have you ever seen such?" one of the men asked as he waited by his horse team.

"Naw," the simple white man answered. "Never did see such, but wouldn't expect less from the Butlers."

"Butlers? I thought it was Lamar's doing?" the driver questioned.

"Better let that Lamar name slip out of your head, boy, if you know what's good for you." The man walked away from the one as if he were asking for trouble.

* * *

The sun rose like every other day, but today was quite different indeed. The clang of the bell gave way to the people of the fields, and at once the plantation's fields came alive with hundreds of workers and slaves. They all noticed the smoke from a distant fire and it raised concern for those who could see it. Cory, at his young age, paid no attention to the unsettled air that was coming over the plantation. With all of the new things in life he took in, he didn't even pay attention to the men gathering in the field.

The women walked as they always did to the kitchen house, and sure enough, Cory sat smiling, as he knew he only had to peel a few potatoes before Chris and Dot came over the hill. Cory's mom watched the excited boy whittle away at the pile, unaware of the irregularities that were around him. As usual, Chris and Dot came towards the kitchen house. This time Chris had a load of men in the wagon. They stopped in a different place than the other days, and the armed men unloaded out of the wagon. Chris turned Dot towards the little house and headed towards Cory.

Dot was uneasy, as was the smile on Chris's face. Cory got up slower this time and walked towards the fidgety horse. "Easy, girl," he said, rubbing her nose. "Easy."

Chris, in a different tone, said, "Come on, boy," as Cory reluctantly made his way to the side of the wagon. "Come on now, boy, let's get!" he snapped at the youngster. Neither he nor the boy were smiling.

"You, nigger bitch! Go get me some food!" rang out over the kitchen lawn.

Both Chris and Cory turned to see one of the armed men grab the queen's shoulder and shove her towards the kitchen door. Cory instinctively began to spring from the wagon. Chris's strong hand held the boy firmly in place. One quick glance let Cory know he would handle this. Chris knew the guards would have simply killed the young boy in a second.

"You boys need some help with something?" Chris asked as he stepped from the wagon. He stared at the boy to make sure Corey didn't move.

The fidgety guard turned angrily in Chris's direction. "You like niggers, boy?"

"I do! I like 'em so much, I convinced Cal Lamar to purchase 'em." Chris's words carried strongly over to the now withering man. "I can't wait to tell him how you think you own his slaves, and how you hit his property."

"I ain't hit no one! Hell you say!" The guardsmen were now retreating backwards towards the side of the field that Chris dropped him off at.

The queen stepped from the kitchen door; the rusty screen creaked as it opened. She held the plate of food for the guardsman in her hand. Chris, without hesitation, grabbed the whip from the seat of the wagon and walked hurriedly toward the queen with the leather whip, uncoiling it in his hands as he paced toward her.

"Get your black ass back in that kitchen!" Chris screamed across the small area where there were a few slaves there peeling potatoes. The whip cracked just a few feet in front of the queen's face. Mortified from the scream of Chris, which she had never heard, she dropped the tin plate and fell backward into the kitchen door that had just shut behind her. "Get!" The whip cracked again on the ground next to the queen.

Her knees went weak and she fell to the ground, then scurried through the doorway, crawling through the dirt.

Chris turned to guardsmen. "Nobody talks to my niggers like that!" He pointed the limp whip at the man, then looped it back into its coiled shape.

The whip cracked and Dot took off at a faster pace than normal, back over the hill. Cory looked back towards the kitchen as two of the armed men dropped in the field retreated away from scene to their assigned post. Cory made his way up to the back of the seat, and placing his hand quietly as though sneaking up on Chris.

"Don't!" Chris snapped. "Just do what you're told." Cory retreated back down into the back of the wagon.

The two made their way to the barn as usual to get the meal load for the next day, but instead they went to the hay barn just to the side this time and stopped next to the big hay pile. Chris knew that Cory had never forked hay, so he grunted as he got down off the wagon. "Now grab that hay up, boy, and put it in the wagon," he said as he drove the fork deep into the hay pile. "Come on, boy, we got a lot to do today." Chris concentrated on his work rather than giving the common explanations he would have given the boy on a normal day.

With the hay filling the back of the wagon, Chris instructed Cory to sit next to him on the bench. Cory knew something was amiss; there was no excitement in the air today as he made his first ride facing forward in the wagon.

The two came over the hill as Dot pulled them and the load of hay up towards the waiting wagons. There were so many men not from there, nothing like he had seen in the past, with wagons of every shape and size. There was a line of slaves from the plantation he had not seen before; they were being walked towards the wagons and men. As Cory got closer, he could see that the field workers were coming in lines from every direction. There were hundreds of people walking towards the wagon teams.

Chris spoke out to the first wagon team they approached. "Y'all been fed yet?" A simple nod as a yes led Chris to know they had. The driver pointed him over to the next line of wagons. "Now get down, boy, and walk behind me and the wagon as I slow down next to these horse teams. You put a big pile of hay in front of each horse, you hear?" Cory acknowledged, and got off the wagon as it approached and slowed.

The sun came up to good morning's light, and Cory watched as the men and women slaves were put into shackles and loaded into the wagons. He heard so many people crying out loud while he placed the hay in front of the waiting horses. He walked slowly behind the wagon.

"Get in the wagon!" one of the wagon team leaders said to the young slave, with a whip cracking to add accent to the command. The whip hit its mark and the young slave girl cried out. "Now get!" The whip cracked again by her head. The others helped her into the back of the wagon, all of them bound in chains.

A pair of horses rode up at full speed. The Lamar brothers were the only ones looking over the mayhem with grins. "Look at the money," Tom Lamar said to his brother. "Just look at the money out there!"

"Missa Tom!" One of the slaves spoke out to the tall horseman, Thomas Lamar. "Missa Tom, why?" Thomas Lamar took the reins of his horse and slapped them on the horse's rear.

"Yah!" was all he said as he jerked the reins hard and rode off. John, his brother, a slight bit more compassionate, looked at the man who had called out to his brother. When their eyes met he looked down, not able to look at the man who had been his trusted house servant for years.

"Yah!" He, too, cracked the reins and followed in the dust of his brother's horse.

Cory watched as the poor man sat back down in the wagon. His spirit was broken again, as well as that of the boy who watched.

Clouds formed overhead and the dark skies, now angry, came in fast. In Georgia, most of the time when it rains it is not a passing shower, and this day would prove to be no different. The big rain fell and the people and horses sat idle in the downpour, waiting for the call to go forward.

* * *

The clouds stretched for miles, it seemed, as the men were putting the final touches on the stables and corrals at the raceway. Several spotter towers were added at the direction of James Bryan as he walked over to the bleacher seats of the racetrack in Savannah. "This rain is going to lighten the viewing days people have if it keeps up," he said as he spoke to the auctioneer under the covered step of the auctioneer's block.

"It ain't going to matter none; people been loading into town the last couple of days! They ain't going to miss the sale, they done come from all over!" the skinny, pale, and frail auctioneer proclaimed as he directed the finishing touches to his podium. "Not going to miss it for the world!"

The day seemed to set early and the giant clouds kept rolling in. The first of many wagons was just seen coming down the small road that led to the racetrack. Behind the wagon were several more that were spaced out as the dust came from the horse teams and wagon wheels. The parade of wagons could be seen coming from the west. The angry skies came from the east, bringing more rain that would meet the arriving group of wagons head-on.

James Bryan watched the clouds and the wagons meet at the fields of the racetrack. The red Georgia clay looked like blood as the rain and the tears of the four hundred sixty people who would be sold there soon hit the ground. These would come to be known as the "weeping times" as so many families were split up, and the hearts of four hundred sixty slaves were broken once again.

In the days to come, all the slaves would be sold and hundreds of families would be separated from their loved ones. The rains would pass, and the records would show that four hundred sixty well-documented slaves would be sold to the highest bidders.

* * *

Cal Lamar came from his offices in the days after the sale and counted the three hundred thousand dollars that poured into his bank accounts The Butler gambling debt had now been paid. The fields of the Butler plantations would not miss a lick, and the four hundred-plus slaves who came from the *Wanderer* replaced the souls of the slaves sold from there. The sun shined after the weeping times on Cal Lamar; his plan went without so much as a hitch.

* * *

The days were few before the final Lamar trial approached. The thought of civil war was thick in the air as the beautiful antebellum city slept quietly through the nights. Regardless of the outcome, the two sides of states were closing down on the dark future that was to come. With the sale of four hundred sixty slaves in Georgia, the eye of the North looked strongly at the second strike, per se. One being the *Wanderer* landing four hundred-plus slaves, two being the largest sale of slaves in American history, and the third opportunity for the South to slap the face of the North was the Cal Lamar trial.

April 15, 1861. The final date was set for the Cal Lamar trial that was to finally convict the fire-eater of piracy, which would lead to his hanging in the streets of Savannah.

Lamar sat in the square just outside the courthouse. The large oak tree cast an enormous web of shadows over the corner of the square where he sat. The erected gallows stood just six feet tall and was arranged under the large branch of the huge oak.

The wood to build the gallows came from the slave auction additions Cal had recently disassembled. The rope came from the dock stowage on the Lamar pier, and the people sweeping the area and doing the new work were Lamar employees as well.

The reporters of the North gathered along the street near the entrance of the courthouse, all the while captivated by the villain who sat smiling at the gallows he was surely to hang from. Cal leaned back and took a deep breath of the fresh spring air that seemed to rock the hangman's noose slightly.

With one smooth spin, Cal spun from the gallery seating there under the oak. He reached into the chest pocket of his jacket and removed the fine leather bag of Cuban tobacco. He then packed his pipe and slowly dragged the match across the slate backing on the pearl matchbox. His eyes squinted slightly to avoid the wisp of smoke that came from the burning match. A long draw and a shake of the match ended in pause as Cal Lamar savored the Cuban tobacco that filled his lungs. He exhaled the large plume of smoke, seemingly at the rope noose, and walked toward the street corner near the entrance of the courthouse.

Cal tipped his hat slightly to the line of jurors who were being led into the courthouse by the bailiff and the two attorneys. All of the jurors looked at the ground in front of them as they walked along the sidewalk on the Bay Street entrance to the courtroom.

Moments passed as the bailiff shut the doors to the side entrance, and a slight shift in the crowd led part of the people outside of the building to move inside the courtroom. The bell of the church steeple clanged loudly 10 times as the trial was about to take place.

As the bell rang, Cal worked his way through the crowded room to the defendant's table and his waiting attorney. With Cal's father in the same law firm as his son's attorney, the smirk of confidence would not leave Cal's face. The biggest of the marionette puppets in this trial were about to be revealed.

"All rise!" The bailiff's voice resonated throughout the courtroom. The entire crowd stood in unison. "The Honorable John C. Nicole presiding!"

The stout man wobbled in from the large mahogany door behind the judge's bench. He motioned with his hands for all to be seated, and immediately the bailiff sternly said, "You may be seated."

There were only about six people in the courtroom that day who knew that Cal Lamar was married to Judge Nichole's daughter. There were exactly nine jurors who knew of the money paid to cement the jury's verdict.

But there was only one who knew the entirety of the plot. He sat twisting the golden ring his father had given him, staring into the sparkle of the diamond at its center. He gazed over his shoulder at the courtroom full of fans being waved throughout the crowd to cool the balmy Savannah weather.

After only two hours of deliberation, the words: "Not guilty!" rang throughout the courtroom. The gavel slammed as the words came from the jowls of the portly judge. Judge Nichole rose as he was striking the wooden disk on the bench. He left the courtroom to the heckling of the Northern statesmen who speckled the room that day.

Cal placed both hands on the desk in front of him and slid the wooden chair back across the hardwood floor of the courtroom. Its noise was second to that of the gavel and just as effective. He rose from the seat and inhaled as he turned around to his loving Savannahians. He slightly moved the one side of the chair and gingerly walked across the center of the courtroom and up to the small wooden swinging doors that separated the gallery. He gestured a thank you to the jury, then parted the gates and began his walk to freedom. The two bailiffs at the rear of the courtroom opened the large, hand-carved wooden doors that had kept the verdict inside. The open doors gave backdrop to the bailiffs as they repeated the verdict that had just been announced moments before to the overflow crowd.

Cal Lamar stepped from the large wooden opening and waved to the loving throng of his Savannah. Several carriers and messengers left the crowd to spread the word of the verdict that was still an echo throughout the azalea-laced square of people standing outside the courtroom.

Within days, the papers throughout the North and South were riddled with headlines about injustice and justice served. It seemed this was the final act that would trigger the impending Civil War, and Cal Lamar seethed with excitement over the thought of his South winning this fight as well.

He had no idea the fight that he'd caused would kill more people than any other battle in history and would unleash a carnage among brothers that would create a permanent scar in this nation's history. It seemed the Southern fire-eater had started his war.

CAMERON

LIFE ON THE SAVANNAH RIVER WAS A MIXTURE OF SEA salt and a symphony of dockworkers as the boats on the Lamar pier were constantly being loaded and unloaded from hold to dock and warehouse to transport. With all the bustle of machine and man doing so, this was no place for a boy. "Wharf rat" was the term given to the small children who were abandoned or left for dead as their parents were shanghaied onto sailing ships from around the world on the docks of Lamar Pier. These rats roamed freely under the docks of the longshoremen above. That term "longshoremen" was ultimately developed for the people who did all the physical labor to move the cargo and cash crops from point to point on the pier.

"Factor" was the name given to the men who were the supervisors of the clandestine group of men working tirelessly on the docks below them. The steel and wooden bridges of Upper Factors Walk stands overlooking the stony River Street in Savannah and the loading operations of the piers to storage warehouses below.

Looking between the wooden boards of the docks and through the gaps of the ships and moorings, the little wharf rats stared in wonder at the riches of the foreign world. "Be careful!" the hushed whisper came from the boy, not even 10 years old. "Don't let them see you," young Kenneth told Cameron as he crept near the dock's edge to steal some of the fruit that had just been set on the dock above their heads.

These strange new items brought here from afar would soon be whisked off to the rich men who were waiting for their prize. These things would often sit on the dock long enough in the Savannah heat that the boys below could fantasize about their use, and often did. The items didn't stay on the dock long as they were delicately moved to the waiting warehouses that would temporarily store the treasures unloaded from the merchant ships.

The wharf rats had no boundaries, and easily gained access from portals unknown to the buildings above in these warehouses. At night the young ones could stare in amazement till they fell asleep in their beds and dreamt of them. In most instances, these beds were bales of cotton and tobacco where they could lay their heads after a long day of playing in wonderment in the underworld of the Lamar piers.

Even though a child's world has in itself a delicate manner simply just from youth, these children had the innocence and wonder in all things the world presented to them. Cameron, being one of the older children, would answer questions that the younger group asked, and improvise answers and logic that seldom hit the mark. The unknowing group of children would sit wide-eyed and listen to the most mystical enchantments that the elder children would lay out as they explained the uses of the items of beauty they had seen on the docks.

An informal rank and file fell upon the militant children. This system of order was derived from watching the factors talk to the longshoremen and longshoremen to slaves, so they practiced the formalities of the social requirements that lived in the world above them. These small children varied in age from six years to fifteen years old. Anyone older would have graduated to the work and labor a young man was supposed to be performing. A fortunate few were taken in by a farmer to help with work on the plantations, but most were shanghaied into slavery by a passing ship. Once you reached a certain age, the choices were sometimes not your own to graduate from the school of life below the docks.

Cameron was a different kind of wharf rat. After all, his father had been a servant to the Queen on one of the finest sailing ships that docked in Savannah. His father was killed in a shipping accident, and his mother was shanghaied onto a ship when he was 10 years old. His astute demeanor gave him the look of determination that promoted him to a natural leader of the group, and five years living in the underworld propelled him to oldest and wisest of the children.

Cameron told the stories of his imagination, which his father used to tell him, of being aboard one of the first steamships that sailed from the aging docks of Lamar. Cameron would go on as the younger children listened about the knowledge that his father passed on to him. Actually, most of his knowledge came from exposure to the riches from afar and the dock men above.

Cameron was fifteen years old now and bigger than the children who were his followers. The fact that he had a father he could remember put him on a pedestal. He knew most of the children didn't have any parents they could recall. He had personally handpicked several of the children from the river as they were thrown in, preceded by the screams of their mothers who were beaten and taken aboard the waiting ships before departing for seas. They were too young to swim, so Cameron or the other wharf rats would come to the rescue of these suddenly orphaned children as the pirates took their moms to be maids to the captain and the sea.

Their mission in life was to save the children as they had been saved by the wharf rats before them. They would cover the young child's eyes and mouth, though the young ones wanted to cry out to their mothers who were beaten into submission in the night air above. Not all children were thrown in the water. Some children were directed by their parents to keep watch as they made company with the seamen who visited the ports.

Piercing young eyes looking from the alleyways of cobblestone watched in wonder, and not a beautiful one. They heard the voices and moans of the concubines behind curtain and candlelight. In some instances, when the parental meeting was over, the mothers would take their earnings and children, then make off into the night so they could provide for the young tormented souls the next morning.

In other instances, the children would stare at the candlelight, hear the noises of childhood confusion, and then hear nothing. Soon the door would open to the secret meeting place in their view, and from the shadows would emerge the laughing men who had entered, walking hand in hand with their mother. They'd receive the secret nod from her as they passed, which meant: "stay in the shadows, these men are very dangerous." The children would follow, scurrying through the shadows of the moonlit cobblestone streets.

Rare as it was, sometimes from the shadows would emerge only one set of footsteps. The tall, shadowy figure would look both ways, giving suspicion that something wasn't right. Then quietly, the single person would pace himself out of the dark place carrying a bag or cloth-made sack from what had been a bed sheet or cotton bale burlap that bore an eerie, elongated, motionless shape. Not seeing the mother appear was sometimes not unusual, as she may stay a moment waiting for the men to leave. Within minutes of the men slipping into the darkness, the child would dart to the waiting arms of their mother.

This time, one of the children, Jennifer, would not find her mother there inside the room. Frantically searching the chamber, she only found remnants of her mother's clothes strewn about. Unlike anything ever seen before, Jennifer saw blood that denoted a fight that was lost.

Running into the night, the young girl panicked. "What direction did they go? Where is my mommy?" Tears filled her eyes, hampering the moonlit race for salvation of the only thing she knew dear in this life.

As the slopes of the landscape descended towards the river in a natural downhill progression, the roads drove the scrambling girl to the dimly lit docks and the moonlit river Savannah. No tears now; wide-eyed, she ran unchallenged by the night. The focus of the horror she was seeking came into the dim light; the man with the sack who had her mother captive. Streaking across the cobblestones the child ran, stumbling on the unevenness of the rounded stones. She never looked down for fear of losing sight of her mother. Closer she came to the scare that the tiny mind imagined. Then from nowhere she, too, was taken prisoner.

The hands reached out from the edge of her sight. Tiny as they were, but strong and dirty, like the hands that had taken their own loved ones away, but these were hands that meant no harm. Cameron and the others subdued the resistance of the child to fight. The wharf rats had saved another little life, as it would have faded into the still, salt air had the little girl made it to the ship of pirates.

Jennifer's mouth was covered by the young captors, only allowing for the horrible scene of the lantern-lit abduction of one she would never see again. Her mom now shanghaied made her an orphan as she lay crying on the ground, feeling like her life was over. It was a new life that was to be revealed to her of scurrying through the shadows of the docks that the other wharf rats had been subjected to.

As Cameron preached to the small children in the dark night air, sometimes pointing to the un-seeable ones above, as most preachers do, he would tell stories to the youngest ones. These were stories of hope the young lads listened to, with the only idea of a wishful life they could have; the stories that their parents may return soon to the docks they had left from. None ever had that reunion, and most of these dreams lasted only a few years, which then yielded to the reality of a life they were to come to know.

Cameron was their temporary parent. He was the oldest of the young band of wharf rats and an experienced teacher to the children. He told of fierce battles from above, which took his father away, and the carnage and bloodshed that put him there with them. It was as horrible as he could make up, because these lies were all that would make these young souls feel better about the torment of their own story. As the children came into the group and told of the horrors that led them there, Cameron and the others would make up more horrific stories of themselves to de-escalate the situation. Soon they would all see that this was going to be their family now, so they might as well be happy.

Cameron, being no different than most, started to believe the stories he told of fighting pirates and scalawags, only to be outnumbered by the forces of evil. His belief in the stories got in his character and he became an astute wharf rat and the voted leader of the youngsters who were in his flock. He also knew from the preachers of the dock's light before him that he was coming to the age that soon would mark his final days.

As the leader of the small group, Cameron often ventured out into the light from the shadows that paled his skin. There were treasures to be had that men would leave, should a coin or small token fall into the underworld. Cameron typically was there to search these shallow waters to find those very treasures thought to be lost beneath the docks. The long-shoremen knew of the children below and would at times provide food and drink to them, much like to a stray dog. As a stray dog would do, the group would gobble these things up with little self-control.

It was a glimmer of light that blasted from the water Cameron spied next to the large sailing ship that was moored at the Lamar docks, under which he lived. All he knew was that it was different than most of the glis-tening he'd seen come from the water. A metallic sparkle perfectly caught the angle between Cameron's eye and the sun between the wide ship and the wooden planks above. It was not more than a few feet below the surface of the murky water that lightly splash against the ship from the incoming tide. The tides in Savannah caused the river to swell twice a day because of the moon's pull on the earth below. As the water rushed into the port city, the current was strong and fast. A lot happened at high tide along the port, because that was when the fully loaded ships could use most of the river's depth and leave the city to make way for the land to which they were sailing.

Daytime was not the hour to venture outside from below the dark boards of the wooden shelter. Nor was it wise to make known the existence of the dark underworld's inhabitants. Cameron knowingly watched as the tide turned and started to rush away to the waiting sea. His wait included the cunning delivery of the night that would help cloak his retrieval of the gold coin he stared at.

The night finally set in and the dirt on his white skin covered him from the eyes of the moonlight that led him out to the water's edge. As he anticipated, the low tide set in at dusk. Cameron ventured toward his prize that the receding waters were beginning to reveal. With the clever crawl that a cat would portray in an exciting pursuit, he inched into the now waiting water to grab the prize that waited below the surface.

The excitement of showing off this grand prize filled his head as he imagined the other children's amazement staring at a seldom seen gold coin. With every step there was excitement, but pause followed caution as he crept towards his waiting trophy. His patience had paid off; the darkness and low tide were a godsend to him as he slowly reached into the spot of water, now only inches deep, to claim his prize.

Without a sound, the net from above surrounded the radius of his quietness. He could feel the dry rope of the web that entangled him burn across his skin as its spun jaws devoured him. Quickly he was whisked upwards and onto the waiting boat's deck above. Within seconds of his being dropped abruptly onto the deck, the thud of a rope bat knocked him flatly onto the surface. The wood of the ship's deck he laid on slowly slipped into the darkness of unconsciousness.

Hours, if not a day, passed as the lifeless body of the young boy lay on the deck of the sailing ship. The whipping sounds of the sails being filled woke young Cameron from his induced sleep. The whistling ropes that supported the sails began singing to him in his somber sleep; his eyes began to slowly open.

"This what you looking for?" roared a loud voice as the sun gave a familiar sparkle to the gold coin in the rough hand just inches from his face.

A giant laugh joined by a chorus of ruffian voices echoed inside Cameron's now throbbing head. Emotions whirling, he drifted back into the dark state of unconsciousness from which he came.

The crash of waves once again woke the boy. An order shouted from somewhere above: "Lower the mainsail!" rang out over the sea's noise as the wind of the approaching storm set upon the ship. Deck hands moved hastily by as focus came to the young lad. He was not with his family of wharf rats at all; he had been shanghaied.

Cowering into the corner of the deck he was laid on, moving like a worm with his hands and feet strongly bound, he curled his way into a fetal position, scared of everything around him. "I thought you would never wake up," a young voice said to Cameron.

The young first mate, Trey, helped Cameron to the dryness below the deck of the ship. Still bound by his lashes, Cameron was led by Trey to the galley, who motioned for him to sit silently on the top of a small barrel.

A gentle hand reached down to cup the face of the young boy and to comfort his shaking body that coldness and horror had hold of. "Don't worry, young squire," the voice of an angel seemed to come. "You're okay." Moist cloths began to clean his face and wipe the tears from his eyes. "Let me get you some water." Cameron felt the presence of the person walking away. The melodic movement of the boat at sea added to the weary stare that young Cameron was able to come up with.

When she turned and walked towards him, it was the face of what Cameron believed to be an angel. The kindness on her face was like no other he had seen in a long time. It was a memory of a dream that he had, when he saw this angelic quality of care.

"Miss Anne," came with a nudge. "Miss Anne is her name. She will clean you up. Don't try anything stupid or I will be back without care for your life," Trey instructed.

From the corner of his hazed view, Cameron watched the galley door open then close with a crash that was amplified by the now raging sea just inches of wood outside the hull. "He's a good boy." The angel spoke again.

Cameron sat motionless except for his drinking lips and his hands that formed a cup beneath them to catch the cool water that relieved his parched mouth. "Let's get you cleaned up some, okay?" The maiden spoke softly to Cameron.

She knew he was scared, and the taunting of the wicked men above was the last thing a frightened boy needed as he awoke from capture. Slowly the cleaning rag became dirty, and slowly the dirty boy became clean. His confusion was understandable; Anne was told of the ploy to trick the young man out from under the docks in Savannah. She knew he lived a life of homelessness and no one cared for him as she wiped clean the little boy's face. She tried to explain that as long as he did exactly what was told of him, the captain would see to it he was well cared for. She also told him of the dangers if he didn't. Her caring words were strong yet compassionate, so as to not give a variance to the boy's understanding. He was cleaned and fed, but not unbound, at the captain's orders. He lay down to sleep as the storm raged on; all hands were on deck throughout the night.

Daylight came through the porthole and the familiar salt air was breathed into his lungs as he awoke the next day. "Did you sleep well?" The familiar woman's voice came from the corner of the room. Still silent, the boy assumed a face of resistance as he stared at his bindings. "No, no, now, that won't do," the woman said. "You are on a boat out in the deepest sea on earth. One look like that at the captain and you'll meet her bottom," Anne said in just a touch above the angelic tone so the boy would understand his predicament. "Listen to me; if you resist your arrest, you will be beaten the first time. If you resist again, you will walk the plank."

The boy's head turned slightly as if he misunderstood what she said. "Walk the plank?" Cameron repeated.

"That means you will be required to walk off of the ship and into the ocean at knife point," Anne explained to the young boy.

The boy's eyes widened as he listened intently now to the angelic figure. "And smile!" she said. "You always smile at the captain."

Just then the iron door handle wrenched back and forth and the door of the galley flew open. In walked a man over six feet tall with long hair, a long beard, and a red coat with gold appointments on the shoulders and big, bright buttons. From the cuffs of the jacket were the hardened hands that held the hat of a captain. Their eyes met, and hearing a very slight ahem come from the lady, Cameron smiled as directed. The captain set his hat on the table and walked towards the now once again shaking young boy, the brief smile whisked away, scared by the man who was walking towards him.

The glimmer of his knife as it was pulled from its scabbard shined in the ray of sun through the porthole that lit the room. The knife was thrust towards the scared-stiff lad with such haste he could almost feel it pierce his skin. "Relax, mate, you keep shaking and I'll cut you. Now give me your hands," the captain said.

The boy's bound hands rose from his lap without his own doing; his body reacted on impulse as the captain commanded it. Swiftly the lashes that bound Cameron's hands and feet fell to the floor and the jeweled knife retreated to the scabbard from which it came. "Come on, boy," the captain said in a normal voice.

However normal this voice was for the captain, it had no normality to Cameron or any other who'd heard it. No one wanted to hear the next level of tone that the captain would make, without proper response to the first. To hear the other would make the strongest of men shake.

As the door opened to the decks of the ship, it gave a sound that all recognized as the double-time command that came without words. The daylight blinded the young boy for a bit, but he could see the men of the vessel scurrying about, most of them in the opposite direction from the towering man who stood next to him.

Life aboard the *Rawlins* was one of a hard sailing life, as he'd heard from the docks above young Cameron's head just a few short days ago. He was among them now, one of them. He had in fact been shanghaied, captured and smuggled aboard a ship in the night. Beaten by sailors, knocked unconscious, and awoken by an angel with skin like that of a porcelain doll. It was not a lie he'd made up, and soon, he was glad that his life as a young man started with such a real adventure.

It was not hard for Cameron to smile now; he had been given a new lease on life, literally. He was fed, he had quarters of lavish comfort—compared to that of the dock life he'd led—and he had freedom to go anywhere on the ship he wished, except of course the captain's quarters. He was also not allowed to go in the first mate's and navigator's quarters, or even below decks to the stores of the hold, where the bales of cotton from the Lamar warehouses were that he had slept on the night before. It didn't matter to him, though; someone wanted him, and that's the way he chose to feel about his new life at sea. He was a sailor now.

James was an old man who bore a leathery, wrinkled face of sailing. His hardened skin and unmanicured look gave meaning to the name Old Salt. It was most likely the salt from the sea's spray and baking it in the sun that gave the man that well-worn look. He was quiet, meticulous, and evenly paced as he followed the orders with deliberation and affect like that of the younger men, just slower and more focused than most.

As the sailors would have it, their language was harsh and their actions were even more so. These men of the sea were steadfast in this hard life, and the life of the sea hardened them. The pushing, laughing, cussing, and fights were had by all, save the captain and mates who stood in uniform on the upper deck of the ship. These men, like the upper factors on the docks that Cameron knew from the Lamar pier in Savannah, were astute, and their posture gave testament to their position next to the captain.

A lot of bustle below the deck was saved for the testosterone-soaked sailors who sought seniority through the toughness portrayed. This was true for the men in whole except for the one old man known only as James.

James walked about the men who scoured over the deck on the *Rawlins*. As the captain or mates shouted orders and summons from above, James was somehow always in motion ahead of the others, starting to perform the task before it left the bellowing mouth of the men from above. Cameron watched as the men jumped to orders that James seemed to knowingly follow in silence before their command was given. Respect was given to the old salt, who was revered, and no one had words with him that were cross.

As Cameron watched the day-to-day tasks of the crew, he was given orders himself and diligently followed them, no matter who instructed him; he was the lowest man on the totem pole and he was told that often. They used the word *man* though, and that in itself made the boy smile.

Cameron's eyes would light up at the end of the day to be anywhere near the stories told during the night as the crew would gather after their work was done. He was proud to be a part of something now, even though he had no idea what it was. The young boy looked at the men and recorded their stories in detail on the notepad in his mind. The old man, James, sitting farther back, watched the young man's animated expressions, and enjoyed the motions and fidgeting that the young lad would exude during tales told by lantern light.

As Cameron worked feverishly to coil and stay the ropes the next day, he was so glad to have been given an order to even touch a rope. He dropped it time after time, trying to perform this simple task. Each time the rope slipped from his hands he would turn to make sure no one saw him blunder the task, his white teeth shining the whole time as he remembered Miss Anne and her advice of a smile. It was easily done now that the sea family he was coming to know accepted him.

The raspy hand touched his shoulder and Cameron snapped his head towards it; it was James. With a gentle demeanor, James motioned with a stay of his hand. He showed the young lad how to secure the rope properly; his cracked lips never spoke. Cameron watched intently as the methodical man artfully twisted the rope into a splendid bind, which was sure. The man finished the lesson, and with a hand on the boy's shoulder, lifted himself up and walked away. Cameron felt his hand press harder on his shoulder on the old man's retreat as he used the boy's shoulder for balance before moving off into the bustling sea of men.

There was another rope that sat untied on the deck, and another beyond it. Soon Cameron worked his way around the ship, tying exactly as shown all of the ropes that lay in disarray. By the day's end, the ropes did not fall from his hands as he adamantly carried out his first order and followed the first lesson the boy ever received from a man. As Cameron tirelessly carried out this simple task, he looked to see if his accomplishments were noticed. Not one man looked back at him as they were doing their work with the same diligence, but without the wanting of acceptance. Reluctantly, Cameron looked up at the main deck to see if the exalted ones were watching him work so earnestly; not one noticed his effort. He moved to the next row and now his focus was so intent that he did not notice the shined boots of the captain standing just feet away.

A glisten of sun coming from the dry wooden deck would not have happened; it came from the golden adornment from the towering figure just to his right. In a mix between horror and excitement, the boy's studied look cast upwards towards the man above him. He stopped just below the neck of the man, at the leather scabbard belt of a musket, as the words came from the well-clad giant. "Good job, sailor."

Cameron's eyes jetted upward to meet those of the captain, his mouth open in awe suddenly shut. The boy could only smile as the man patted his head and walked away. His walk towards the front of the ship parted the sailors as they moved in respect from out of his way. He made straight for the old man, now sitting on a cask, and touched the old salt on the shoulder, same as Cameron's head. Brief words were spoken between the two and they both laughed with a similar tone.

Cameron would learn much in the days to come from the old man as the lessons of seamanship were unfolded in front of him and to no other. James saw something in the young man now, a natural leader of men with a thirst for knowledge that he knew would help him gain respect of the men who made up the world he knew on the sea.

Slowly at first the lessons played out from the old man, then finally words were introduced between them, and the bewilderment of the young sailor kept him quiet. No other on board the ship was privy to these seldom words except for one, the captain.

The young men on the upper deck watched below as the men scuffled to the reaction of the captain's words. They, after all, did not have to follow these orders; they had been told what to do by the captain himself, and they would not waiver from these orders previously given. Standing at attention, the few well-appointed men stood with chins high as the *Rawlins* broke the sea. "Turn the ship 10°, present our position, and forecast the path that is to Jamaica!" the captain barked.

Without legislation, the tasks were followed immediately as commissioned. Then, upon completion of the tasks, the young men stood and looked ahead at the broad sea, almost envisioning their destinations, which were days and miles away. Without moving their heads too much, these young squires of the sea would catch the sight of the old man James and what was now his apprentice, methodically working together as the man spoke to the young boy quite frequently.

The young men on board could only imagine what was being said by the once silent man and the wharf rat who had been pulled aboard the ship. They all wondered except one, the captain; he knew exactly what the words were that were being said between them. He had heard these very directions from the same old man many years ago.

CIVIL WAR

April 12, 1861, the Civil War.

THE LAWS OF THE PRESIDENT AND THE LEGALLY POWER-
ful Union having been denounced, the secessionist fire-eaters of the South
had the war they were hoping for. The war was a terrible mix of the entire
North wanting to abolish slavery in the South and make a comfortable
home for the new president. The South's few wealthy wanted to keep
things the way they were, while many wanted to hide behind the beauty
and splendid life with no consequences. These few Southerners against the
entire half of the states in the North would prove to be a hellish battle
that would kill more men than anyone could imagine. A civil war, or "war
amongst ourselves," is the most grotesque; and in many instances, families
and brothers fought against each other. Many thought that the exact cause
was slavery. However, slavery was a front for the greed that most all the
white men shared.

Word spread quickly throughout the country that shots against the
sides had been fired. The trading commerce set just as fast to the shipment of
guns and gunpowder and tools of war. The cultivation of field crops slowed
down, as the South would only be trading cotton and other cash crops to
the islands, held mostly by the Spanish, in the Southern Hemisphere. The
most southern port closest to these islands would soon become a bustling
war trading post.

Charleston and her sister city, Savannah, were the primary shipping
infrastructure of the Confederates. The blockade runners, small as they

may have been, supplied the shipments of cash crops for guns and ammunition with the islands. The Lamar ports were busier than ever now. There were no more pretty strolls along River Street, and the exotics of the world were not the imports left on the dock to see. This was a time of war.

Colonel Charles Augustus Lafayette Lamar had the slave ship *Wanderer* loaded with the precious white cargo of sugar and cotton. There was enough white gold loaded aboard to secure a nice armament of supplies in trade. As civilian turned military leader he, as many of the key figures in the South, paced the floor of not knowing. The new boots of his uniform could be heard several floors below in the Lamar warehouses as he watched the *Wanderer* being loaded. He knew his ship of speed could run a shipment of guns from the islands and back to the Southern port. He detested the fancy hypocrites of the South who wanted nothing but her money. He himself thought of that hypocrisy and its boundlessness as he watched his money fund the war.

His plan was to deliver the goods to the islands, then speed the *Wanderer* north up the Savannah River to the waiting men on the line of the War between the States. He planned that once the heavy load of guns was delivered, he would race up the river and fight behind the lines of the newly heavily fortified Confederate Army.

The North knew the *Wanderer* was the fastest ship in the South, and that it had actually been made for a commander of the South on the docks of the New York Yacht Club. It would figure heavily as part of the South's military might. The Northern spies lay in wait for her on Hutchinson Island across the Savannah River from the Lamar piers and watched her every move.

The cunning Northern commanders knew that they had most of the artillery, and that the South badly needed the guns of the islands. Upon the word of the *Wanderer*'s loading, they deployed their blockade. As soon as the *Wanderer* cleared the watchful guns of Fort Pulaski, now under the Confederate flag, the artillerymen of the fort watched through the spyglasses as she was captured. With her mainmast barely full of Savannah salt wind, she would become a prize of the North once again.

* * *

Cuffie worked hard in the northernmost Butler plantation. He knew that the tobacco being picked was under a less watchful eye. He had also heard rumors of a terrible battle, and that the men in the North in blue coats were opposite them. The watchmen and slave masters of the tobacco fields told the slaves, "If the white men from the North get you, they are going to chain you back up and make you work in the mines beneath the ground." The wide-eyed groups of slaves gasped. They could feel the scars of the chains that were on them ache as they listened to the men who had barely spoken to them before. They were scared, but they listened as the men went on with the plan of how they were to be a part of the aid to the brave soldiers out fighting for what was the slave's freedom to work in the sun.

As devised, the Butler plantations came together as one large plantation. The crops that made money for guns were tended to, and the lesser money crops were left to die in the fields. The white man's power had been cut in half by the displacement of the able-bodied deployed to defend the South. The main Butler plantation was strategically placed to provide logistical support for the Confederate troops. The small kitchen house where Cory's mom worked was added onto by double, if not triple. The production of meals for many army men now was a daunting battle in itself, and the work would be around the clock to supply these men.

As the quiet queen worked adamantly in the renovated kitchen, she watched as the kitchen staff tripled in size to that of before. With all the old cooks gone now because of the big sale of document slaves, most of the women were Congolese, and she informally knew them as villagers from within or around her old Congolese home. The women cooked and tended the fires in the ovens and the cook pot areas, while the men and boys of the kitchen chopped wood for them and peeled the potatoes outside to be cooked. The kitchen itself was quite a large production, as well as the number of men outside prepping the wood and food for them. Chris was appointed to oversee the kitchen grounds and was responsible for the women inside as well. He'd never carried a gun in his earlier role, but with such a large crowd under his direction and war in the wind, he kept his sidearm and rifle close.

The roles had to change with the times now, and with so many slaves familiar with the kitchen missing from the sale, the queen was in charge of cooking. Chris was now having to oversee a large number of slaves in the process, and that left Cory and Dot to distribute the food to the outposts that were scattered throughout the Southern local region.

No more were the wondrous rides in the back of the old wagon, nor the wide-eyed and taking in of all the hard workers, new places, and scenes of peaceful times. It was a time of war. Cory often saw the fires and smoke of battles as he ventured far away into the areas near the front lines. He would often return by day's end and tell his mom as he used to of the daily adventures, but this time without the excitement he once had. His mom still managed a smile as she listened, and she spent her few hours at home cleaning her own dirt-floor confines to provide the best she could for her boy, who was quickly becoming a man.

The bell still clanged every morning as it used to when he was younger. These days, though, it woke him up from his well-deserved sleep. He, as did the others, all headed down the dirt paths that led to the day's work. Cory headed to the stables to fetch the wagon and Dot so he could perform his task of delivery throughout the Southern lines. He was performing his ritual as normal one day when he noticed a boy his age staring at him. He turned quickly to the person and their eyes met.

Cuffie remembered almost a year ago the same gaze that he and Cory had shared as they were marched aboard the *Wanderer*. With war in the air around them, the conditions were similar in feeling and fright;

however, without the chains, and both unsupervised at the time, now it was different. Both young men smiled as they remembered each other.

"Brother!" Cory said to Cuffie as he stopped his chores and tied Dot to the post for keeping. "Oh, my brother!" His sentiment came in voice.

"Is it you?" Cuffie softly spoke as he set down his pitchfork and moved to meet his childhood friend.

Cory, being much better dressed, and on his own guard for longer, still had his princely qualities as Cuffie admired him. "Look at you!" he exclaimed after a brief hug. He stepped back and looked Cory over from head to toe. "Shoes? They gave you shoes?" He thought he must live in a much nicer place, and his life was so much better than his own.

Cory looked down at his feet to see the old leather shoes that were well worn. He stopped and looked at the pair of shoes and went back to the day not a month ago that he saw a dead soldier in the field. With no one around, he removed the dead man's shoes and belt as the open eyes of the dead soldier seemed fixed on him. The dead man's eyes, wide open, told a story of the horrors of war. Cory snapped from the story being told yet again in his mind as he looked to Cuffie. "Yes, I gots me some shoes."

The two, quiet now, relished in the moment over cheap leather shoes. "What do you do now?" Cuffie asked as he touched Cory's shirt like it was beautiful.

"I drive this old wagon here and deliver the foods and all to the fighting men," Cory said with some assuredness in his voice.

"You get to leave here?" gasped Cuffie.

Cory was about to carry on with an elaboration but the white guardsman yelled at them to go back to work. This cut short his response with a quick, "See you tomorrow." Cuffie knew he would, as he lived above the barn in the loft.

That day came and went like most; both young men had a brief moment of happiness and some aspirations to see each other the next day. Cory made his way out of the tin barn to fetch a load of potatoes from the stall. The workers there stopped their construction of the addition to the barn and helped the young man load the potatoes. "What y'all building?" Cory asked the men.

"We's building more rooms on the barn. Dey is gonna make a hospital for the mens dying out there." Cory's thoughts kept him quiet.

Where are we going to put the potatoes? he asked himself.

Cory left the building men at the barn to deliver the potatoes, still pondering where on earth they would put the potatoes from now on. He promptly delivered his load to the kitchen and began loading the pans of food that had been prepared by the women inside. The men from the yard were directed by Chris to help with the pans, as the wagon would be filled as high as the sideboards. Cory set off by the same path he'd traveled a hundred times before towards the north, where the skies turned gray with battle smoke.

Cory neared the area where he'd heard the distant cannons blast before. He knew something was amiss, as there was an eerie silence over the fields. He pulled back on the reins cautiously and steered Dot down the long dirt road.

The oaks and pines seemed thick as the scared two plodded down the road, slower than days before. Cory stared through the trees to the left, as he thought he saw something move in the dark woods. There it was again! His eyes wider, he pulled the reins close to his chest. His heart was now beating in his chest harder than ever; it was the loudest thing in the quiet woods.

The sudden and loud snap of a twig to his right caused him to turn his head in that direction with lightning speed. In one motion he cracked the reins onto Dot's back and fixed his eyes into the direction of the noise. The horse, scared as he was, jumped into action. The pans clanged loudly as the jalopy lurched into motion. Cory's head whipped backwards with the force of Dot's canter; he could just make out the raccoon sniffing about on the roadside behind him that had made the noise. He pulled on the reins but the horse barely slowed from the immediate signal. Dot eventually slowed, and the pans then drifted back to quiet. He breathed a slight sigh of relief. "Whoa down, girl, whoa down now," he said to Dot as the wagon slowed down to walking speed. "That a girl. It's okay." It was as though he was reassuring himself as well as the horse.

The moment of silence was immediately shattered. "Charge!" The bloodcurdling scream came from his immediate left.

"Charge!" he heard from the right as guns fired and men in uniform sprang from the cover of the woods on both sides.

There was no crack of the whip necessary as Dot now jumped to full cantor from the men's screams. She was running for her life, and poor Cory was in for the ride of his. His soul jumped back into his skin as the two sped down the road as fast as possible. Cory instinctively laid flat on the wooden bench after hearing the gunfire. He peered over the top of the back of the seat; through the jumping pans of potatoes, he saw the two sides of Confederate and Union converge on the road just where he had come from. Smoke from the muzzle blasts, cannon fire, and the glimmer of bayonets shone through the mayhem as the men fought and killed each other on the once quiet roadway.

Dot ran all the way to the military encampment they were headed to. She knew the way from having traveled it so many times. The gates began to open as always, and the wagon and Cory flew into the safety of the camp with about half of the intended load of potatoes, most of which were not in the pans anymore. The Confederate soldiers shut the fort gates behind the frightened guest.

Cory was given a map of the roadways and new places and stops to deliver food. The marked roads were far out of the way for him from what he usually traveled, but out of the line of fire, and not close to the front, where he would deliver the Confederates nourishment. The fort soldiers detained him overnight for safety until the scouts came back into the camp later that day to report the battle news. The Union now held that road, as Sherman's March was progressing through the South. The Confederate supply lines were slowly being dismantled.

It was the following day when Dot and Cory, along with two guards, made their way back to the Butler kitchen. The two well-heeled Confederate soldiers would now ride escort for Cory, as the nourishment of the troops was most important next to weapons.

The Rawlins

WITH THE PRIDE OF THE CONFEDERATE FLEET, THE *Wanderer*, now in Union hands, the need for blockade runners and privateers to haul the much-needed loads of guns to the weapon-starved army was crucial. All available ships were commissioned by the money of the South to help fight for the cause.

The sails of the *Rawlins* were full of Jamaican breeze as Cameron looked out over the bow of the ship. The *Rawlins* was making good time, he could tell by the split of the water as the ship sailed towards the waiting Confederate states. As one of the first mates now, the young man had learned a lot of the sea from the time he'd spent on the deck under the watchful eyes of James, which gave him great knowledge.

"Ship's speed?" the captain inquired as he yelled up to the front of the ship.

Cameron, stationed at point, was there, as James was; always ahead of the men for the commands given. He sheepishly grinned as he grabbed the bucket in front of James. Carefully the rope was rolled up, so as not to tangle when the long rope that held the speed bucket was deployed. Along the rope every three feet was tied a small knot. Cameron looked back towards the second mate at the rear of the ship.

"Time!" the captain said after looking to see if the sails were full.

"Time!" the second mate shouted loudly to the waiting Cameron on the ship's bow.

Cameron threw the small wooden bucket over the edge of the ship. Its splash and partial sinking pulled the bucket briskly to the rear of the ship. He counted to himself as the knots raced through his open hand.

"Time!" the second mate shouted as the bucket passed the rear mark of the ship's stern.

"Ten knots, sir!" Cameron shouted to the captain fixedly staring at the young man, in wait of his count.

"Two degrees port, fly the jib hard starboard!" the captain shouted as the crew of men scurried about. "Aye...move, ye scallywags," he told the crew and smiled as the wind blew the sea spray in his face.

Cameron pulled the bucket back up to the ship's bow. He carefully placed the bucket to the left, and starting with the rope on the bottom, he carefully coiled it for his next reading. He slightly twisted the rope to make it lay flat; in his mind he could hear James's instructions, as if they were being told to him again.

The sails popped with the new deployment of orders from the captain and the ship split the seas and the waves now roaring off the front of the wooden hull. The captain, now facing the wind, looked slightly to the second mate. Quietly he said, "Time."

The second mate shouted loudly, "Time!" as the entire crew watched in anticipation. Cameron threw the bucket over the ship's rail and watched it race backwards towards the rear of the ship. Cameron closed his eyes as he concentrated on the knots; he knew from the counts before that the speed of the knots was greater this time. He focused intently. "Time!" yelled the second mate from the stern as the bucket reached its mark.

All the eyes on deck looked to Cameron and awaited his reply; the orders had been followed and the sails rose to order, the ship fullback at the wind.

"Fourteen knots, sir!" Cameron said. The crew erupted with a cheer. The second mate smiled, and the captain registered the wind speed on his competent face. Cameron, having given the great news, hauled the bucket back to the front of the ship. He carefully placed it back in wait and looked west into the wind. They were going back to Savannah.

* * *

The Butler plantation was in full swing. The production of the kitchen and its crew of forty-eight cooks kept a full staff of men busy peeling potatoes and shucking corn. The queen watched over the production now; she was once again able to walk amongst the people she knew and oversee the operations of the small village of people that it formed. She had the look of a queen and the astute ambience that came with that title. The other women looked up to her, not just because she used to be the queen of the tiny Congolese village, but because her gentle touch and care set her apart from the others. She always would stand next to anyone who struggled with his or her chores and help them.

Chris watched over her grace from the outside. He saw her as she seemed to float behind the others, her gentle smile and perfect skin; he thought of the sweet corn bread that she had given to him and his mind played it over and over, each time a more elaborate version of the story than before.

* * *

"Yah!" Cory snapped at the horse. Dot and he now followed the scouts on horseback as they sped into the grounds of the kitchen. The men stopped briefly at the outside work crew as the slaves grabbed the load of empty pans from the wagon. The queen motioned for one of the girls to take them some water while she watched from inside the kitchen. The young girl ran with the bucket and ladle to the waiting horsemen.

The two white guards drank from the ladle to quench their thirst. When they were finished, they threw the ladle back at the girl and laughed as the ladle hit the ground. She backed up slowly and bowed at the men in reverence before she picked up the now dirty ladle. Wiping the dirt from the drinking spoon, she walked towards Cory. She watched as the white men seemed to be so war-hardened that they did not appreciate the kindness of the young girl. The two smiled as Cory drank from the water. He could taste the Georgia dirt that remained on the metal spoon. As he crushed the gritty dirt in his teeth, he seethed at the white man with a smile.

"Move out!" The two horsemen slapped their reins on the horses. Dot jumped a little as Cory handed the young maiden the ladle. "Thank you," he smiled, then cracked the reins in pursuit of the horsemen.

The girl backed away as the queen watched the two smile at each other. She thought back to how her husband, the king, high on his throne as Cory was now in the wagon, had that same smile. She blushed while the moment came back to her of her husband's gentle touch. From staring off into nowhere, she regained her composure and turned, surveying the grounds of the kitchen yard. Chris was staring intently at the queen as their eyes met. She turned her head down and walked into the kitchen.

Cuffie stood at the barn as he put the finishing coat of paint on the new addition. The hospital was now complete. Cuffie received the riders and grabbed the horses' bridles to lead them to the new lean-to just a short distance away. The dismounted men gave orders as Cory pulled up next to the two. "We leave at first light. Have the horses ready then, boy!"

"Yes, sa!" both Cory and Cuffie said in unison.

The two young men walked a short distance to the new feeding and watering corrals built for the horses. "You still live above the barn?" Cory asked as the two walked along towards the corral, Cory now pulling Dot by her bridle, too.

"No, dey is done made it a nice place for the doctors and nurses up there," Cuffie answered as he removed the saddles and put them under the new cover.

"Where do you stay now?" Cory asked his friend.

"I stay under here with the horses now; me and Dot both done lost our home," he chuckled as he hung the bridles up on the post.

Cory sort of chuckled with him as he thought how his life had changed so much as well. "Oh!" He snapped from his misery. "I got you something!" Cory lifted a small cloth wadded up under the seat.

Wrapped in the cloth was a pair of shoes and a belt. Cory retrieved the items and thrust them at Cuffie. He had never received anything nice from anyone since the time they shared as families in the peaceful Congolese village miles—and years—away. He went there in his mind as his mother would give him little things and say, "Your daddy would want you to have this."

His tears played the recorded memory of his mom and her nice gestures when he was a boy. The memory quickly went from enchantment to horror as he remembered the God-awful splash when they cast her dead body to sea aboard the *Wanderer*. Looking back at Cory, Cuffie smiled with tears of what Cory thought were joy and in a small way, they were. "Thank you," he said softly.

The next morning, Cuffie awoke to the movement of someone in the makeshift lean-to. He quietly rose to see Cory in the dark, preparing the soldiers' horses for the day ahead, new shoes already on. "What you doing up so early?" Cuffie asked of the known silhouette.

"Those men said to be ready when the sun come up. That means be ready!" Cory spoke with confidence without breaking from his task.

The two made ready the horses, Dot, and the old wagon. Cory knew it was a big day today, as his mother had been ordered to the kitchen with the entire staff under her at 3:00 a.m. so they could have the meals prepared for lunch by daybreak, before the men and Cory rode out.

At first light, the scouts made their way towards the lean-to. He could tell that the two men were clean and shaven and their clothes look pressed as they made their way from the barn. He supposed they had slept in the loft that was once Cuffie's. The two men laughed slightly as they neared, tugging their sleeves at the cuff of their newly pressed jackets. Cory saw the young slave girl who had given him the water step out of the barn doors from behind the two men and run towards the kitchen. Her torn dress was barely covering her naked body.

Confused by seeing the kitchen girl in the barn, Cory walked the two horses to the soldiers and handed them the reins. He was greeted with a stern look, which immediately sent him in the other direction towards Cuffie and the waiting Dot. Without a word, Cory stepped to the wagon seat and followed the soldiers towards the kitchen.

Being more of a stagehand now, he knew that he didn't have to load the pans in the wagon, but he got off anyway and walked inside, being that there were so many to move. He saw his mother comforting the young girl who had just been raped by the two soldiers in the barn. She was only twelve years old. His mother motioned to his stare to go and follow the others who were silently loading the pans. The young girl moved as the queen made the motion, following the queen's hand with her eyes. The young girl's face met Cory's; her eye was swollen shut.

* * *

The Tybee Island lighthouse blinked in the dark as the *Rawlins* made way through the sea to the lower east coast of the Confederacy. Young Cameron came up from the lower decks as the spotter yelled, "Land ho!"

The haze of sleeping snapped immediately from him as the ship entered the familiar waters of his childhood home. An experienced seaman now, Cameron looked into the dark to see the lighthouse beacon. He thought as he slept that night how proud of him all of the little wharf rats would be when they saw him return to the docks of Lamar Pier. He knew that after the years of his being shanghaied, they too might be gone, or might not recognize him with the beautiful clothes he wore now as a first mate. He was at home on the ship; the crew was his family, and the captain was just like a father. He looked forward into the morning's dark air as the cool ocean's spray touched his face.

The morning's sun barely popped up behind them as they snuck past the blockade of ships that waited for her. Flying the Confederate flag, matching that of Fort Pulaski, the *Rawlins* dropped sail in the presence of the mighty Confederate fort. Several cannon shots sailed a safe distance over the *Rawlins's* mast towards the waiting ships of the blockade enemies that circled about like sharks in Savannah's gray sea. The morning sun shone brightly now on the green marsh grass of the Savannah River. Cameron was home.

In short order, the *Rawlins* swerved past the sandbars and made her way by some of the homes and plantations along the Savannah River. Most people came to the shore to wave at her as the one sail now slowly propelled her through the winding river. In the distance, Cameron could see the Lamar rice tower, a 60-foot monolith that once held a fortune in rice. It had been destroyed by cannon fire that made holes in the great tower. The buildings started to come into view of the River Street young Cameron used to call home. The words "Lamar Pier" came clearly into view as the *Rawlins* made her way down the muddy river.

The sound of a steam whistle broke the silence of the still sleeping city, its sound bouncing off and along the stone-faced buildings that lined the city's shore. The mast of the *Rawlins* now stood still as the steamship SS *Lamar* roared to life and came towards the sailing ship. The *Rawlins* would be towed upriver by the steamship *Lamar*.

Cameron looked under the pier at his old home under the Lamar docks he'd left as a boy. There was no one to be seen. His gallant return in his full regalia was not to happen. The *Lamar* cut off his view as she pulled up next to the *Rawlins* and gave the towlines to the waiting crew on board.

The steam whistle broke his gaze when it sounded. He turned and slowly lumbered up to the bow to watch. The men tied the lines to the heavy wooden cleats of the ship. Still somewhat disappointed, he watched the towlines tighten. He turned and walked towards the rear of the *Rawlins*. He noticed that his pace was the same as the Lamar docks that were now moving backwards as well. For a brief moment he walked the familiar path to the rear of the ship and the mainland stayed still with his pace. Not looking anywhere but the docks, he made the stop at the ship's stern. Savannah was disappearing in the background behind the *Rawlins* now. Just as Lamar Pier started to fade from view, he saw a tiny image of a child under the dock. The two disenchanted people looked at each other as Cameron's heart leapt. He smiled and waved, and the little girl waved ever so slightly back. The captain looked back to see Cameron waving at a shadow as it disappeared in the dark of the dock's shade.

"Come on, boy!" the captain spoke as he patted Cameron on the back. "So much has changed with time." His seldom-heard and raspy voice cracked. "And time has changed so much." Cameron knew it was true.

He looked up to the captain and gently asked, "Where is your home, Captain?"

"My home? Well, my home is here with you on the ship, same as yours now," he said, looking slightly down at the young man he'd watched grow aboard the *Rawlins*. "Same as yours."

Cameron looked from the captain again out over the fading city, and then with a hardness he looked forward to the unknown waters of the Savannah River. He noticed that James was looking at them both. He wondered what secrets the old man held of captain and sea as Cameron saw James smile and turn towards the bow.

* * *

Cory noticed that blankets were added for stealth in travel now to quiet the pans. Laying the blankets over the pans in the wagon was smart, he thought to himself as he and Dot poked along the trail. He was alone again in his travels, as the guards were only there with him briefly to establish a new supply route and would not have given a slave a map of such importance. The road forked and turned. He noticed notches that the three had cut into the trees to remind Cory which way to go; there were no battle sounds this time while he traveled along the seemingly deserted road.

On the times when he saw a raccoon near the roadway, he chuckled and looked immediately behind it to see if an army of men accompanied it; there never was. He made his way to the Confederate hold and was greeted with a long stare from the guards as he approached. He thought, *How do these men not know this horse? She brings them lunch every day.* He laughed to himself and smiled at the guard's stone face.

The gates of the fort opened, and the inner city of the pointed-cut tree makeshift fort was bustling like never before. There were people immediately at the front of the wagon today who grabbed Dot's bridle. "Whoa, girl," the Confederate soldier said.

"I got your lunch today again, sir," Cory said, smiling briefly. His words were met with a simple nod from the soldier. Cory was starting to move from the seat to grab the old pans from the place where they were kept.

"Stay right there, boy! Hold them reins tight now, you hear?" the soldier demanded.

Cory sat motionless as the men started to unload the food from the wagon and carry it across the dirt yard of the fort grounds. From inside a small shed, men carrying a stretcher made of wooden planks walked towards the wagon. On the board was a mortally wounded man, the red blood shining brightly in contrast to the perfect white cotton linens that were wrapped around his wound. The men carrying the half-dead soldier came around to the rear of the wagon and loaded the man into it. He moaned with every movement they caused. Then came another; the wagon was filled with men laying on the wooden deck covered with the blankets. He knew what the blankets were there for now. There came another few soldiers who could walk, but their heads and eyes were bandaged, and some men were leading them as they made their way like blind people, reaching out in front of them. The injured people climbed into the back of the wagon.

The man holding the horse led her to turn around; the cargo moaned with each movement. "Slow now, boy," the man said when Dot was released. "No empty pans today," he added as Cory rode softly through the wooden gates.

Almost scared to turn around, Cory did look back to see the young men lying there. He watched them rock slightly and moan as the movements of the wagon and the relentless dirt road steadily moved the men from side to side. He thought how they looked lying there and how they hurt. He turned around, facing the road, and remembered how he got to the Butler plantation too, and the relentless rocking waves of the *Wanderer*. This trip would be a long, drawn-out reminder of his earlier years coming here. The smile he always kept was gone as the sun started to sink in the west.

Cory made his way slowly until the night caught him. He peered closely at the trees to see the notched marks that led him back to the Butler plantation. Everything seemed to be a movement in the darkened woods and Cory studied them well. The moaning of the men in the rear of the wagon made the ride even scarier as the shadows of trees looked down at the passing crew. He saw in the distance the glimmer of the Butler plantation's lights set on the gate for his late arrival. He made straight for the barn, where he knew a medical staff was waiting in the new field hospital. Dot came to a stop in front of the old barn doors as she had done many times before.

The doors opened wide and a number of people dressed in white came forward to the wagon and started to carry or help the wounded men into the brightly lit room. He noticed that Cuffie was one of the people helping. "Where did you—" Cory started to say, but he stopped himself halfway through the sentence. He knew they weren't to talk in the company of whites. Cory dismounted the wagon after holding the reins during the unloading. He knew that the people he worked for would want someone on the wagon in case the horse got spooked.

Cory walked around to Dot after the barn door shut and the ailing men were inside. He and Dot walked alone to the shed out back to break the wagon down for the day; without Cuffie, he unbridled and corralled the horse and put the wagon away. Walking back by the barn on the way home now on the moonlit dirt path, his shoulders were down and he was tired, dragging his feet. Just then a bloodcurdling scream came from within the barn. "No! Not my leg! Not my leg!" the unknown soldier pleaded over and over again.

Cory regained himself and walked towards the barn where he'd heard the scream. The cracks in the boards admitted light, and a knot in the wood siding gave a perfect view of the scene within. He saw the doctor in white surrounded by mostly women, a soldier lying on a table with a piece of wood in his mouth to bite down on, and then the doctor turned towards the lying man with a silver saw. His view of what was about to happen was obscured, but he could see Cuffie standing in the corner watching with the widest eyes ever. The man screamed through the wood in his mouth and

Cory saw Cuffie shut his eyes as hard as he could. Cory saw the blood drip onto the hay of the floor from the table.

* * *

The thick, black smoke from the steam engines poured onto the decks of the *Rawlins*. The captain looked downward at the deck in disgust at the brown, muddy water the men were dishing from over the side to use to clean the deck; his boat was a mess. The red Georgia clay infused in the water left a brownish haze on the wooden decks of the fine sailing ship. Black specks of the coal within the fire aboard the *Lamar's* engines added to the disarray. The deck of the *Rawlins* was simply a mess. The sailors peered through the smoke, thick like a sea mist as the *Rawlins* was dragged through the meandering river. The steamship slowed and rounded the corner in the shrinking Savannah River, and Cameron saw the first signs of life as the sawmill came into view a short distance ahead.

"All hands on deck!" the captain ordered, and the crew came from the hold doors below. Not under speed, the thick, black smoke of the *Lamar* rosé skyward.

Aboard the *Lamar*, the men were already on deck, ropes ready for tossing off the lines of the towed ship. The captain of the *Lamar* was to pass the dock slowly and allow the *Rawlins* to untie the lines and dock, since she had no power. The captain of the *Lamar* noticed that there were no dockhands as usual on the lumberyard wharfs when the ships approached; only a ghostly silence. His senses perked up with the anticipation of something wrong.

The doors of the dock house flew open just thirty feet from the bow of the *Lamar* as she slowly passed. The black cannon rolled forward and turned straight for the pilothouse of the *Lamar*. The *Lamar's* captain hit the deck just as the cannonball ripped through the wood of the captain's perch and took the top of the steering wheel with it. All of the glass was gone now from the concussion of the blast. The dazed captain's eyesight came into focus slowly, the blurry wooden deck inches from his face. He noticed the small pool of blood contrasting on the wood that was now in his focus.

The deafening sound of the cannon blast left his ears ringing loudly; the gunshots were coming into audible focus now. His mind racing, he knew the ship would hit the bank of the river if he did not steer away immediately. He stood amidst the gunfire and turned the wheel wildly. "Full port!" he yelled as the wheels spun round.

One-quarter of the wooden wheel was missing. "Cut the lines!" he gasped. "Cut the damn lines!" He ran to the opposite side of the wheel-house. From the captain's deck above, he could see the mighty swing of the axe as the lines were cut to the *Rawlins*. "Full steam ahead!" he bellowed as the dense, dark smoke from her stacks spewed out.

The crew of the *Rawlins* was speechless. Cameron couldn't believe the happenings as the cannon's roar and the gunshots ripped through the *Lamar*. The taut towropes snapped backward at the *Rawlins*'s bow when they were cut; he could feel the boat's speed slow to a crawl. They were sitting ducks. The *Rawlins*, under no power, drifted straight into the waiting cannon's view.

The long stick rammed another cannonball down the barrel and the striker came downward to the top of the cannon to light the beast again. The small flash of the primer gunpowder flashed and the cannon roared again. Out of the cannon's mouth came the exploding steel ball, followed by a thick stream of white smoke and fire like a dragon had just spit death onto the scattering decks of the *Rawlins*. The crack of wood and the creaking of timber could be heard as the mainsail's mast fell into the muddy water of the river.

Gunshots from both sides could be heard now as the *Rawlins* crashed into the docks of the Lamar sawmill. The seamen poured onto the docks. Knives and cutlasses high, the gallant crew leapt to the broken docks of the mill. The impact of the large ship shuddered the dock with such force that the man loading the cannon and the gunmen in the shack lost their footing. The captain of the *Rawlins* pulled the pistols from his holsters as Cameron watched from behind the ship's rail. Steadily he aimed; the pistol's hammer dropped. The smoke and fire like that of a cannon shot forward, and Cameron watched the man loading the cannonball fall from the shot's impact. The smoke from the captain's pistol blew slightly backwards and the captain grabbed his chest. The ever-powerful legs of the captain buckled and he dropped to his knees on the deck. Face forward he fell as the Union rifleman's bullet took his life.

Without regard for his own life, Cameron ran to the only man who ever loved him. Shots flew over his head as he stared into the open eyes of the man he loved and respected. Such disbelief; the thick smoke poured over the blood-soaked wooden deck as he knelt, crying.

"Go!" was the last word the captain spoke. The captain was dead.

Cameron grabbed the captain's sword lying on the deck and ran to kill the man who had struck him down. He jumped over the tangled mast and sails, then leapt from the bow of the *Rawlins*. He watched as one of the crewmen slid his sword into the chest of the man with the rifle. There were no more gunshots now and the small puffs of white smoke lifted.

The sounds of swords were gone; the small force of Union soldiers were all dead, and the silence of the Georgia pines looked down on the injured and dying crew. The only sound was the moaning of the injured and the boots Cameron wore as he made his way to the dying Union soldier who leaned against the wall. The fear in his eyes met the rage in Cameron's. Cameron, standing before the man who had just shot the captain, looked down on the man as the fresh blood oozed from his stomach. Cameron's face, hardened by the salt of the sea, and without mercy, stabbed the captain's blade through the dying man's heart.

He walked through the dock house onto the land as the smoke cleared. He saw his crew slowly make their way up the docks as the smoke of the *Lamar* rose across the tree tops while she ran away back to Savannah.

A squad of Confederates charged into the still camp on horseback, and the slaves then emerged from the thick woods. Cameron would have his revenge on the Union that killed his family.

He and the other crewmen, after clearing the decks and steadying the crippled ship, took the bodies of the captain and James across the river. They were laid to rest under a 100-year-old oak with beautiful weeping Spanish moss casting a shadow on the graves of the two.

"Atlanta is lost!" the Confederate commander led with as he spoke to the surviving crewmembers and Cameron. "What's onboard your ship?" the uniformed Confederate commander asked.

Cameron, being first mate and now the captain, spoke to the crewmen of the ship. "Mr. Lloyd, report the holdings!"

Mr. Lloyd began to read from the ship's log the hold manifest for the *Rawlins*. The list was long, and the colonel knew from hearing the list that the artillery would have saved the stronghold he once commanded.

"We must all fall back and reset the battle lines south of the river," the Confederate commander instructed.

"Wait, sir! I will not be fighting in this war!" exclaimed Cameron. "Me and my men will unload the weapons and leave this godforsaken place here with you." His crew grumbled the acceptance of his plan.

"Oh, I guess you and your men will *paddle* your ship down the Savannah River and right out to sea," the Confederate jested. The other soldiers laughed at the colonel's remarks.

"We will wash her out with the tide and fore-sail, thank you!" Cameron whipped back at the officer.

"Oh well, sir, let me tell you!" The colonel peered closer to Cameron. "I just told you Atlanta is lost. Sherman's march is headed to Savannah now, boy!" The colonel leered at the wide-eyed young captain. "As you pass Savannah, the guns of the fallen Fort Pulaski will blow you to pieces. Your bodies will be the only thing that washes out to sea." The band of Confederates laughed as the colonel made his point firm.

"Savannah is lost too?" Camera shot back.

"No, but her people will surrender the city to Sherman without a fight. They will leave their homes and land so Sherman will have a nice Christmas gift for the Union president," the officer next to the colonel stated as he waved his pipe at the group.

"But we were just there!" Cameron responded as he remembered the hollow streets of Savannah.

"Yeah, and your captain was just alive, too!" The Confederate chuckles caused Cameron to stand. He heard the pistols of the Confederates cock as he moved. The commander said straight-faced, "Boy, this is a war! For every foot forward we take...they take two. We've lost hundreds if not thousands of lives trying to fight a war without guns enough to match theirs. You will help us get the guns that are in your hold and you will join us now or you will die here in this spot!"

Cameron knew they were outnumbered. He knew that Pulaski's ominous fort, if held by the Union, would surely kill them as they tried to make sail. He knew with Savannah under Union control he would not even make it past the city port or the blockade boats that would be at the river's mouth. He looked at the *Rawlins*. "She is lost." The crew sank with the realization, as did Cameron.

"We make for Butler plantation at daybreak. There will be food and medical attention there. We will set the *Rawlins*'s artillery in the fields and hold our ground there," the commander said and turned from the teeming men. "Now get some sleep!" he shouted back as he walked away.

***

Cory was stopped halfway to the outpost that he was headed towards. A finely appointed Confederate commander and several soldiers on horseback led a tattered squad of a hundred soldiers down the road Cory was on. "Whoa down there, girl." Cory spoke to Dot and she began to slow down.

The group of soldiers stopped in the road, as did Cory, Dot, and the fresh load of cooked potatoes. "What you got there, boy?" the commander said to the young man, now facing an army. Dot, at a stop now, stepped backwards as the man approached young Cory.

"Speak up, boy!" the captain next to the commander said, and pulled his sword from its scabbard.

Pointing the sword at Cory, the man and his horse walked beside Dot and along the wagon. Cory couldn't talk from fear. The horses were so tall compared to Dot. The man looked like a giant to Cory. He turned his head and faced away from the steely blade.

"What you got hiding under them blankets, boy?" the captain demanded, now moving his sword tip from the boy's head to the blankets in the rear of the wagon.

The captain gently lifted the edge of the blanket closest to him with the tip of his sword. His movement with the blade was slow and meticulous. The commander pulled his pistol and pointed it at the rear of the wagon, which from his point of stance was directly at Cory's head. Cory wanted to say potatoes so badly but his jaw was frozen in fright. The captain's blade flipped the blanket back, expecting nothing less than an ambush of men to jump from the wagon.

"Food, boys!" the captain yelled back to the following men. "Come and get it!" He backed his horse up two steps. The army of men converged on the wagon.

"Where you from, boy!" The captain now had the sword in Cory's face again.

"Ba-Ba-Butler," was all the frightened young man could say.

"Butler plantation, boy?" the captain snapped.

"Ya, Ya, Ya, Yess, sa!" He could barely be heard because of the pans clanging and the men yelling in cheer. "Butler plantation...sir!"

"Good." The captain retracted his sword. "Good answer, boy!"

The commander then turned to the officer on the left of him and said something. Cory could not make out a word the men were saying. The famished army of men had left one pan of potatoes in the wagon as they sat along the roadside and in the field eating like a pack of hungry dogs. The commander and his mounted men got off their horses. "Come mind these horses, boy!" said the officer, gathering the reins from his commanding officers.

Cory's knees shook with his own weight when he jumped down from the wagon as the men like giants walked by him. He grabbed their horses' reins and watched the men converge on the last pan of potatoes. These men, unlike dogs, ate like wolves as they looked over the men and land while they stood over the pan of potatoes.

"There's a hospital at Butler," he heard the men speaking.

"And more food, too!" another added to the almost growling mens' conversation.

"We should rest up there and get ourselves ready, sir!" the captain suggested.

The commander nodded in agreement as he stuffed the food in his mouth. The wolves and the dogs finished devouring the meal in minutes. Cory realized they'd left the pans lying in the road and throughout the field. He couldn't believe the heathens these men had become.

The commander and the officers mounted up after snatching the reins from Cory's hands. "Boy!" the commander ordered, "You get your wagon turned around and lead us back to the Butler place right now, you hear?" Without a word, Cory turned away and walked Dot to turn around with the wagon.

When he finished, he started to climb back up the step to the seat. "You walk that horse, boy! These soldiers are going to be riding in your stead," the captain commanded. "Put the injured in the wagon." This caused a dozen bandaged men to come to the front of the pack. Cory could hear the boards creak as the heavy human load filled every place to be had on board. Dot moaned with the strain as she barely got the wagon wheels to move.

"Yah!" the officer yelled at his horse and rocketed forward to scout the way for the walking troops.

The march seemed to last forever while the boy led the army into the west. The sun beat on the brigade all day as they walked in the red Georgia clay. Day turned to night as the tattered group entered the gates of the Butler plantation. The army of men converged on the plantation one hundred strong. They passed the kitchen and began starting fires and eating the potatoes and corn raw. Cory watched as they ransacked the kitchen in starvation. There was no one there from the plantation as darkness had the plantation quiet. "Where's the hospital, boy?" the officer asked Cory.

"It's up the hill, sir, right up dey," Cory responded.

"Take them in there for attention." The officer turned toward the heathens who stripped through the kitchen.

Cory heard the men claim each find as a prize. The yells and howls of the pack of dogs were heard across the field. Cuffie, hearing the commotion, opened the big barn door as though he was looking for a bear or a group of them. He saw Cory barely able to walk headed toward the light of the doorway. "You okay?" Cuffie asked as he took the reins from the boy's hands. He could see that Cory's walk was that of exasperation. Cory could not manage a word.

The wounded soldiers climbed out of the wagon and lumbered into the barn. Cory was able to see the doctors and nurses get up from their sleep and come down from the loft to help the injured men. Cuffie put a hand on Cory's shoulder. "I gots her," he said, leading Dot off to the shed. Cory, now admitting defeat to a long day, turned to the path towards the shacks where he lived. His feet would barely carry his exhausted body.

The screams of a woman shot down the hill at Cory. His head went up from the ground and locked in on the sound. The woman's screams were terrible; his feet froze as his mind put together the chaos. He started running towards the screams in the dark. He heard Cuffie yell, "No, Cory!" Cory paid no attention, running straight at the noises in the dark. Cory topped the small hill and saw the lights from the little row of shacks where the slaves lived. He froze for a second as he saw the Confederate heathens from the kitchen now walking into the small shacks. The screams were clear now as his heart leapt from his chest. He ran harder than ever towards the shack, the third one from the end, his home. The door was open; he knew his mother would never leave the door open while she slept. He heard, above all, the screams of his mother come from the doorway in the shack. The dim, candlelit, one-room shack rang with the terrified screams of his mother. The white man, on top of her now, punched her in the face as she screamed in the dim cabin. The tearing of her clothes and the thrusting of the soldier's pelvis could be seen by the terrified boy. The man turned and smiled at Cory, It was one of the scouts that had raped the girl in the barn just a few days before.

He ran to save his mother, with no regard for his own life. He sprang like a cat onto the back of the white assailant. He punched the man wildly and then froze in mid-swing. The blade of a sword ripped through his side and upwards to his chest, leaving his body frozen in pain. His open mouth couldn't yell as the man in the corner of the room who was next to rape the queen turned the sword's blade sideways in his body; it was a military-style kill. The man then lifted the boy, blade still impaled in him, and threw him to the floor as he retracted the blade from the dying child in one fluid movement.

Cory lay in a pool of his own blood, looking up at his mother as the room started to darken. His mother's screams were the last thing the young prince would ever hear as the soldiers continued to rape her.

* * *

The last of the munitions were unloaded onto the work carts of the sawmill from the hold of the *Rawlins*. Cameron, watching closely, surveyed his options. He did not want to be in this war, nor did he answer to any other commander, other than the two men he'd buried across the river. He found, as most men do, that those gone before you still lead you in mind and spirit. The old man James was on his left shoulder and the steadfast captain on the right. Harmony and heresy went through the young man's mind. It was something he had heard all along from the two, but in passing;

their voices were louder than ever now. "Not now!" both seemed to agree as Cameron attached the rigging to one of the wagons. The horses of the soldiers were used to pull the wagons, and there were more wagons than horses. The Confederates had an easy solution; the slaves who returned to the campsite would pull the remaining wagons.

Cameron couldn't believe the hatred between the men just because of the color of their skin. He had been at sea for years throughout the islands; the old salts with their dark, cracked skin were one shade lighter than the Jamaicans and Cubans he had come to know throughout his travels of the Indies. He seemed to relate to the workers of the group because he, too, came from nothing and was forced into the life that he led. There was one difference though, between the slaves of the sea and those of the land. You realize on a ship, in an ocean, that you can't run very far, and the people there with you came from a world of spurn and rejection by most too, like yourself. So you sit and listen to the stories of their lives and you realize that they are not so different from you, regardless of what color they are. There was no color in rank, and they were all outcasts and slaves of the sea.

The outcast part is what gave the Confederates their distaste for the sailors aboard the *Rawlins*. They also looked down on them as pirates of sorts. These men hailed from the most exotic places in the world. Their skin was fashioned by Mother Nature to make them survive the conditions she'd dealt them. To have white skin, Cameron learned, gave tale to his lack of sea experience and not being an islander. He remembered being aboard the *Rawlins* looking out over the bow, hoping the sea salt and hot sun would make his skin closer to that of his brothers of the sea and islands. It didn't, however; his white skin was from Savannah, and he grew a dislike for his own color. He wanted the look of a hardened seaman and the skills of an island survivor.

His mind's wandering was brought to an end as the Confederate captain yelled to the other soldiers: "Lash the slaves to the wagons!" The smiling white soldiers obliged.

As they came towards the seamen from the *Rawlins,* they walked among the ranks of them and pulled out the Jamaican man, a fine sailor with great ocean skills who was respected by the crew of men of the *Rawlins.* The crew's family nature caused them to step towards the white Confederate as the man put his hands on the Jamaican seaman. Cameron, being the whitest of all the sailors and still with a slight Southern twang in his words, stepped forward. "Unhand him." Cameron was now at the face of the soldier. There was no waver in his voice.

The soldier pulled his bayonet from his leather belt. Cameron pulled the captain's sword from his side. Both sides of men noticed the fine blade of the islands as it trumped the confederate man's tiny bayonet. Most of the Confederates now turned towards the skirmish as the tiny band of seamen grouped for a fight. There stood young Cameron, longsword in hand, arm outstretched and ready with almost twenty guns pointed back at the unwavering group. The Confederate colonel stepped up on his horse. "Quite a show, young lad," he said with a look that told the small group they were all about to die. "Quite a show indeed." He dismounted his horse and walked between the lines of men.

"You know you will all die here today, if that's what you want!" He surveyed the group. "It doesn't matter to me. I could simply say the word and you would be shot before your knives met their mark!" He walked towards the sword he saw was now slightly shaking.

He stopped inches from the boy's face. "I will give you one chance to drop your weapons, or you will surely die here today. I will leave you dead where you stand and have the animals clean the flesh from your bones!" His tone left no one to question the threat, not even the Confederates. "Now drop your arms, sir, and since you want to defend this black's life with your own, step lively to his side and haul that wagon, you pirates." Not even a blink came from the colonel as he made his ultimatum.

Cameron, hearing the weapons of the Confederates being cocked, also heard the knives of his crew drop to the ground. He lowered his shaking sword and put it back in the scabbard of its keep and handed the pair to the colonel. The voices of the captain and James said once again, "Not now, boy!"

Cameron placed the harness over his head and his crew followed his lead. The Confederate soldiers uncocked and lowered their weapons. "That sure is some purdy horses," he heard a Confederate say as they laughed at their humiliation.

The colonel slid the sword under the saddlebag of his horse and mounted his saddle. High above the crowd of men, the only man on horseback, the commander gave the orders to move out. The men pushed the wagons as they followed the other horses and men in front. Cameron looked at the red dirt and wondered, *What kind of hell is this?* The dry, red clay was uneven and billowed dust while the weary crew pushed one of the last wagons in the train.

After hours of pulling the wagon, he saw the horses' dung from the wagons ahead. He could tell by the big, round clumps that it was horse manure that had been trampled. He then saw human feces on the ground. The smell of human waste was so different than the other smells he encountered at the rear of the pack. He looked up to see the men in uniform dance through the thick grass as the train moved forward. They passed the squatting few more frequently now as the men using the bathroom would look back at the moving human train, each holding balance on their rifles as they relieved themselves. They ran double-time back into formation and rejoined the marching troops.

Cameron was not about to soil his pants in front of his crew. His stomach ached with pain; the feeling was about to overcome him. "Halt!" the colonel said as he held his hand in a stopping motion. The train of men stopped. "Take a break!" Cameron heard from the front of the line. It was all he needed to hear; he flew to the road's edge in the high grass and grinned with a slight sigh of relief.

* * *

The Butler plantation was a scene of havoc. The slave masters and white farm hands came from their cabins and houses at the clang of the morning's bell. They made straight for the tents erected near the kitchen.

"Commander!" William Quintus demanded as he led the group of irate owners' representatives. The men by the fire outside did not stand. One soldier pulled his pistol and pointed it straight at William as he cocked the hammer back. The other soldier there said, "Lower your tone, mind you." The tent's flap shot back and the well-appointed colonel walked out to see the unsettled group. William immediately addressed him.

"Colonel, I demand to know what gives you the right to waltz into our home of the South that has been in constant support of your troops. Your men have ruined our kitchens, supplies, and have destroyed the tranquility of our help. We strive to provide you and your men—" William was rudely interrupted. The gloved finger of the colonel touched his lips as if to seal them.

"Let me tell you something! The hundred men you see out there is what's left of a thousand! Your food you were to provide never made it to the battle lines. My men were starved in the field of battle and haven't eaten in almost two weeks. We walked without water over a hundred miles to get here. The forts and outpost you provisioned are all gone. They are the smoke of burning timbers and men that filled the air as we walked here. You want to know what right I have? I'll tell you. It's the right that I have as I watched the hundreds of my men die protecting people like you. The right of life each gave for the Confederacy. I say! Now where is your honor and support for the remaining brave souls out there?" He pushed William's face with the finger he had on the man's lips. "Where?" he demanded with the gloved finger still pointing in the man's face.

William was speechless with dishonor. He stepped back and bowing his head said, "I apologize. I will have my staff make ready for you and your men a fine meal. Soap will be brought up for you and your men and you can bathe in the pond at the rear of that field." He pointed over the colonel's shoulder. "Your clothes will be cleaned, washed, and pressed. Your wounded can seek help at the hospital over there." He pointed in the other direction down the hill. "I apologize, sir. We are here to serve you, as you and your gallant men have served the sons of the South," he said, and placed his hand on his chest as he bowed.

William then turned to the others behind him. The angry mob looked all flushed as he spoke. "You, go get several cows from the ranch for cooking. You, go to the field stores and get the potatoes and corn. You, reassemble the kitchen and start the fires. And you, go get the soaps and make ready bathing for the men in the field. Gather their clothes and have them cleaned at once." He clapped his hands twice and the group dispersed at the direction of his orders. William turned back to the colonel. "You, kind sir, can make residence at the main house. I will have your hot bath drawn and meal readied," he said with the utmost respect to the colonel.

"I will be eating with my men." He turned and looked at the soldiers now standing next to the fire, and motioned his hand for them to sit again. The soldiers looked at William like they knew what answer was coming from their commander. They shook their heads and put their pistols back in the holsters. William heard the uncocking of the hammers as he turned back towards the main house.

"Colonel, some of the forces that just came into camp said there were two well-clad scouts that had been murdered, and they matched the description of the scouts staying in the barn here at Butler," the commander said as he returned to his seat next to the fire.

"Murdered, huh? Ya get to still murder people in a time of war?" the colonel said.

"Colonel, they was scalped alive and left to die. They's didn't get killed by no Union boys; they say Indians got 'em." The commander sadly moved his head side to side. "They pulled their guts out of 'em alive, Colonel!"

"It's gonna get real interesting fighting two different enemies at once, but I guess we'd best be getting ready," the colonel said, moving the flap to the tent with his hat and walking inside. "God help us!" he seemed to say to himself as the cloth door fell back into place.

* * *

The day cast downward on Cameron and the men who pulled the wagons down the endless Georgia road. Heading slightly south caused the feeling of retreat in the spirit of the men as they followed their commander. The wagons creaked and moaned at the weight of the munitions they held. On top of the crates and barrels of gunpowder were the wounded soldiers who could not walk; their moans were as loud as the creaks in the wagon wheels.

Cameron heard in the distance a horse coming at high speed. Its speed was contrasted by the slow clopping of the horse-drawn wagons. Hours had passed since any break had been given; the commander on horseback up front raised his hand to stop. Cameron dropped to his knees, as did most of the other men in the weary parade.

The rider approached fast, while the commander pulled his brass spyglass out of his leather pouch. He studied the rider, then said to the captain on foot, "It's one of ours."

The gray jacket and sloped hat with the Confederate markings came into view. The man and horse slowed as he approached the weary group. He saluted with a taut look at the colonel as he stopped his horse. "Colonel, sir!" He snapped as the colonel saluted back. "Colonel, I rode from the Butler plantation. Food and provisions are there for you, sir!" he said with a straight order of words.

"We are headed there now," the tired man responded. "How far till we make camp?"

"Just down this road, sir!" The officers on foot smiled with the news.

"Yes, sir!" the captain shot back. He turned to dispatch the orders that the perilous journey was almost over.

* * *

Cuffie came from the barn where the hospital was set up. He saw to it that the doctors there treated Cory's mother. She was unable to speak from the terrible beating she had sustained and was in shock. Tears were her only words as she lay there. Cory's body was wrapped up in a sheet and put with the other bodies that were casualties of war. Cuffie remembered the look Cory had when he walked up to the barn leading Dot. His spirit seemed broken by the men he'd led to the hospital. He still did not stop though until he led them to the doctors. His tired eyes told Cuffie that he could go no more as he handed the reins to his friend. Cuffie thought, *why would these men do such a terrible thing?* He hated them all.

The young man walked towards the place in the shed where he would sleep. He plopped down on a log he had fashioned as a seat and stared at the fire in the lantern there. The fire danced from the wind, and he started to cry tears for his friend who was lost.

The tears blurred the flame when he looked into the fire. "Boy," he heard the words of Kia Longo speak to him. The old adviser's voice was clear. "Boy, you must not harbor hatred, for life is not fair. The prince is here with me and we all are watching you."

Cuffie spoke to the flames. "But these men...I want them to die a thousand deaths."

"They will, my son, they will. You are not the one to take this upon yourself to give them these deaths, for you are the only wise man left of the Maliki tribe," the old adviser comforted. "The prince is with the king now. You are the only one left to save the queen of our people."

"How will I do this? How can I survive this journey?" He began speaking to himself.

"You must, for all of our people who have passed before you, for your friends, the king, and young Cory. Keep your anger away, boy, and go to her, for them." The wise man spoke through the flame.

Cuffie thought of the horrors he had been through. The people killed, and the people who died. He thought of the old man as they dragged his dead body past him on board the *Wanderer*. He heard the splash as his mentor was thrown into the sea. He saw the faces of them all clearly.

"You must use your head and your heart, together," the old voice said. "You will be free, my son; I have seen your future. For this day is why I trained you as a boy. This day you will carry the Maliki tribe with you. Their spirit rests within you, and you will set your people free!"

Cuffie spoke out, "But how?"

"Not now, my son," was all he heard as the old Maliki warrior's voice faded into the flame.

Cuffie could not sleep after the apparition and voice that came to him. He left the shed where Dot was and went to the hospital barn to check on the queen. He walked in to hear the conversations of men asking why a slave woman was amongst them.

"You should get that slave out of here!" one of the wounded soldiers said from his cot.

"Yeah, something bad is going to happen to her for sure," one of the others grumbled.

The doctor met Cuffie at the door. "Son, we have to move her; these men are dangerous," he said as he placed his hands on the young man's shoulders. "I will come tend to her in her home; she'll be safer there." The doctor spoke with care. "She's going to be fine, son."

Cuffie appreciated the doctor's kind words. He turned to the staring soldiers and shot them a look to kill. Kia Longo's voice from his shoulder reminded him, "Not now."

"I'll have the men carry her up in a moment. Go on up to her house and make it ready," the doctor added.

Cuffie turned and ran up the hill to the small row of shacks. He noticed the women going into Cory's home. He stopped running when he got to the door to see several women cleaning and bringing flowers into the room. He noticed one young girl, the one with the black eye, sitting on the foot of the bed. The little girl had a single flower in her hands. He turned and knew that these women would care for the queen. He felt the spirits of the men past, smiling on the goodness of the people. He started to make his way towards the kitchen.

As he walked up the hill towards the kitchen, he saw coming through the gate of the plantation another long line of men. Fear raced through his soul as he saw the men and thought of the heathens who had killed his friends.

"He was my friend, too," a voice came from the shadows. Chris stepped lightly towards young Cuffie. "Don't worry, I've already taken care so's nothing like that will happen again." His compassion convinced Cuffie to listen to the voices that began racing through his head.

"You stay right cheer," Chris said. Cuffie surveyed the lay of the land. The kitchen was in full swing. Confederate guards watched as the men of the kitchen prepared the huge meals. The women worked away inside. Others were stringing up clothes to dry by lines drawn between the huge pecan trees that were evenly placed. He looked back as the men approached and the commanding officers rode in on horseback to give instruction. The two colonels met in the driveway and talked briefly. He couldn't hear the instructions but he saw the hand gestures pointing their way around the Butler lands.

The caravan of men and wagons began to move again. He knew that the wagons and horses were to be attended to so, with a sigh, he turned toward the barn.

"Don't worry, son, I got guards down there too!" Chris said, and then he patted Cuffie on the back. Cuffie started walking down towards the barn. He picked up his pace to get in front of the men he knew were headed to the pond to bathe. Since he was quickstepping, he jogged down towards the barn. He waved his arms while he ran to stay ahead of the wagon teams headed his way towards the barn, so they would follow. Being ahead of them by a good distance, he opened the barn doors and told the doctors, "They's mo men coming!" Then he shut the door.

Cuffie stood next to the barn as if to direct traffic of the wagons that approached. The horses were to be unhitched and corralled, and the wagons placed neatly on the side of the barn. He heard the sound of clopping horses coming from the area of the pond. It was the colonel who had made camp the other day. He rode straight at Cuffie, almost as if he didn't even see the boy; his horse sped towards the front of the barn. The wagon train approached and the commander spoke. "Take the wagons down the side here towards the field. Stop them over there by the line of trees." He turned and looked down at Cuffie. "Mind you, boy, when them wagons get stopped, you unhitch, feed, and drink them horses." The commander raised his voice.

"Yes, sa!" Cuffie responded as the giant horse partially blocked his view.

The wagon procession began to lumber by. Cuffie noticed the wagons were loaded to the high point with crates and boxes.

The colonel, with the simultaneous opening of the barn doors, said, "Stop here and unload the wounded." The doctors and aides walked out to grab the few men on top of the wagons. Cuffie stayed back out of the way, as a lot was happening around him. The man on horseback was definitely running the operations of all. "Move out!" the colonel yelled, and with a turn of his horse, he began to canter off.

Cuffie started walking by the wagons in front, and told the drivers exactly where to put the wagons. After his direction, he stood and surveyed the train of wagons and counted the horses he was to corral and feed. He stood frozen as he saw the next few wagons. Exhausted men were pulling the wooden wagons, having been shackled to them, with cargo piled as high as possible. These men were almost dead. He stood speechless as he counted four wagons pulled by humans; he had never seen such horror. These white men were heathens, too.

He quickly ran to the back of the last wagon and began pushing with all of his might. "Whoa!" The voice came from the front of the train. He walked cautiously around to the front of the wagon as the men pulling it fell to the ground. He frantically tried to undo the leathers that were fashioned around the men, their limp bodies too tired to help.

"Water," the man said, lying on the ground. Cuffie took off with lightning speed to fetch a pail of water for the men. The Confederate drivers of the horse-drawn teams walked towards the pond as he ran the pails of water to the men. He turned to fetch two more. The men staggered towards the boy, an angel in their eyes. In a panic he left the horses tied up to the wagons in front as he raced to help the men.

"Y'all go into the corral. They's water in there and a place to lay down." The panic-stricken boy darted from man to man. "I'ze go get you some food," he said, and started to run to the kitchen. Just then he realized he couldn't carry enough in his hands. He turned and raced towards Dot, and in seconds she was hooked up to Cory's wagon. He jumped in the seat and slapped the reins down; Dot took off towards the kitchen.

Chris saw the wide-eyed boy and Dot flying up the hill towards the kitchen. He knew that Cuffie was trying to help the distressed men he saw pulling the wagons by. He motioned for the boy to come towards the back of the kitchen. "Right cheer, boy!" Chris directed Cuffie with one hand and put his finger in front of his mouth as if to tell the boy to be quiet. The two guards stepped forward. "He's going to take this to the main house; they eat first," Chris said as he walked right past them with all the authority of a commander. He in fact was the commander in charge of the kitchen, and the two men were instructed to follow his orders. "You's gonna take this down to them fellas?" Chris said quietly when the two got out of earshot of the guards.

"Yeah, they's almost dead!" Cuffie said as again Chris gave Cuffie the sign to be quiet.

"I gonna get you loaded, but you head towards the main house as you leave, so the guards don't think much a difference."

"Yes, sa!" Cuffie said with a conspiratorial response.

With the wagon loaded full of the best meals for the main house, Cuffie snapped the reins and slowly headed towards the big house at the end of the pecan tree drive. With a dastardly look, he turned the cart and slipped quietly behind the cover of the confederate jasmine that hid the path that led to the servant's quarters.

It came to him suddenly as he drove Dot down the row of small houses where the slave quarters were. In front of Cory's house came the loud call, "Whoa!" Cuffie sprang from the seat and ran to the back of the wagon. Just then the door of the queen's house opened and two ladies walked out to see what the matter was. "Come and gets some of this food!" Cuffie exclaimed to the women. He walked in with a pan full of the finest roast beef, and presented it to the queen.

He felt like he was back in the old village and meeting the queen for the first time. He bowed upon presentation. He was followed by the women carrying bread and fruit who laid out the meal fit for a king at the feet of the queen. She smiled as if her royalty was restored, and motioned for the young girl with the black eye to grab the orange that she was fixated on. Cuffie knew the past elders were smiling down on him as he backed out of the room slowly and shut the door.

Within seconds his thoughts snapped back to the starving, half-dead men behind the barn. He slapped the leather reins down again and sped towards the waiting men in the corral.

He undid the corral post and walked Dot straight back to where the men were lying in the hay. He tied Dot to the corner post and all the men got up to see what had just arrived. Cuffie had such a good feeling of feeding the hungry men, especially the food fit for the master's house. He walked away and looked at the setting sun and imagined if Cory felt like this when he did that job every day. He could feel Cory's spirit with him as he went to unlatch the gate and care for the horses and wagons.

Cuffie had such an enchantment within him when he took the horses to the corral. He could see the men eating like kings, and some in their weary state even managed a smile. He thought the queen was happy some too, as the food was such a gift. He finished loading the horses into the corral for the evening.

As the sun started to set, Cuffie went with a lantern he fetched from the barn to see the men, and give them some final instructions. He walked across the dim corral with the lantern leading the way. All of the men who were a horse team for the day looked to see the approaching lantern. When they saw the young man's face they all smiled, and several got up to pat his back in appreciation. He noticed the one smiling white boy sitting across him in the group. He instinctively moved the lantern closer to see the young man his same age. The young Cameron stood at the obvious gesture of awkwardness. He approached Cuffie and stood motionless. "Thank you!" the young Cameron said.

Cuffie looked him over, his skin white and accented by the lantern's flame. He saw the fire's light dancing in the boy's eyes. He glanced at the flame as if to hear Kia Longo's voice. What he heard was the old man's voice as it seemed to come from Cameron's moving mouth. "It's not my war," Cameron said.

Cuffie told the men where to bed down and that he would be back tomorrow early to take them down to the pond to get cleaned. He turned, haunted by the words from Cameron. He played them over and over as he stared at the fire of Kia Longo in the lantern. "It's not my war!" He gathered himself into the stables and faded off to sleep.

* * *

The two colonels of the first and second regiments of the Confederacy made their battle strategies in the commander's tent. They would stage the cannons along a pecan tree's base and in the cover of its shade. They would place the riflemen along the fields 150 yards out into the cotton fields. The cannons would easily fire their shots over the riflemen's position as the Union advanced onto the riflemen. The two squads made ready for war as they loaded the munitions into the tree line as directed. The riflemen all loaded powder, caps, and shot for their rifles and sharpened their bayonets for the battle.

Well-fed and clean, they were the best they had been in a month. With the troops at the ready, they waited for the scouts to report Sherman's position. The Union knew right where the Confederates would be, and they were coming.

With the speeding clop of the scout's horse, the Battle of Buckhead Creek was close at hand. Just as planned, the Union was coming from the west, straight into the sights of the waiting Confederate cannons. The nervous yet courageous Southern armies now formed one wall across the field as they waited for the Union to advance into the Butler fields.

The wise Union generals were not winning the war by fighting hand-to-hand. They were well armed with the mighty cannons that were produced in the steel mills of the North. They also knew of the blockade that the *Rawlins* slipped past as it ran the guns north up the Savannah River to the troops. These island cannons they imported on her were lighter and designed for ships. The Union knew they would not shoot half the distance of the black steel beast that they possessed. Unfortunately, the Confederates knew this too.

The Southern colonels needed a plan to get the Union to advance into the range of their artillery. They knew that their riflemen could draw out the Union riflemen as the Union waited to advance the big guns a safe distance away. The plan was to remove the jackets of the Confederate soldiers, place them on the slaves of the Butler plantation, and march those poor souls out into the field to draw the Union riflemen's fire. The Confederate colonels set their plan into action.

Cuffie, the field slaves, the barn hands, Cameron, and the men of the *Rawlins* were all gathered at gunpoint and forced to put on the Confederate gray jackets. Each person was handed a stick while being told to hold it as if it were a rifle and walk into the fields. They were informed that if they did not, they would be shot on sight. They were also told of the row of 150 riflemen that they would be walking towards, that lay in wait out in the field. If they did not walk in a straight line, the men in the field would kill them. They were to walk past the riflemen in the field, not to look down at them, and walk 150 yards past them. Any further and they would be shot by the snipers behind them. The somber group of men and slaves did as they were told. The only chance they had, figured Cameron, was to go into the fields, out of the riflemen's range, take cover in the cotton and crawl south, away from both armies.

They walked straight out, sticks high, and into the pointed rifles of the field riflemen. They walked as instructed past them and without looking down. The riflemen followed the line of men. The eyes of the marching men were wide; they knew they were going to be shot in the back, and they could easily see the Union forces in the distance. There were thousands of them, it seemed.

Cameron, without turning his head, discussed the plan to duck down on his command and run low as they got a hundred yards away from the rifles behind them. He passed the plan down the line. Cuffie was only three people away from Cameron as he listened intently to the man's plan. He thought it would work; he was thinking of running himself. He was told that on Cameron's command, and not a second before, to duck into the cover of the bush cotton and head left, or south. Cuffie passed the plan on. Cameron knew the Union commanders had spyglasses, and he held his stick high so they could see he was unarmed.

Hearts racing, with their plan passed down the line, the brave souls waited for the command as they walked straight at the mighty guns of the Union. "Now!" Cameron yelled from deep within him. All the men dropped to the ground and climbed low through the cotton.

The nervous field of riflemen shot at the scared group as instructed. They were never meant to do that. Their positions were given up by the few shots that were let out by them. The Union gunmen who had been crawling through the cotton fired at the riflemen's position. The riflemen of the Confederacy shot back.

The Union generals fired the smaller cannons, hitting their mark as cannonballs blasted the Confederate riflemen in the field. The smaller Union cannons roared, and that's when the Confederates made the final mistake; they fired their cannons back at the Union riflemen in the fields. The Confederate cannons' positions were given, and the mighty Union grand cannons roared to life, flying over the heads of all the men in the fields. They hit their marks on the line of pecan trees.

The Union fired shot after shot from the mighty cannons; there was soon no response from the small guns of the Confederate Army. "Charge!" the lead riflemen of the Confederacy yelled out over the roaring cannons, and the command was echoed down the line. The gallant soldiers of the Confederacy made it almost a hundred yards towards the Union before being shot down by the snipers of the Union soldiers.

Cuffie and Cameron, as well as the other decoys in the line, could hear the men fall in the cotton around them. The field was silent except for the moans and cries of the wounded army.

"The war is over!" the Union army commander cried through a huge wooden horn. "Walk away from your post and do not resist any further. All the slaves are now free men!"

A New Lease on Life

Before the Civil War was over, the Union states had passed a law that all men would be freedmen. The North thought that turning the slaves against the Southern masters would further deteriorate the already weakening Southern armies and their support. It would also cripple the economy when millions of dollars in assets—which were the slaves—left the South. The news of being free never reached very far South though, and most Southern slaves did not hear that their freedom was available.

Cuffie lay in the field of cotton; his ears rang with the loud blasts of the enormous cannons and gunfire. All the noise seemed to stop at once. The wooden horn sounded again, "You are all free! The war is over!" Cuffie couldn't believe what he was hearing. Slowly he began to rise from the ground as he saw the others coming up from the cotton in the battle's smoke. He noticed the man next to him, colored as he was, and wearing a Confederate coat. Still disoriented by the commotion, it came to him that he too was wearing the same type of coat.

He tore the jacket off and threw it on the ground. Hatred of the colors that had taken his freedom, raped and killed his friends and family, not to mention that most of the people wearing them now were dead...he stood staring at the gray coat and the tears of remembrance rolled down his face. He stomped his feet down on the colors of the South with scorn for their horrible acts of inhumanity. A movement just in the bushes broke his sorrow.

Cameron lay on his back in the cotton fields. The thick smoke of cannons and gunfire had settled into the branches of the cotton. The Georgia sun's rays shined through the smoke like rays from heaven. There was a silence through the ringing in his ears as he was starting to come to. Cameron thought to himself, *Am I dead?* All he could remember was a blast right in front of him. He could feel the pain in his entire body from the explosion having occurred just a few feet away. His whole body hurt as he moaned in pain. What his eyes could see seemed to freeze like a series of photographs. His eyes tried to focus on the scenes while they were mixed with the images of remembering the cannons' blasts and the moments that led up to him lying on the ground. The pictures were playing too fast now, and the cotton seemed to blur and streak in front of his eyes. His heart raced and he felt coldness and tremors start to take over his body.

Slap! Cameron heard the slap of skin. *Slap!* There it was again. The pictures in his mind seemed to freeze while he figured out where the noise was coming from. The third slap was felt on his cheek, and he opened his eyes to see the smoke-laden bushes.

Cuffie was standing over Cameron. "Hey!" He slapped his face again; Cameron's eyes shot open. "Thought youz wa' dead," Cuffie said to the groggy sailor. "I saw a cannon blast hit right in front of you." Cameron tried to move but the concussion from the cannon blast made every action hurt. "No, no, now you just sit still," Cuffie said with a big smile, glad to see his friend move at all.

Just then, several of the other sailors from the *Rawlins* came towards the spot where Cameron lay. "Sir!" one sailor exclaimed as he knelt over Cameron. "Sir, we thought you were gone. Your body was thrown in the air when the cannonball hit just feet from you." To Cameron the voices meant he wasn't dead. He looked at the familiar faces around him and couldn't appreciate them more. "Sir, we have to get this coat off of you. We don't want the army men coming to think you're a soldier," the sailor said as he grabbed his shoulder to help Cameron up to a seated position. "You okay?" the sailor asked.

"I don't—aaaauugghhh!" Cameron screamed out in pain as the men were pulling the Confederate jacket off of him. Cuffie grabbed the jacket and stuffed it into the base of one of the cotton bushes. Cameron rubbed his eyes. "What happened?"

"Boy, you were blown to smithereens!" the sailor said laughingly. "I mean, that cannonball hit right in front of you!" Cameron, now blinking the dirt out of his eyes, could barely hear anything as the men gathered around him. "Let's get him up!" The sailors picked him up off the ground. He was shaken, but everything seemed to work okay. The group of men turned back towards the Butler place and walked out of the battlefield.

As the tattered crew made it to the edge of the cotton field, they could see the carnage of the big gun's damage; holes in the earth fifteen feet wide and six feet deep were all over. The wounded Confederate soldiers lay screaming in pain as some of their comrades tried to give them aid. Broken pecan trees, destroyed artillery, and men lying dead in the grass were highlighted by the smoke that rose from the Union's cannon blast holes in the earth.

Amidst the smoke and despair, in the distance stood a horse alone, still tied to a tree. His presence there was odd as Cameron noticed the majestic animal calmly standing there in the scene. Cameron couldn't help but notice that the smoke had cleared around the tall brown horse and the sun seemed to reflect off of his shiny coat. Then the horse raised his head and looked straight at Cameron.

There it was again; a twinkle, but it wasn't a gold coin in the Savannah River this time. It was the sparkle of the handle, one of a sword that shined straight into Cameron's eye. He broke free from the help of the men and ran towards the glimmer in hopes of his wildest guess. It became more and more in focus—it was the captain's sword.

He approached the horse slowly and noticed it didn't startle when he ran up. "Easy, girl," he said as he slowly reached out his hand towards the horse. He patted her side and made his way down the length of the fine horse. He pulled the beautiful handle and case from underneath the horse's saddlebag. He couldn't believe it. He slowly put his gunpowder-stained right hand into the handle, and grasped the leather scabbard with his left hand, carefully pulling the two apart. The beautiful silver blade and fine golden handle both sparkled in the beautiful Georgia sun. He could see his reflection in the blade as it glimmered. He saw the image of a blackened, hard-faced young man, eyes wide, as the mirror-finish blade came from its cloak.

"Cameron." He heard the voice from behind him "Is it the captain's sword?" the sailor asked.

Turning with military excellence, Cameron spun around and faced the men. "Yes, sir, it is!" He pulled the sword fully from the scabbard. "Indeed." Cuffie felt a sense of nostalgia come from Cameron while he watched him stare at the beautiful sword. He saw a more stately man looking at the blade, with a wanting look; the same that Cuffie had when he stared at the flames of the fire while talking to Kia Longo. Cuffie knew that the look Cameron gave the sword was one a boy would give at a prize from his father passed down to him.

Cuffie quickly spoke. "Hide that!" He tapped on Cameron's shoulder. "Hide it now." Cameron snapped out of his daze. He knew Cuffie was right. The descending army of the Union would surely take it away, and it would probably never be seen again.

"He's right, sir!" one of the sailors said. Cameron's mind raced; where could he hide such a long item from the eyes of the army coming across the fields? Cuffie patted him on the leg. "Puts it downs ya pants leg and hold onto me like you're lame." It was a perfect idea. Cameron quickly slid the sword down his pants next to his leg. He pulled his shirt over the handle of the sword and put his arm over Cuffie's shoulder. Walking with a straight-leg limp wouldn't stand out a bit in the war-torn battlefield.

"Wait there, boy!" A voice came from behind the men. During the excitement, no one noticed the man leaning against the broken tree the horse was tied to. Sitting with his back against the tree was the Confederate commander who had taken the sword from Cameron days ago. His hand was over his chest and his gray jacket was soaked with blood.

The men turned around as if a ghost had spoken to them. The commander's left hand took his pistol and pointed right at the group. *Snap* was the sound the hammer made as the commander pulled the trigger. The slap of the hammer was the only sound the gun made. The blood-soaked cartridge in the gun used to discharge the weapon had caused it to misfire.

The entire group of men stood wide-eyed as they all watched what would be the certain end of their lives, each thought to themselves. The commander dropped his pistol arm to the ground in despair and coughed; blood came from the lips of the mortally injured man. Each man thought the bullet was meant him.

Cuffie turned to the commander and, taking a few steps towards him, kicked the dying man squarely on the chin. The boots that Cory used to wear burned an image in Cuffie's mind as they met their mark perfectly. The commander was knocked out cold.

"Thanks," Cameron said as he put his arm around Cuffie and began to fake his limp away from the horse.

"You are all free!" the loud wooden horn broadcast across the field. "Soldiers, put down your weapons and disband. The war is over!" The message repeated itself as the men walked through the smoky shambles of the plantation.

"We'z free?" Cuffie asked the others of the group. "We'z free to go from here?"

"Yep! Just like that, you're free!" Cameron said. Cameron and his men had no other intention than to go back to the ship, make ready, and sail her out of the wretched South. They did not plan on pulling a wagon back down the long Georgia road like a mule this time, either. The group of men gravitated towards the gated entrance of the Butler plantation. "Where are we going?" Cuffie asked.

Cameron responded, saying, "We are going to go back to our ship and leave this place."

"I, I can't go without the queen of our people of Maliki," Cuffie said. "I must take her."

"Well, I'm not going to be able to stop those men from heading to the ship, I tell you. But if you can get there, to the sawmill, we will sail you and your queen away to a safe place," Cameron responded as he stopped walking. "Cuffie, do you know where the lumberyard is?"

"I do," Cuffie said.

"Tell us how to get there, then go get your queen and meet us there," Cameron instructed.

Cuffie took a piece of a fallen limb and began to scratch out a diagram of the properties. He meticulously drew the roads from the front gate to the river where the lumberyard was. He told them what the notch marks on the trees along the way looked like to go to the lumberyard. He laughed as he watched the sailors swat at the Georgia mosquitoes like they were bees sent from hell.

"We have to get out of here. What's with all the bugs in the air?" one of the sailors asked.

"The big ones are mosquitoes, and the little ones are gnats. If you keep moving or if the breeze blows they won't bother you," Cuffie chuckled his reply.

"I'll take the wind at my back any day over this!" the sailor grumbled.

"Aye, and the sails full!" another added.

Cuffie watched as the group of men took off in the afternoon sun towards the gates of Butler. He wanted so badly to go with them as they crossed the gates' threshold and freely walked down the road. The young sea captain who could have been Cuffie's only friend, even though they'd just met, was leaving. Cameron looked back over his shoulder as they walked away, draping his arm across the shoulders of the nearest sailor to continue the disguise of the hidden sword. The sting of the mosquitoes' bites snapped Cuffie out of his gaze and sent him running to the slave quarters where the queen was.

Cuffie ran now as fast as he could towards the slave quarters. While he was running down the main road towards the house, he noticed the Union Army just coming up to the fields and at the line of pecan trees. He did not want to get caught up in any change of plans to be free. He felt like the mentors in his life were pushing him as he ran.

"Where you going, boy?" He heard a deep voice come from the side of the main house. Chris walked out onto the path where Cuffie was running.

"I's going to get Miz Cara," Cuffie said, using the name the whites had given his queen.

"Well, I was on the way there myself," Chris said. "I wanted to make sure she was okay, too."

"I don't trust them army folk. Dey say we was free!" Cuffie panted as he replied.

"I don't trust them either," Chris replied. "I am a Southerner, and, well...they just killed all the people we have been supporting for years. They probably won't take kindly to the whites here now, either." Cuffie was completely caught off guard by the conversation between the two. Chris had a tone in his voice of concern, and had not said many things to him in the past. His voice was shaking, and Cuffie knew that he too shared a concern for the chance at freedom they seem to have been handed. Chris knew that the Confederate Army had run through the plantation with little regard to people or property. He also knew that the opposing army might very well ransack anything left and burn it, as was the way of Sherman's scorched earth policy. This kept any supplies from getting to the remaining Confederate troops.

"Go down there and get Mrs. Cara. I'll meet you behind the quarters at the little pond in just a bit. I will have Dot and the wagon down there waiting so's we can carry Mrs. Cara," Chris said as he looked Cuffie eye to eye. It was an awkward stare the two shared, but Cuffie could tell that they both were scared and were on the same path to get out of the way of the war and the armies, and the destruction that both brought. Cuffie turned and continued to run towards the small shack at the end of the road.

Out of breath, Cuffie rounded the corner to see the slave shacks now. There were people gathering their belongings, and most of the shacks seemed to be empty already. The door on the third shack from the end was open. *Oh no, she's gone!* Cuffie thought as he sped toward the small, white one-room shack. He ran up to the doorway at breakneck speed.

There lay the queen in her small bed, motionless. Her hair was let down and flowing over her shoulders, eyes closed, and hands locked by crossed fingers on her chest. On the bed around her were wildflowers and in her hair, small daisies. Kneeling next to the bed was the small girl the queen had taken to after the Confederate soldiers had hurt her.

"What happened to her? What did they do?" Cuffie slowly entered the room. Reverence was seen on the little girl's face.

"She's couldn't make it. Her heart hurt so much." The little girl began to rise from a kneeling position. Cuffie walked slowly to the bedside. He placed his hand on the little girl's shoulder. They both knelt down at the bed where the queen's body lay. Tears rolled down Cuffie's face as he looked at the peaceful face of the queen. He turned to the little girl. "We must leave here. We have to go."

"No, I won't leave her. She's the only one left. No one...I have no one!" the little girl cried as she looked at Cuffie.

Cuffie wanted to reply that he had no one either. His friend's mom, the queen, was the only one he'd had left as well. He turned from looking at the queen and noticed a candle burning by the bed. He stared into the flame, like he would do when he needed the advice of his elders. The flame did not speak to him this time.

He turned to the little girl. "I will take care of you," he said. "Come on, let's go." The little girl got up with Cuffie and hand in hand, they walked out of the little shack.

There comes a time in a man's life when the thought of being a child forever is the safest place one could be. Often, when someone dies, the people closest to them get stronger. Almost twenty now, Cuffie knew that he had to be the adult. He knew the little girl was lost and had no one to hold onto, like him, years ago. The pain they both felt was horrible, but Cuffie knew he had guidance from his forefathers and was raised up to be a proud young man.

Cuffie could see that her heart was broken and she was dressed in rags, which were made into a small dress. He turned to the little girl. "What's your name?" he asked as they entered the dirt roadway in front of the shacks. The little girl, almost twelve years old, still holding Cuffie's hand tightly, looked up at him. "You da only otha person ever ask me ma name," she said.

"The only *other* person?" He hunched his back, to seem shorter as the two walked so she'd feel more comfortable.

"My name is Tia Longo. Dey call me Tia. I was named afta my grand-father," the little girl said, looking back. "That lady is de only one who'd ever asked."

"That lady?" Cuffie said. "That lady was a queen." He stood tall now, at attention, while he was walking. "Queen Cara of Maliki, the mighty Congo people." He knew that if the girl did not know who the queen was that she must be from another place and not from the *Wanderer*. "Where are you from?" Cuffie asked.

"I'm not so sure; dem people who raised me took me in after my momma died aboard some ship. She was all alone with me on dey. I was just a young girl when I came to this plantation. The people who raise me told me I was'n named after my granddaddy, Kia Longo. Both dem people who raised me just gots sold when they were taken away to Savannah. I was not old enough to go or be sold with them. So I hads to stay here until I was olda."

Cuffie couldn't believe what he was hearing. Was this his old mentor's grandchild? It seemed things were falling into place, and the voices that spoke to him were guiding them through some plan. The two turned off the main path that the others were walking on. "Where are we going?" the frail little voice asked.

"We'z going to the little pond. I done been down there by the fields where thems army folk headed. I don't want to be near anymore fighting or army folk no mo," Cuffie said.

"Me neither," Tia responded. The two picked up the pace and made their way through the thicket of woods behind the shacks. The ground was sloped downhill and made slick by the thick coat of pine needles that covered the ground. Tia slipped a little, and then fell flat on her back as the Georgia pine needles made her feet lose traction. Cuffie, in reaction to her falling, leaned back while the two still held hands and he fell alongside her.

"You okay?" he asked.

Tia, still emotional from the death of her new mother, replied with some tears, "Yes..."

He said, "It's okay, Princess," as he picked the pine needles from her hair.

Her look went from sad, to perplexed, to a smile as Cuffie stood up and offered his hand out to her. "It's okay if I call you Princess, ain't it?" he asked.

She smiled and took his hand. She had never been called a princess.

Dot's familiar snort led the two to look in the direction of the small pond at the bottom of the hill. There sat Chris, perched on the old wagon that Cory used to drive. The horse stood ready as the two approached. "Where's Miz Cara?" Chris asked.

He could tell from the smile that disappeared from Tia's face that something was terribly wrong. Cuffie looked up at Chris and shook his head.

"Ahww, sweetness, I'm sorry," Chris said as he hopped down from the front of the small wagon. "She loved you, little girl, I know it!" Tia's head sank towards the ground and she was about to cry again. "It's okay, Princess," Chris said. The little girl's head shot up without a tear, as if she had just seen a ghost.

"See, I told you that you were a princess!" Cuffie said with a big smile. Tia smiled back at the two.

Chris held out his hand and bowed as if escorting royalty onto a coach. The little girl smiled as she accepted his hand, then she daintily stepped into the wagon. Cuffie patted Dot on the head between the ears and jumped into the back of the wagon. Chris climbed aboard and with a light slap of the reins and release of the brakes, the three took off, away from the small, quiet pond.

* * *

Adventuring across the short distance of the Georgia countryside led to some marvels that the boat crew had rarely seen. The long, winding limbs of the mighty oaks rose up from their base and cascaded back down to the earth. In some instances, the huge limbs touched the leaf-covered ground, relieving the limb of its overbearing weight. The limbs would then take back towards the sky like the spires of a crown. The squirrels played throughout the majestic beings, briefly stopping to look at the gazing humans below. The red Georgia clay added a beautiful contrast to the green and brown monoliths that lined the way to the ship.

The now captain, young Cameron, and crew, walked in bewilderment through the unknown environment. They were not worried so much about the wildlife of the woods but the mosquitoes that Cuffie had warned them of. That's what kept them moving. Soon the winding road began to slightly descend downhill, and the geology led them to know they were approaching the river. Carefully the men pursued their final yards, as they had no idea of what lay ahead at the old sawmill. They hoped the *Rawlins* was still there and not under guard or sunken.

Stealthy movements between the trees led the captain and crew to the edge of the pines and the muddy banks of the Savannah River. Hidden in the marsh grass, the crew surveyed the river for any movement. She lay still, as the change of tide had the current midway between coming in and going out. The woods across had no movement, or at least no sign of it from the men's vantage point. They, too, lay motionless in the tall marsh grass; the cattails swayed above them in the light breeze that blew down the Savannah. "The current is turning," Cameron said quietly to the crew. "The camp is just upriver. We should cross here and approach the camp from the woods over there."

The men agreed, since the mosquitoes had been the only ones to spot their position. They happily submersed themselves in the water to escape the mosquitoes' attack. Once across the river, the small band of sailors began their advancement towards the sawmill. Constantly quieted by the hand gestures of Cameron to remain stealthy, the group eased upon the edge of the trees that ran around the saw camp. Not one motion or movement was seen. The camp lay silent in the deep Georgia woods.

Just past the docks, the foremast of the *Rawlins* could be seen. Cameron's eyes lit up. "Let's make our way to the ship," he said in a loud whisper. "You two go over to the stack of logs there. You and you, go around the edge of the woods and come in past the small shack. The rest, follow me towards the saw building. We will proceed to the docks from there." Cameron gave the orders, and the men quickly followed them. He pulled the captain's sword out of its scabbard and silently motioned for the men to follow him as he left the cover of the woods. Quietly, he took the group across the still yard to the mill building; no movement was seen in the yard at all.

Cameron not only knew where he'd sent the others, but he could easily hear the clumsy sailors crackling through the woods as they made their way to the points directed. Over his shoulder, he saw the men behind the pile of wood signal the all clear. Cameron looked over the huge saw table to see the docks and to survey the conditions ahead. Like a mouse, he climbed across the big machine. A slight slip and movement of boards under his feet caused him to turn and press his fingers against his lips, as if to tell the others behind him to be quiet.

The dead bodies of the Union soldiers in the dock house were still there; Cameron knew nobody had been there because they still lay in the positions in which they'd died. Cameron stood up on the saw table and motioned to the two separate groups of men to come on into the camp center as the area was clear. "First, let's get the bodies cleared from the dock and yard. I don't want anyone to come up and think we killed any of these men. Take any weapons, papers, and money they may have and put their bodies on the wood line over there behind the stacked wood," Cameron commanded. The men all followed their orders.

Cameron walked through the dock house towards the *Rawlins*. He passed by one of the dead Union soldiers and noticed that he, different from the rest, was dressed in tall boots and leather cross straps carrying holsters and two pistols. The dead man, about Cameron's size, was obviously a mounted Calvary officer. Cameron sat on the floor of the dock next to him and put his foot up to the bottom of the dead man's boot; a perfect fit. After his collection of the apparel and weapons, he made his way towards the *Rawlins*.

The docks were quiet, and the boat seemed anchored by the falling mast that plunged into the murky water of the Savannah. In reverence he stepped aboard, immediately remembering the captain's last stand. He stood aboard the ship and looked at the spot where the captain had last stood. In a memory clear as day, he could see the captain as he fell upon the deck.

"Tie her up, sir?" Cameron was snapped from his daze.

"Yes, secure the front line and tie the rear loose. We will need to pull down the mainsail and loose the rigging before we bring her alongside the dock full," Cameron ordered. He made his way towards the captain's quarters. He entered the stateroom and was struck by the items the captain had collected from the foreign lands. A small, ivory tusk-handled magnifying glass sat on the writing desk atop the map there. The map's edges were curled and worn, as though it had been rolled a thousand times. A pair of glass water pitchers from her sister ship *the Wanderer* provided bookends for several bound books that sat perched on the end of the desk. Cameron gently ran his hand along the items, as that of a child admiring a new toy.

In the corner sat a wooden chest next to the bed. Cameron slowly stepped towards the rounded-top wooden box.

The hasp of the strongbox was not fastened. He opened the box with as much delicacy as he could, trying not to disturb anything in respect to its owner. The top was held by a small chain to keep it from falling backwards. Its opening revealed an inset tray of what seemed to be personal belongings; a tiny diamond ring that would have been made for a woman in marriage. He picked up the item and held it to the light coming in the stained-glass window. Next he found a small roll of paper with a silk ribbon wrapped around it, tied in a bow. He gently pulled the ribbon to release the scroll.

Written in perfect penmanship was: *Establishment of Privateer – Savannah, Georgia. This grants right of person to Aaron James Jamison, A Free American Citizen.* There was no date by the name, but the document was presented with a seal of wax from the presiding President Jefferson Davis. The paper was fine parchment and granted the owner *Right As Captain.* Cameron had never known the captain's real name. He released the bottom of the paper and the fine parchment recoiled to its original shape. He re-tied the silk ribbon and placed it neatly into the box again.

Cameron shut the lid of the strongbox and continued to survey the other contents of the room. On a shelf above the strongbox were the books that Cameron saw when he'd first entered the room. He looked intently at the names and titles of the books that sat dusty on the shelf. One of the books was named *The Captain and the Kid.* Cameron slowly pulled the book from its position. He began to open the old book and noticed that the pages were stiff, as well as the leather binding that kept them together. He delicately flipped through the pages of the book. He skimmed across several of the pages and noticed what looked like one of the pages slowly slip out of place a little bit deeper into the book. He turned to the damaged page. When the book opened to the area where the page had slipped down, he noticed that it was slightly different on the edge; he made his way to its exact location. Upon revealing the page, the loose paper slipped from the book and cascaded like a feather to the floor. Cameron watched as the paper landed softly on the wooden deck. There was no writing on the paper. He bent down and picked up the blank page. He turned it over to survey the oddity of a blank page and noticed that the other side did indeed have writing. He flipped it over to reveal a finely detailed map. He could not believe his eyes.

He put the map back in front of page number sixty-nine, where it originally came from. He remembered James commonly using the number sixty-nine and remembered it was the old man's favorite number. He placed the book back on the shelf and went to help the men ready the ship.

Escape from the Deep South

The men began the repairs on the *Rawlins* so they could escape the Union Army and the Georgia sun. The army of mosquitoes and tiny gnats had found them though, and the group of men found no relief from their invasion. The wood yard, set deep in the tall Georgia pines, was cast with shadows from the wooden towers. Occasionally the breeze would whisper through the pine needles and shew the winged invaders away with it.

Cameron wiped the sweat from his forehead as he continued to work on the repair of the broken ship. With the mainsail mast broken at the base, the mighty ship was rendered helplessly stuck in the river Savannah.

The clop of horse's hooves came from the distance, which brought awareness to the crew and new captain of the marooned ship. Silently the crew laid down their tools of work and made way for the weapons they had salvaged from the dead Union soldiers and several small arms they had stashed aboard when they crewed the ship.

Cameron silently pointed at the positions in the mill yard for the men to take in ambush of the oncoming visitors. Several men made for the cover of the woods at the camp's entrance; a few others hid under the dock. Cameron and two others positioned themselves near the saw machine in the camp's center. The hooves grew louder as they made a hollow sound on the hardened red Georgia clay.

Dot rounded the last of the majestic pines towards the wood camp's main road entrance. Sitting high on the front seat were Chris, Tia, and

Cuffie. "Whoa, girl," Chris told the horse with a light tap of the reins. "Whoa...now," he said as he pulled back on them and grabbed for the wooden brake lever.

The sailors by the front entrance, realizing that the invaders were three in number and only one horse and wagon, came from the woods with guns raised.

Cuffie immediately realized that the men had never seen Chris or Tia and had no idea that he would be coming with a white man. The smile went from the three riders' faces.

"Hey! Whoa! Dey is friends of mine!" Cuffie said to the approaching sailors. "Dey okay!" He leapt from the wagon to the ground.

Cuffie made his way around to the front of the wagon and grabbed the bridle of Dot. "Whoa now, girl," he said, and he patted her soft snout and forehead.

"He's okay, men!" Cameron declared, appearing from behind the steam-powered saw. "Lower your weapons!" He put the sword back in the scabbard next to his pistols.

"Look at you!" Cuffie said, now smiling again as he stared at Cameron's fine captain clothes.

"Who's your friend?" Cameron questioned as he approached the frightened two still seated on the wagon.

"Dat Mr. Chris, and dat's little Tia." Cuffie quickly introduced them to the group of men now all coming from their hiding places.

Tia was scared even after the introduction and her eyes darted from the different positions the men were coming from.

"How you doing?" Chris said as he climbed down from the wagon.

"I thought you were bringing the queen," Cameron remarked while he was approaching with a perplexed look.

Chris turned back towards the wagon and stretched his arms towards the little girl. "We brought a princess instead." He smiled like a father at the little one. Tia lit up with a huge smile and seemed to fly down from the wagon in the strong arms of Chris.

"Cuffie, you ever sail a ship before?" Cameron asked intently, then realized the irony of his words.

"Na...no," Cuffie replied.

"Well, it's not that hard. You just have to follow orders and work with the crew. You think that's something you can do?" Cameron said as he sized him up for a sailor's position.

"I...I...guess's so. Didn't never get sick when I was on the last boat I rode on," Cuffie replied.

"Well, that's a good thing," Cameron said as he patted Cuffie on the back. "And you, sir...you ever sail?" He directed his comment towards Chris.

"Yes, I have. I was quartermaster aboard the SS *Savannah*," he replied when he set little Tia down to her feet. The sailors now gathered in tighter around the wagon, hearing the words from Chris with amazement. Grumbling amongst the men was heard, and Chris looked over his shoulder towards the two crewmen who were talking low behind him.

"You know her? The SS *Savannah*?" Chris asked the two men.

"Aye. We've heard tell. She's a steamship, but not much of a sailing ship, is she?" one sailor answered.

It was apparent that Cameron and the other crewmembers had no idea what the ship was. Cuffie turned towards Chris in amazement, as he had only seen Chris drive a wagon on the farm.

"On the contrary!" Chris shot back. "Aye, she was of steam," he said to the two, now speaking like a sailor. "But she was a three-masted ship and used the wind as much, if not more." He turned towards Cameron. "Sail her a lot, we did. Across the Atlantic and to several ports in England and Ireland."

Cameron, with his mouth slightly open, looked at Cuffie, who immediately smiled bigger now and shrugged his shoulders upwards as to being unaware as well to the news.

Chris smiled. "Aye, I'm a sailor."

Cameron was relieved as he heard the man. He leaned forward towards the little girl and slightly down to her level. "And you, Princess. You ever sail?" he said with a big smile.

The little girl never lost eye contact with Cameron as he leaned toward her. She said, "No, but I can cook! Can you?"

Cameron rose up from his lowered position with a big laugh at the firmness of the young girl's statement. He began to laugh heartily and was joined by the laughter of all the towering sailors around her.

"Well, we need one of those, too, to make a whole crew," he said as his eyes twinkled. "Don't we, men?"

A huge, "Aye, Captain!" came from the chuckling group of men. "That we do!"

"Cuffie, you and Princess go over to the house there and see what kind of food stores and cooking tools you can find," Cameron began in a captain's tone. "You'll find some other items below in the galley of the ship." He pointed from the small house to the ship now tied neatly to the docks. "The quarters next to the galley are for the cook. They were the quarters of Miss Anne. You'll see Princess here to her new room." He squatted down next to the girl. "We are all hungry!" he said with a smile as he patted her back and the two took off.

Cameron rose, his tone changed to a deeper, more direct voice. "Before we can sail, we have to repair the mainmast," he said.

Chris said in response, "You're gonna have to do more than repair the mainsail to get the *Rawlins* down the Savannah."

"You know her?" Cameron asked Chris proudly.

"Aye, I know her...and so does the entire Union Army," Chris said to the group of men. "You'll never get her past the port of Savannah or the guns of Pulaski."

Cameron's hope sank, as well as that of the crew. They knew in the back of their minds that the port would be controlled, and they had forgotten the mighty fort that protected its entrance from the sea. The men all looked to Chris for more information.

"This ship was to deliver the artillery that was brought in from Jamaica," he said as the men now listened intently. "She was to be reloaded with fine timber and oak beams and deliver them to the shipyards in Jamaica for another load of guns." As he spoke, the men looked towards the finely milled stack of oak planks that sat stacked neatly under the shed area of the lumberyard. "That oak is worth its weight in gold to the Jamaicans," he said, as if already counting the money of its worth. "The trick," he said, "is to get it out of the port. The problem," he continued, "is that now the Confederates are not in control of the Savannah port and the *Rawlins* will never be cleared to pass." The emotions of the men seemed to sink even lower with the truth of the statement. "They will know—her as she sits." He motioned towards the docks. "She'll have to change."

Cameron and the men listened along as Chris directed the group with authority and past experience. His knowledge of the Lamar operations and shipping was well appreciated. The plan was laid out to change the *Rawlins* and her rear quarterdeck enclosure. Build the rear deck higher and on top of the old one, and carve a beautiful wooden maiden to lie just under the main front spinnaker mast.

Chris drew out the ship in the dirt with a small stick. The crew beheld the plans. The resemblance to the *Rawlins* was striking at first, then it seemed to change as the additions were added to the decks and running lines. He took the small stick and said, "And all the wood you need is right there." He pointed to the various piles of milled lumber.

The men all seemed to like the idea of changing the ship's look and noticed that Chris's plans left out one key element. "What of the mast?" one of the sailors asked as he looked up from the ground to the architect.

"Ahhh...the best part!" he exclaimed. He took the tiny stick and drew three very long lines from the deck of the boat plan to the dirt sky above. "Three new masts, twice as tall as the old."

"Three new masts! Twice as tall as the old ones?" Cameron exclaimed as he seemed to marvel at the plan being drawn.

"Yes, twice the size," Chris confirmed.

"These numbers will not do; they are sixty feet at best!" Cameron stood.

The other men followed in stance. "They look too big, Chris," he surmised, as if the final drawing was now an undoable task. Chris took the stick and stood next to Cameron, pointing at the towering pines just a few feet away. "They are right there!"

The men began the plan for the rebuilding of the ship. Chris noticed a small stream of smoke that came from the *Rawlins*, giving sign that Cuffie and Tia were making the kitchen ready. He headed to check on their progress.

"Little Tia?" Chris called as he stuck his head through the doorway in the galley. Tia, small as she was, had rekindled the fire under the large pot of water. "What did you all find to eat?" he asked in a very pleasant voice.

Cuffie looked up from his potato peeling and smiled. He replied for the busy chef. "We'z found a mess of potatoes by the barn over there."

Tia never looked up as she was reorganizing her new kitchen. The determined look on her face was just like that of her informal adoptive mother, the queen.

"Princess," he said, "Miz Cara would be proud of you." She stopped her reordering of the spices and gave Chris a huge smile. She liked being called Princess.

It was not long before the smell of the spices drifted through the lumberyard and the sky began to darken with the setting sun. The men all started to head back to the ship, to their familiar surroundings after a hard day's work. As the footsteps of the men were heard walking above, Tia put the top back on the boiling pot and walked from the galley to the upper deck. "Y'all wash up!" she said with her tiny hands on her hips. "Dinner is almost ready!"

The weary men smiled as they walked past the four-and-a-half-foot-tall young woman. "Yes'm," Cameron said, then he turned towards the rear of the ship. He walked into the room of the captain and plopped down on the thick featherbed, noticing that the lantern in the room was lit and that the bed was made. He sat up slightly to look over the rest of the room.

In the corner was a small table with a round hole cut in the center; placed in the hole of the table was a beautiful china bowl. Under the table was a matching pitcher of water, and a small cloth folded neatly was lying next to the table. He laid his head back down on the bed and thought how lucky he was to be sitting in such fine surroundings. The bed was not a rough, old bale of cotton or the hammock that he was used to.

He laid back and slowly sank his head further into the soft cotton pillows on his new bed. He stared up at the wooden ceiling and watched the shadows cast from the lantern's flame dance on the wooden beams above. He wondered how many times the captain had done the same. The lantern's dance before him began to blur as the young man started to slip into sleep.

The clang of the pot's lid and shutting of the doors leading to the deck brought Cameron from his well-deserved sleep. He sprang up from the bed as though he had no idea where he was. His hand grabbed the fine linen on the mattress and he realized it was not a dream. He could hear the men talking on the deck, and knew that dinner must have been served. He spun around to a standing position and walked towards the washbowl and pitcher in the corner of the room. The moment was surreal as he poured the fresh water from the pitcher into the bowl for him to wash his face. He plunged his two now weathered hands into the bowl to bring the fresh water to his face. Behind the bowl of water and mounted to the table was an oval mirror. He looked into the eyes of a man as the water dripped from his face. He had made it.

Remembering the look he gave to the mirror, Cameron walked out of the stateroom with a straight back and to the double doors that led to the open ship's deck. He had never walked out of that room before, and neither had he ever had the feeling of a king walking onto the deck of the *Rawlins*, but he felt it now.

The tiny sparkles flew from the fire the men had made in the steel pot from the mill's boiler. The fresh-cut oak crackled as the dried wood burned a rich orange glow. The men sat around the burning flames, plates in hand, scooping away at the potatoes the young princess had prepared. They all seemed to like the meal immensely.

"There he is!" Chris said as he looked up from the meal on the tin plate.

The others looked up too as the captain stepped on deck. From behind them a tiny figure's silhouette appeared with both hands stretched out in front, holding the plate of the captain. Almost like an apparition, the little girl came floating towards him. He watched the figure turn from the ghost of the ship's Miss Anne to the little Princess Tia.

"I...I...found this dress in the room next to the kitchen there." Little Tia spoke softly, still holding the food out towards Cameron. "I'z hopes it's be okay I wore it," she said with the biggest, brightest eyes a little girl could have.

The smell of the spices in the food brought his mind back to the days when Cameron was a boy. His mind went to the day he first woke up aboard the *Rawlins* and saw the face of an angel wearing the same dress. She was cooking that day, and the lovely smell of the spices in the food was just as they were now.

"It was Miss Anne's," he said as he reached for the plate of food from the little girl. She turned around to show him the dress he knew all too well.

"It barely does fit. I had to take it up with some string in the back," she said, truly feeling like a woman now.

"Do you think she would minds if I wo it?" she asked as she stopped, facing Cameron again.

"Not at all." He smiled. "She would love to know a princess wore it so well." He placed his hand on her shoulder and walked towards the men on the deck by the fire. The men noticed his puzzled look when he sat next to the fire with the others. "You know it's not that cold out, there's really no need for a fire," he mentioned as he stuck the potatoes into his mouth.

"Keeps the bugs up away," Cuffie responded, all too eager to tell the captain it was his idea.

"Hmmm." Cameron continued to eat like a starving man.

"You like it?" Tia quietly asked as she squatted next to Cameron. She placed a cup of water on the deck at his feet.

"It's very good. I haven't had food like this since Miss Anne left us," Cameron replied.

The little girl looked somberly down at the deck. "I'm sorry to hear about Miss Anne. The men told me she passed."

"It's okay, Princess. We've all lost someone close," Chris said as he looked at Cuffie, then her. Cameron raised his head, a slight glimmer of tear in his eye.

"What's wrong? You didn't like my cooking, lad?" one of the sailors shot out to break the somber setting.

Slightly startled by how loud the sailor was, Cameron smiled and said, "I think she's bested you! And...she's prettier than you as well!" he chuckled. The men all laughed and continued eating.

"You know, we'll have to rename the ship," Chris said, dragging the wooden spoon across the tin plate, trying to get every drop of potatoes. Cameron's eyes shot up from his food as if to protest. "They will be looking for her," Chris added.

"I've got some more food if you would like it," Tia offered to Chris. "Let me get that pot for y'all." The little girl drifted across the deck of the ship. Her tiny feet were hidden by the long dress that gracefully dragged along the floor.

Cameron watched the girl in the dress of the woman he had considered an angel float across the smooth wooden timbers. He knew Chris was right. The Union forces would be looking for the *Rawlins*.

"*Princess Anne*," he said as he looked across the fire at the men. The glimmer of a tear reappeared in his eye with the mention of the name that combined the two women's names who had worn the dress.

"Hear, hear! The *Princess Anne*!" the men all exclaimed like an army in service to a queen.

Cuffie looked at Chris with a big smile as the flames jumped in his eyes as well.

"Hear, hear!" he said.

* * *

The daylight crept slowly through the towering pines of the mill yard and the morning's sun began to rise slowly on the newly commissioned *Princess Anne*. Cameron had never slept so well, with the light tapping of the river water that washed against the wooden hull of the ship. Getting out from under the linens, he was very well rested. He rubbed his eyes as he heard the activity of the day begin. He walked towards the washbasin to freshen up and get the sleep out of his eyes when he noticed the boots that he had been wearing were neatly placed by the door, shining like a new coin. He cleaned up, got dressed, put his new-looking boots on, and made his way towards the doors of the deck. The sun rising from the east was very bright and it shined across the deck of the transforming ship.

"Captain," Chris greeted, sitting by the coals of the fire from the night before. He took a couple of pieces of wood to rekindle a small flame and put a large piece of Spanish moss on top of the fire to create a smudge pot. The thick smoke poured over the pot's edge and around the area of the deck. "Keeps the bugs away and the fire from getting so hot. You don't want to give off big smoke signals right now, and this stuff will smolder for hours and keep close to the deck." Chris slapped the dirt from his hands and continued. "I will need to ride to Savannah to make ready a berth for the ship," he said, looking out over the rail of the deck.

Just then a towering pine tree fell through the rays of the morning's light and displaced the twilight. "Timberrrrr!" yelled the man as he pushed the tree's bottom, like he was toppling the tree with his bare hands. The tree came down with a thunderous crash. Both men stopped as the huge monolith fell to the ground. "I was saying, sir. I must ride out in front of the ship and make ready a birth for the *Princes Anne*," Chris said.

There was a lot happening now. Cameron looked through the smoke at Chris. "Why berth there? In Savannah?"

"First, they won't let you sail by without a port stop. Second, you can't sail by anyways," Chris responded, standing and walking towards the young captain. "You'll need bigger sails. Those new masts will dwarf your old sails."

"Where on earth will we get sails and rigging in a port that has no use for us?" Cameron asked.

"Well, we are going to be delivering this milled oak to Jamaica. The people in the port will know where the wood is from." Chris moved a little closer. "We'll just tell the port smith on the Lamar docks that this is directed by Cal Lamar. The refitting of the ship and new changes to her are a disguise plan from the boss himself." He finished with his hands almost touching in prayer as in the hope that this wild scheme would work.

"I think that they will hang us as pirates!" Cameron said. "But I agree, we will never sail by the port or the cannons of Pulaski without permission."

"It's true. But once you're past Pulaski, you will be greeted by the blockade. Without papers to the transport they will seize the ship," Chris added.

The two men looked over the busy sailors in the yard. The work was going all as planned. Another mighty pine tree fell across the yard with a *whoosh* of fresh air accented by the fresh, green pine smell.

* * *

The lights of Savannah twinkled in the distance as Chris came from the north. The setting sun gave a blood-red aura to the tranquil city, and the closing darkness covered the colony and matched the darkness within. Chris, having not been to the city in a few months, started to get into character. He had always transported slaves from Butler to the City Market, and into the waiting hands of Joseph Bryan. The slave trader's post was on the north side of the city. It was the darker side of Savannah.

At night, Savannah's air changed from that of the daytime, when she was a Southern charm with mannerism and grace, to the darkness that underlined the city like the cold gray cobblestones that formed her streets. Only a few lights burned, drawing sailors and such where drinks and women could be had. This was the part of the city that Chris was most familiar with. With its veil of Southern charm down, the wretched face of the Southern belle could be seen.

Voices came from the doorways and the torches crackled as the soot raced up the whitewashed walls of the pub. The thick smell of rum and tobacco was emanating from her streets now; not the beautiful smell of confederate jasmine that most knew of in the daylight. Chris put on the practiced steel face of a pirate and a seaman, and then he stepped down from the carriage. He made his way across the stone walkway towards the noise and torches.

The striking of a match from the alleyway caused Chris to jerk his head sharply towards the sound. The sulfur burned brightly as the match exploded in an orange glow. The steely eyes, dark hair, and top hat were briefly exposed in the alley's darkness as the match's fire was pulled into the black pipe the man held. Chris stopped and faced the now darkened alley. "Bryan!" he said, with no crack in his voice.

The dark silhouette of a figure stepped from the alley just off of Bull Street. The thin figure moved into the flame's light that lit the pub's entrance and danced on the stones of the cobbled street below.

"Ahh, Chris." Bryan's voice slithered from the dark; the white eyes of the two dark figures behind him stayed fixed on Chris. "What brings you here?" The smoke poured the words from the man's mouth.

"Let's go somewhere we can talk," Chris responded. He couldn't stand the pasty little slave salesman.

The shadowy figure turned without speech into the blackness. Chris stepped into the darkened alley and could barely see anything; he followed the thick smoke of the Cuban tobacco. Just ahead he heard the creaking of a hatch, and the underground stairwell and tunnel under the door began to glow. Chris watched as the two goons lifted the heavy doors that led to the underground world of Savannah.

The walls were formed of Savannah gray bricks, and the stairs made of the same, which led into the red glow of flames. The black smoke from the torches below led its way along the arched stone ceilings that were well sooted from the smoke's travel. Chris stepped down into the room that narrowed and formed the tunnel under the streets of Savannah. The heavy wooden doors slammed behind him, causing the torch flames to flicker on the walls. "How did you escape Butler?" Bryan turned and asked.

"I was instructed to secure the ship docked at the mill," Chris quickly responded. "She was to be loaded with oak and returned before it could be lost to fire from the oncoming army."

"Sherman burned everything as he came through the South," Bryan responded.

"He did not burn Savannah," Chris quickly shot back.

"True indeed," Bryan answered with another draw from the black pipe.

"This ship is leaving the docks of the mill. I am under orders to cargo her to Jamaica," Chris replied in a militant voice.

"Jamaica, huh? Why you?" Bryan questioned.

"The captain was killed when the *Lamar* was fired upon as she towed her up river," Chris explained. Bryan pondered his answer.

"Why would I not hear from the messengers of this plan?"

"All dead in battle. This mission is about to be compromised as soon as Union forces find the *Rawlins* missing," Chris retorted.

"You plan to sail the *Rawlins* back down the Savannah? The Union forces will quickly snap her up!" Bryan replied, as though the plan was a fake.

"I was ordered to refit her as I did the SS *Savannah*," Chris answered. "New lines, new decks, and three new masts. The colonel's plans were well thought out. She will be coming as the *Princess Anne*."

Bryan's eyes lit up. "Now that sounds like Cal," he snickered. Joseph Bryan led Chris down the darkened tunnel. He grabbed a torch from the cast iron wall hold and led the way through the underground labyrinth of Savannah. Within a few city blocks the men came to an intersection in the tunnels. Another set of steps led up to a thick wooden door, much like the one back on Bull Street where they'd entered.

The torch now lit the stairwell and the black iron rings cast into the bricks that led up to the wooden door. Bryan took the iron rod out of the holder on the wall. The ten-inch-long black steel shaft had a three-pound cannonball fashioned onto its end. He slammed it against the wooden door in a coded knock. Soon footsteps could be heard above and the mechanical sounds of the lock being pulled from its hasp broke the silence.

The door, cracked at first, was then pulled open abruptly; the spiders and cockroaches fled from the spot they held there. The police magistrate leaned the door against the wall, making the steal hinges wail, then a rush of air came through the tunnel and Chris could smell the salt air of the river overtaking the dank odor in the tunnel. "What have you?" the magistrate asked as he squatted, blocking the top of the stairs.

The pasty face of Bryan appeared from the darkness below. "Meet me at the Pirate's Pub," the screechy voice cracked. "I have orders from Lamar." The magistrate stood back and sneered downward at the darkened hole. Without a word, he slammed the door back down. The locking of the hasp was clearly heard while it echoed through the tunnel.

The four men pressed on down the brick-lined catacombs towards the Pirate's Pub.

"Broad," Bryan said as he walked into the intersection of two more tunnels.

"Huh?" Chris responded.

"Broad Street," Bryan said, thrusting the torch into the hands of one of his thugs. He pulled a match out from his black coat pocket and with a swipe on the wall, the match exploded into a bright flame. He pulled the flame down into the pipe with several long draws on the bowl; it began to glow with an orange light. "The Pirate's Pub is above us," he said in another puff of Cuban smoke.

The man with the torch walked through a doorway and around the corner. Bryan stayed in his spot while the second thug watched the man with the torch go through the opening. The small chamber off of the tunnel was well lit by the torch as the first man ascended the rounded stairs to the Pirate's Pub. The familiar slap of the steel ball on the oaken doors again echoed through the arch of bricks throughout the tunnels. The air of salt water and marsh grass came quickly through the tunnels as the doors above were opened.

The calm of the dark tunnel was quickly dissipated by the loud voices that came from above. The first man passed the torch down to the second in the tunnel and he ascended the stairs. The man with the torch now motioned with his hand that the way was clear as Bryan drew from his pipe with the face of an aristocrat. He knew that the smell of Cuban tobacco would set a precedent for his ascension into the Pirate's Pub.

The man with the torch pushed Chris's shoulder when he passed by the torch and Bryan smiled slightly at the two, disappearing up the stairs into the room above. Chris's head came out of the tunnel opening in the floor and into the well-lit room; the noise of drunken men and women was almost deafening. His eyes burned, as the room was laden with thick smoke from the crowded bar. For a brief second the chatter stopped and the people of the bar watched the men ascend from the floor's tunnel entrance. Only pirates used this passage, and at least two of the men were definitely not pirates.

The noise started up again soon and the bar master shouted, "Aye... Bryan!" The door shut swiftly behind them. Chris noticed it matched the surrounding floor perfectly as the pirates resumed their positions standing on the door. "What brings you here?" John said from behind the bar, slamming down a small glass and pouring Bryan a shot of rum.

"John, I will need to use the room," Bryan said as he purposely pulled again from his pipe. He picked up the glass and in one motion drank the brown liquor down. He slammed the glass down. "Another!" The barkeep poured the liquor, and Bryan explained that he was meeting the chief magistrate and would need some bread and drinks. With a simple nod of the head, the barkeep motioned to the doorman as to the arrival of the magistrate. He grabbed the drink maiden's dress at the shoulder when she walked by; her soft dimples disappeared from her cheeks as the hand spun her around.

"Aye, take them to the back," he said, shoving her in the direction of the meeting room. She recoiled and solemnly curtsied for the men to follow.

The four men walked towards the back of the pub, following the tattered red silk dress of the woman to the doorway. She entered first and lit several lanterns inside the small wood-clad walls of the room. She turned and wiped the table off, straightened the chairs, and motioned for the men to step inside. Her beautiful smile returned to her youthful cheeks. "I'll get you some bread and beer rightly," she said, exiting the small meeting room.

Bryan motioned with his head for the two goons to remain outside while he and Chris walked into the room and shut the door. Bryan set his hat on the window ledge, then made his way around the table's opposite side so he could face the door. He motioned for Chris to take the seat to his left. "Jamaica...huh!" Bryan rubbed his chin as though he had a beard, which he did not. "The cargo is fine oak timber for the ships there? Correct?" he said.

"The cargo is timber, yes." Chris acknowledged. "I'm not sure what Colonel Lamar has planned for it," he added smartly.

The maiden opened the door again and set down a plate of bread and a pitcher with three mugs. Bryan reached his pasty white hand out to touch the maiden's when she set the plate on the table. "Bring some rum!" The maiden turned in response as if to move away from Bryan but his clammy grasp covered her light skin. "What's your name, little girl?"

With despair, she pulled away from the unwanted invasion. "Jordan... sir," she cooed as the man held her.

"Jordan..." He slithered the word with an illicit Southern drawl.

She pulled her arm away from the invader and with a slight curtsy, left the room.

Within a few moments, the magistrate was escorted through the pub and into the back where the two goons sat in front of the door. One man stood as he approached the two, the other sat still on the wooden crate, seemingly doing his fingernails with the silver blade of his knife. The doorway to the small wooden room opened. "Ahhh, Chief. How have you been?" Bryan said, standing and greeting the man with both arms outstretched over the table of food and drinks.

"Get to your business, Bryan! Why did you ask me to come to this hellhole?" the magistrate asked.

"Ah...come now." Bryan motioned to the chair and pulled it back away from the table. "Don't seem so frustrated. Have some rum." Bryan slid a small glass in front of the man. "Our old friend, Cal Lamar, has another boat that wishes to pass through your gates of Savannah." Bryan's eyes twinkled as he poured the rum from the bottle.

"Can't do it!" The magistrate slapped his hands down on the wooden table. "The Union ships still dock at Lamar Pier. It can't be had."

"Well now, I'm sure our Colonel Lamar will be quite displeased with your insubordination. After all, he left you his job as magistrate and deputy of police for just such an event," Bryan admonished, striking another match on the table to light the black, Cuban-filled pipe. "I'm sure the docks of the privateers aren't crawling with Union ships," he said as he laughed alone and blew the Cuban smoke in the magistrate's face. The magistrate seethed at the man. "He's asked me to personally deliver the load directly to Jamaica," Bryan added. Chris's eyes darted wildly; this had not ever been a part of the plan.

"You are getting on a ship to Jamaica?" the magistrate asked.

"Yes," Bryan replied. "There's a fortune in sugar and oak to be delivered. The Union has already seized twenty-five thousand bales of his cotton under your watch. I personally won't be letting my friend Cal down." He glared at the man. "Are you going to let them take the last of his possessions?"

"Not when it comes to putting you on a boat and sailing you away from Savannah." He chuckled and drank the rum that sat in front of him. Chris listened to the two men make the plan for the SS *Lamar* steamship to tow the *Princess Anne* from the mill camp upriver to the privateer's dock. Bryan explained how the ship would be loaded in Augusta with wood and then in Savannah with sugar. He also explained that he and the two men outside the door and one woman would join the ship's crew and they would make their way south to Jamaica. The magistrate agreed, knowing that a heavy movement of aristocratic Southerners had recently relocated to South America in retreat of the Union progression. He agreed to have the papers approved and dispatch the SS *Lamar* to receive the *Princes Anne*. The magistrate left after the plans were complete.

"Sugar?" Chris asked.

"Yes. White gold!" Bryan said. "You won't be making a trip to Jamaica without it." He pulled a pouch from his jacket pocket and packed a small wad of the Cuban tobacco in the end of the pipe. "And you won't be making off with any of *my* white gold without me riding on top of it," he chuckled.

Chris's face remained unbroken by the laugh. "What's your trade in Jamaica?" he asked.

Bryan, in his best pirate voice, replied, "Aye, matey, we'll be trading sugar and running rum ashore." He scooped up the little glass and butted it to the glass of Chris for an unmatched toast. "Come now, Chris," Bryan said. "Let's head back to the City Market. You can stay in the loft of the barn there, it's quite nice." He stood and dragged another match across the table and slowly walked by, lighting the black Cuban pipe of distinction.

* * *

The clopping of horse hooves on the cobblestone streets of the City Market woke Chris from the sound sleep that the few shots of rum had caused. The streets of Savannah were at her best now. The dark shadows of night gave way to the new sun's rise and Chris rose from his bed of hay, climbing down the ladder to the stables below the loft. There stood his old friend, Dot. "Hey, old girl," Chris said with a smile; the horse moved her ears about at the familiar voice. "You got your belly full and rested up?" he said as he tilted the bucket he'd filled with oats that was now empty. Chris's gaze rose up from the bucket to see the steely face of Bryan.

"You sleep well?" Bryan asked. Chris noticed he looked even more like a snake in the bright of day.

"Yep. I was just asking Dot here the same thing. After all, it is a barn," he smiled in reply.

"The papers for travel will be drawn up today," Bryan began. "The sugar will be delivered to the docks by nightfall," he said. "How worthy is the ship?"

"Not too!" Chris said. "The sails were destroyed by the Union cannon fire; we have rebuilt the masts, but we will need new sails and rigging from the shipyard." He knew that Bryan was too committed to even balk at the idea of not providing the support to make such an overseas trip.

"I will accompany you to the yards," Bryan replied. "I know some people there." Chris led Dot from the stalls. He hooked her back up to the wagon and adjusted the leather straps so they rode on her just right. He felt the wagon shift as Bryan climbed aboard. "Come along, we haven't all day," Bryan said, once again smoking his pipe. Chris ignored the aristocratic nature in which Bryan poised himself and held his head stiff with his silken top hat perched attentively upon his black hair. All the black made Bryan's skin appear all the whiter. "So you're a capable soul who can sail this vessel to Jamaica and back?" Bryan asked.

"Well, let's see...I sailed the SS *Savannah* from here to London, then went on up to Scotland, Belgium, and across the Baltic Sea to Russia," he remarked. "I think I can handle a little hop down to Jamaica," he said slightly sarcastically.

"But the *Savannah* was of steam, not of sail!" Bryan replied as he pulled from his pipe.

"Yeah...yeah, they put that steam engine on her side so they could say it was the first steamship to cross the Atlantic." Chris looked over to Bryan's unmoving head. "But the truth of the matter is, the sails got us there. The steam engine just pulled us into port." Bryan's head turned, as that was the first time he'd heard that version of the story. Chris cracked the reins and watched Bryan jerk his neck as they headed down the street to the Lamar warehouses of shipbuilding.

The Princess Anne

Cameron had done exactly as he was told; the masts of the newly designed ship were in place, and the tiny sails were tied to the cross rigging to look like full sail appointments. They were barely big enough to pull the charade off. The brown water of the Savannah River and the silt mud made for a great wood stain for the new oak appointments that had been added to the old *Rawlins*. The exotic sculpture of a river maiden's bust adorned the foremast and bow of the ship. Her beautiful features were sculpted by one of the crew from the memory he had of the lovely Anne, who used to walk her decks.

"Is that Miss Anne?" Tia asked Cameron as they walked along the dock, admiring the new renovations to the now tall sailing ship.

"It's as close as you're going to get." They made their way to the ship's stern façade. "That right there...is for you." He pointed to the marquis and name on the rear of the ship. He knew the little girl could not read the words that were carved out of wood and infilled with bright, shiny copper. "It says *Princess Anne.*" His voice cracked slightly. "You are the princess, there." He pointed to the name in large letters.

The girl stood in a motionless stare at the word she had never seen. A tear rolled down her cheek as she pointed at the golden letters. "Princess," she said.

"Yes, honey, Princess. That's you," Cameron said gently.

Just then the whistle blew on the steamship *Lamar*; the black smoke from her stacks rose up in the clear blue skies above the Savannah River amongst the pines. "All aboard, men!" Cameron yelled to the men in the yard and on the docks. In a softer, gentler voice he said, "You too, Princess." The little girl scampered up the ramp and below the decks of the now *Princess Anne.*

The boat had been turned so that she was ready to sail. Her lines hung from the bow rails in ready for the toss to the *Lamar*. The boat had been built just as it was drawn out in the dirt. She stood tall and grand, presenting herself to the steamship that came around the final turn in the river. Another loud blast from the steam whistle bellowed across the quiet Georgia landscape. Cameron ran to the upper deck, sword mounted securely to his side, cross strap leathers holding the twin pistols. The tall, shiny boots accented the new captain's outfit.

"Cast off the main lines on my command. Make ready the towropes for throw; secure the main deck." The orders came smoothly, as he had practiced them all day. He stood proudly as the men scurried to their positions. The *Lamar* rumbled, and the motors poured smoke in her turn to position. Cameron could hear the *Lamar's* captain yelling the orders out to control the boat.

"Starboard all ahead! Port engine full reverse, rudder starboard full!" the captain yelled above the mighty engines. The *Lamar* swung full round and moved just in front of the *Princess Anne*. The men aboard the *Lamar* moved as a symphony of carefully orchestrated maneuvers; they had done this many times before. "Starboard now reverse slow, port reverse to slow, rudder straight as the keel," the orders came. The *Lamar* began to back towards the *Princess Anne*, its thick, black smoke drifting down onto the decks of Cameron's new ship. When the two ships got within ten feet of each other, the *Lamar*'s captain yelled his orders. "Engines to neutral!" The whistle sounded.

Cameron, now louder and with more bass, like the *Lamar*'s captain, called out, "Cast the front lines!" In an instant, the small ropes sailed high from the front of the *Princess Anne* to the rear decks of the *Lamar*. The men aboard the *Lamar* tied the heavy towropes to the thinner ropes.

"Heave ho!" they yelled back to the *Princess Anne*. The *Lamar* captain came from his pilot's house on top of the ship and walked with his hands behind him, worthy and content watching the men work on the decks below.

"Secure the main lines!" Cameron now yelled towards the front of the ship. He wanted the captain of the *Lamar* to hear his orders. Once the men aboard the *Princess Anne* secured the heavy tow lines to the main front anchor cleats, Cameron gave the orders to the man at the boat's dock edge. "Cast off the dock lines!" The men loosed the dock lines while still on board and pulled them into the *Princess Anne*. She was free. "The *Princess Anne* is yours, sir!" Cameron yelled with all his might to the captain on the aft deck.

The *Lamar* captain tipped his cap and turned. "All ahead full!" he yelled as he walked back towards the pilothouse.

Cameron was so proud of himself. He repeated the commands in his head as he smiled, looking out over the decks of the *Princess Anne*. He placed his hands on his hips and braced his stance; the towropes tightened with a slight jerk, causing him to take a half-step back because of the jerk that the lines had caused. In doing so, his right hand moved slightly back, hitting the handle of the captain's sword. His eyes immediately shot to the bank where he had buried the captain and his mentor, James. He saluted to the grave markers where both men lay. The black smoke from the *Lamar* drifted across the decks of the now *Princess Anne* one more time.

* * *

Chris had watched the *Lamar* take off in a stream of black smoke as directed early that day. He and Bryan had gone through the warehouse along the wharf owned by Cal Lamar and acquired the sails and rigging for the ship. They had also gone by Bryan's house and picked up the two large chests that held Bryan's personal belongings. Chris thought to himself, *how did one man need so much stuff to travel at sea?* All he wore was the same black outfit every day. He smiled at the joke he made to himself.

"Something funny?" Bryan exclaimed.

"Naw...no, sir," Chris replied. "I just love this town. It makes me smile." He raised his head and smelled in hard the beautiful salt air and confederate jasmine Savannah smelled of. Bryan took a look at Chris, then turned back towards the front of the wagon to see the bustling longshoremen working like ants on the busy seaport. "Ahh...Savannah," Chris said with another deep breath.

The curators of the piers walked along the Upper Factors Walk high above the warehouse men below. The two men bobbled in the wagon down the stony road. Their heads seemed to jerk with every rock the steel-wrapped wooden wheels hit. Dot's hooves clopped and made an echo that bounced from the stone buildings that lined the river's street. Soon they neared the south end of the street and stopped in front of the last roadways of stone that led up to the beautiful city above. The long bridge over the roadway was made of steel and oak planks.

The factor above them stopped his pace and stared at the wagon that was now sitting in the way of the warehousemen. Bryan turned to the man on the thin steel bridge above him and raised his silken top hat. The factor, recognizing Bryan, turned to the workers below him. "You there!" the factor yelled out to the warehouse foreman below. "Run behind that wagon and find out where the berth is to deliver the bags of sugar!"

"Yaaah, sa!" the black slave shot back immediately. Bryan tipped his hat to the factor, then he motioned for Chris to continue south along the river street. The buildings in this part of the street slowly began to disappear as the wagon kept on. The huge granite walls of the city's bluff took shape from the buildings they had just passed. Several tiny and very steep stairs led down to the street from the wrought iron gates forty feet above. They were headed to the lesser end of the pier, the one of the privateers and pirates.

The steam whistle sounded as the SS *Lamar* passed the Lamar piers. The long blast from the whistle echoed down the stone street to the waiting ears of Chris. "Whoaaa, girl!" he said with a small tug on the reins. Chris turned back in his seat to see the tall new masts of the ship. The *Princess Anne* began to tower above the other smaller boats along the wharf.

"Is that her?" Bryan asked as he pulled the top hat from his head.

"Aye, it is the *Princess Anne*," Chris said, smiling, like an architect seeing his masterpiece for the first time. The tall masts moved slowly by the others as she made her way along Savannah's best. "Let's get!" Chris said with a snap of the reins. Dot lurched forward down the darkening street and Bryan's head snapped backwards as the horse and wagon leapt to meet Chris's friends.

The tide sat still in the Savannah River, which was a relief for young Cameron as they neared the docks. Coming in on a gallant tall ship would mean no room for error as the boat docked, especially on the south docks in front of the most revered seamen and privateers in the Atlantic. The *Lamar* crept up to the docks at a very slow speed. The weight of the *Princess Anne* would drift her hard into the docks if the speed of the ship was too fast.

Cameron's position on the main deck was nostalgic. He remembered the captain's stance when they made harbor; his chin high and eyes straight ahead. But he was scared to death. All eyes were upon the now great ship as she docked amidst the blockade runners. "Prepare the starboard dock lines!" he yelled.

"Aye, sir!" the men said as they leapt into action.

"Prepare to cast the main tow lines!" Cameron said in full voice. "Rudder now straight as keel!" the ship slowly crawled towards the docks.

The captain of the *Lamar* yelled, "Engines to neutral!" The large steamship slowed and presented some slack in the lines that towed the *Princess Anne*.

"Cast the tow lines!" Cameron said, and the huge ropes flew over the bow and into the muddy water of the Savannah River.

"Rudder 10 degrees to port!" Cameron yelled.

"Full ahead starboard engine, full reverse port engine, rudder full port!" the *Lamar* captain yelled.

The men's voices echoed between the ships. The *Princess Anne* drifted along towards the waiting docks of the Lamar southern piers. The *Lamar* had once again spun on a dime with her twin engines, which only a dual steam engine could do. She made her way slowly back by the *Princess Anne*. "She's all yours, Captain!" the captain of the *Lamar* yelled to Cameron.

Cameron tipped his captain's hat as the *Lamar* let out a long blast from the steam whistle. "All ahead full!" the *Lamar* captain bellowed.

"Easy, men...port rudder twenty degrees; port rudder...now fifty degrees!" Cameron yelled as the boat floated into position. "Full port rudder! Cast the main lines!" The *Princess Anne* softly touched the docks and made her first berth.

The men continued to tie the boat down to the dock while Cameron walked down from the upper deck. The section of railings was removed and the gangplanks were installed from the ship to the dock. Cameron walked as royalty down the wooden ramp and onto the wooden dock of the Lamar pier. He could not help but look down and see if any children were looking up between the slats of the wood where he used to live.

"Aye, Captain!" Chris exclaimed as the young Cameron turned to inspect his beautiful ship.

Cameron's head turned back to the familiar voice. "Aye, ye!" Cameron replied in a deep tone. Chris smiled at the obvious deep tone the nostalgic young man had developed.

"That's the ship!" Bryan turned and said to the slave behind the wagon. "Now get!" The slave jumped and ran across the stones, back up the river street to the warehouses.

Both Bryan and Chris stepped down from the wagon. "All as planned?" Chris said to Cameron as he walked up the dock from the roadway.

"Yes, sir!" Cameron replied. He then looked to the pasty white figure walking around the horse to make his way for an introduction. Chris winked at Cameron. "This is Joseph Bryan. He will be joining us as we sail to Jamaica."

Cameron's look was that of slight shock. He turned from the trusted wink of Chris and stretched out his hand to shake that of Joseph Bryan, who entered the conversation. Bryan pulled his clammy hand from the thick wool jacket pocket and shook Cameron's hand. "Captain Cameron Michael Montgomery, at your service, sir," Cameron exclaimed. "I'll see to it that your items are stored in the guest quarters."

"Very well!" Bryan replied. "I have other business matters to attend to. We should leave at first light, before the Union ships at the north docks wonder why such a grand ship is docked at the privateer's port," he said, then he turned and left up the Liberty Street ramp from the river.

"What's that all about?" Cameron asked as he turned to Chris.

"Well...I began to lay out our plan, when Bryan stepped in and, let's say, sweetened the deal!" Chris said, grinning.

"Permission to come aboard, sir?" The voice came from behind the two men admiring the ship. Cameron turned and saw a chain of men carrying hundred-pound sacks of sugar; his eyes widened.

"Ah, yes!" Chris responded to the slave chain. "Right this way." He led the men up the wooden gangplank aboard the *Princess Anne*. Cameron stood in awe as at least 100 men lined down the street along the river.

Once on board, Chris smiled and turned back towards Cameron. "Hey, Captain!" Cameron was still staring at the long line of men bringing the bags of sugar on board. "Your sails and rigging are in the wagon," Chris added with a laugh, descending below the decks of the *Princess Anne* to lead the men to the storage hold.

The crew of the *Princess Anne* worked under the hot day's sun and into the night, while the sun seemed to lower into the river. The crisp, white sails were all hung from the towering masts and were readied for deployment as the night set in on the docks of Savannah.

Waiting till nightfall to enter the underworld of the docks he knew all too well, Cameron remembered the last day he'd spent in Savannah, staring at the gold coin just at the water's edge. He could see it clear as day, even though it was years ago. The low tide that night exposed the rocks and mud, just at the dock's edge. Cameron walked across the deck of the *Princess Anne* towards the gangplank.

"Where you going?" Cuffie asked as he sat in the shadows of the railings.

"Uh! You startled me," Cameron said with a gasp. He did not see Cuffie in the dark. "I...um, well, I am going for a stroll along the docks there," he said nervously.

"Hmmmm. Why you'z so jumpy?" Cuffie inquired, and emerged from the shadows of the masts. "You knows Misa Chris saids it way too dangerous to be about," he added.

"Trust me...I know these docks all too well," Cameron said smartly. He walked up to the gangplank and down to the docks below. He then looked both ways and squatted next to the dock's edge. With one final look back up he saw Cuffie's wide eyes between the rails of the ship. He put his finger in front of his lips as if to tell Cuffie to keep quiet, and with one swift motion, he swung around the dock's piling and onto the rocks and mud below. He vanished from Cuffie's sight in an instant.

Cameron crept quietly along the muddy shore under the docks. The moonlight shone through the long gaps of the dock boards, casting light on the well-traveled path below him.

He had traveled halfway down the wharf towards the North-held docks when he heard footsteps behind him and slid behind one of the wide wooden pilings that lined the informal path. He heard the steps get closer as the mud and the sand crackled with each tread. The dark silhouette crept by Cameron. When he saw the figure's face in the light between the boards, he spoke. "Cuffie!" in a yelled whisper came from behind the post. Cuffie froze; his two white eyes flying open were the only movement. "What are you doing here?" the hushed yelling continued.

"I-I's...uh...you'z scared me to death!" Cuffie answered back.

"Shhh!" Cameron quieted him.

"I wanted to make sure the new captain was safe," Cuffie admitted.

"Safe!" Cameron exclaimed. "I used to live here. It's *you* who isn't safe.

"You liv—" Cuffie went to reply but was interrupted.

"Come on!" Cameron said as he jerked Cuffie's shirt by the sleeve. "Follow me. Closely, and don't make a sound."

The two young men scurried like rats under the wooden pier. The path was well worn as it led to the Lamar pier next to the warehouses. Voices could be heard above them as they got near the Union-held docks of the pier. Cameron stopped and motioned for Cuffie to follow him and be very quiet. He pointed above to the voices and shadows of the men just over their heads. Cameron then slipped between the cracks of the seawall stones, where the docks overhead met the land. The space between the walls opened up and a small light could be seen just ahead in the distance as the two made their way through the mud-lined cavern.

"Thomas?" a small voice whispered. "Thomas...that you?" The little girl, about ten years old, scampered from one corner of the room to the other when she saw Cameron's face appear in the light. She cowered into the corner and put her arm over her face to hide from the unknown invaders.

Cameron moved very slowly. "It's okay," he said in a calm, quiet voice. The little girl crept an inch deeper into the corner, her eyes peering over her arm covering her face. "I used to live here," he said. The little girl slowly lowered her arm to reveal her muddy little face. She didn't make a sound. "I used to live here, when I was your age," he said with the most caring voice. "See?" He reached towards the corner of the room. The little girl jumped again, scared, and put her arm back over her face. "It's okay, sweetheart, I'm just going to show you where I hid my toy when I was your age and I lived here too." The little girl again slowly moved her arm down to see what Cameron was doing. She watched as he felt along the row of bricks that made the seawall. Towards the top, his hands stopped and both met on one brick near the corner. Carefully he slid the brick from its place in line with the others and pulled it out from the wall. The little girl sat amazed as Cameron gently set the brick down and reached into the hole now in the wall. Like a surgeon, Cameron gently pulled his hand from the secret spot. The light danced on the gold chain as he let it dangle from his hand in the little room. A golden pendant slipped down its length and came to rest at the bottom of the chain.

The necklace sparkled in the dimly lit room, its beautiful gold reflecting the lantern's firelight and casting sparkles on the muddy walls of the room. "I'm Cameron," he said to the little girl, now staring intently at the gold necklace and pendent.

The soft voice gently spoke. "I know that name," she said as she lowered her arm and turned slightly out of the corner.

"Oh yeah? And how's that?" he questioned the little girl.

"Ta-Thomas used to tell us stories about a boy who went off to sail around the world. Is that you?"

He replied, "I don't know about going off to sail around the world. But I did leave here on a ship," he chuckled.

"It's you then," She calmly said.

"Yes, ma'am. And who might you be?" Cameron asked as he moved a little closer to the child.

She flinched at his movement and said, "I'm Jamie...Jamie Foster."

Cameron stuck out his right hand. "Pleased to meet you, Ms. Foster." She reached out to shake his hand and retracted it suddenly. Her eyes shot past Cameron as Cuffie's face came into the light. "It's okay, love, he's my friend," Cameron comforted.

The three sat there in the dark, underground room where Cameron grew up. Cameron told both Cuffie and Jamie about the time he'd spent in the underworld as a wharf rat. He watched as they both listened like the other children used to when he told his stories by the light of a lantern.

Cuffie could see his younger days too as the flames from the lantern jumped and their shadows danced on the walls. He thought of Kia Longo and his life stories he'd heard as a child. Cameron was just finishing the story of the day he got taken away on the *Rawlins* as Jamie sat straight up. "That's what happened to Thomas!"

The little girl nodded her head and began to cry. She remembered back on that day with all the clarity in the world. "When was this?" Cameron asked.

Her sobbing voice said, "About one week past." She continued to cry.

Cameron put his arm around her to comfort her. "Now, now, sweetness, we can't have all that," he said as he held the little girl. "If you'd like, we can take my boat and see if we can find him."

The little girl's eyes shot up to meet Cameron's. "Really?" she gasped.

The three made their way back towards the ship. The girl moved like a cat on the little road and maze of the pilings that lined the path through the mud, back to the south docks. Once safely on board the *Princess Anne*, Cuffie introduced Jamie to Tia and the girls became instant friends. Cuffie told them both that they needed to stay in Anne's room until he came back down and got them the next day once they were at sea. Tia showed the little girl to her new quarters and said, "Now let's get you cleaned up a bit."

The next morning came all too fast for Cameron. He tossed and turned all night from the pictures that raced through his head while he slept. The footsteps from the sailors on the deck above his bed let Cameron know he had overslept. He opened his eyes and sprang from the bed with the urgency of oversleeping. He was the captain; his mind raced as he clumsily put his attire together. When he reached for his boots and they were not by the bedside where he'd left them, a short panic led him to glance at the door and there sat his boots, once again cleaned and polished for his presentation. He quickly splashed water on his face and patted his hair as he headed to the door. Just as his hand touched the knob he paced himself, gained his composure, and stepped slowly through the door to the main deck.

The decks of the *Princess Anne* were quiet; the moon still was high over the Savannah River and no movement could be seen on the river street below. Almost the same time that Cameron realized he had not been woken up by footsteps above his bed from the sailors making the boat ready, he turned to hear Chris's startling voice. "Late-night stroll through the mud?" Chris said, knowing the voice would have startled him.

"I...ah...what mud?" Cameron responded.

"The mud and the footprints of three people who clearly walked up our gangplank and across the decks there. In fact, one of them was wearing boots and walked right up to your door...Captain," Chris said with a stern look to Cameron.

Cameron spent the next couple of hours explaining where he had been and where he was raised. During the time the two men talked, Captain Cameron cleaned the decks and gangplank of the muddy footprints as the sun began to slowly peek over the eastern horizon.

"The little girl, I have no problem with. I know why you would want to save an innocent soul like that," Chris began. "To let an undocumented slave loose under the dock or to be found with one would be piracy!" He spun as he talked. "They'll hang you for that one," he said, then he stopped in Cameron's face. Cameron swallowed deeply as the thought of the noose around his neck scared him. "But you," Chris continued, "why would you go on an adventure to your old boyhood home, under the taken docks of the Union, nonetheless? If you had been caught and mentioned your connection with the new ship on the privateers' dock, you could've compromised all of us." Chris's tone was now one of aggravation. "What have you to say?"

Cameron pulled from his pocket the long, golden necklace. He held it out towards Chris as the pendant swiveled with its movement. The moonlight pierced the golden surface of the medallion. Chris swiftly grabbed the necklace from Cameron. He knew immediately upon sight what the necklace was. "Where did you get this?" he insisted.

Cameron couldn't believe how fast the necklace was removed from his hand. "Give it back!" he exclaimed.

Chris stood staring deeply into Cameron's eyes. "Where?"

"It was my father's...now give it to me!" Cameron stepped toward Chris.

"Easy, lad. Do you know what this is?" Chris asked in a calm voice. Cameron stood waiting for the answer. "It's a mark of the queen's counsel. Issued to the few men who were to come to the New World representing the Queen and England as a secret royal guard in the battle of 1812," he said as he handed the golden necklace back to Cameron. "These men on either side of the docks would not take kindly to the bearer of this royal guard emblem. Maybe you'll wear it when we head over to England?" he chuckled.

"We are going to England?" Cameron responded.

"You never know as a man of the sea, especially a royal guard. But it would seem more fitting over there."

Just as soon as the men finished talking, the morning sun came over the eastern horizon. The docks were still, and no movement was seen except a tiny horse and carriage that came down the Broad Street ramp to River Street towards the pirate docks. The well-dressed coachman pulled the covered carriage down to the edge of the wharf. The driver made his way from the front of the carriage to the door and placed a stepstool at the foot of the carriage door. He opened the door and a beautiful white glove led its way out of the door and grabbed the coachman's outstretched hand. He bowed as the woman gracefully stepped from the carriage.

The young Southern belle stood silently as Joseph Bryan exited the carriage. Her wide hoop skirt and layered lace added a beauty to the Savannah docks that had left when the South conceded in the war. Bryan stood there in his normal black attire, pointing at the coachman.

Chris looked at Cameron and rolled his eyes. Just then the iron gate of the tunnel in the tall stone wall opened with a slam and the two goons to accompany Bryan made their way from the Pirate's Pub secret entrance. Chris whispered, "This is going to be an interesting voyage."

Cameron, in fact, didn't think *interesting* of any sort was a necessity on the voyage. He watched as the newcomers made their way down the docks and towards the *Princess Anne*. Chris stood on the lower deck to welcome the variety of guests who were walking the docks toward the gangplank. Halfway down the gangplank now, Chris's outreached hand waited for the beautiful gloved woman to help her aboard. "Milady," he offered. With a slight look of concern, the pale Southern belle gently took the hand of Chris and smiled for a moment, then carefully looked back down and placed her feet on the wooden gangplank. "Easy," Chris said as she intently focused on each step.

Cameron could smell the perfume the minute she got near the edge of the ship. It added a beautiful start to the day Savannah would bring. He was in the middle of his second big breath of perfume as she made the deck of the ship. Awkwardly, he repeated Chris's salutation, "Milady." She smiled at him with the satisfaction of having navigated the ramp and now standing on stable footings.

Chris reached his hand to help Bryan; he, too, seemed to awkwardly be aware of the ramp's slight movement as the current gently rocked the boat. The wood squeaked as the additional weight was added. Not wanting to seem needy, the scared Bryan refused Chris's hand; but just as he passed Chris in the middle of the ramp, he slipped on some of the morning dew that seemed to cover everything in the port city. Chris immediately grabbed Bryan's sleeve at the shoulder to catch his unbalance. "Whoa, there," he chuckled. "I've got you."

The two thugs made their way to the end of the ramp. Chris, in jest, offered his hand as help for them to board also. With an awkward look and a smirk of rejection from both sides, Chris turned and headed up the ramp, smiling.

"Welcome aboard the *Princess Anne*," Cameron said to the new group on board. "Milady and sir, your quarters are below, just there." He motioned to the main door. "And the crew quarters are located just past the cargo hold there," he offered the two men. "Chris, would you see to it that everyone is placed, sir?"

"Aye, Captain!" Chris answered sharply.

"We will be leaving port soon and the decks will be full. Please give us some time to pair with the steamer tug as you make yourselves comfortable below. Once we are safely underway, I will send for you as we depart," Cameron said with authority, and then turned to show off his captains' ability for the young lady. "Make ready the lines, men!" he shouted to the crew just now making their way topside. "Port lines be ready!"

"Aye, Captain!" responded the crew.

The decks were now bustling on the *Princess Anne* while the passengers went below and the crew followed the orders given. Just then the *Lamar's* steam whistle blew. It was time to leave the beautiful port city. Cameron could still smell the perfume of the beautiful woman as he looked over the working decks of the ship and at the new sun's rise on Savannah. Within a short time, the *Lamar* was slowly steaming along the Savannah River with the *Princess Anne* once again in tow. The tall marsh grass of the river seemed to slowly pass as the beautiful tall ship headed towards the mouth of the mighty port and Fort Pulaski that guarded it.

Cuffie could see, from the porthole below the deck, the familiar scenes of the riverbanks. His memory played an all too familiar scene of the first time he saw the banks of the river. He looked down at Tia and Jamie. "It's going to be okay," he said.

The two girls were all smiles. They both had met a new friend and were aboard a ship that was much nicer than a slave shack and the muddy riverbank homes they knew. Cuffie smiled back at them and turned to the porthole again. The tall walls of Pulaski began to fill the portholes of the *Princess Anne*. Cuffie noticed that its walls were crumbled, and black powder blast marks ran around the huge holes in the fort's brickwork. She looked badly beaten.

The *Princess Anne* had just passed the sand bars that lie off the inlet of Tybee Island. The *Lamar's* work was done. The black smoke that poured from her stacks slowed, as did her speed, and soon the two ships entered the Atlantic Ocean at the Savannah River's end. "Cast the tow lines," Cameron said as he stood up on the main deck, ready to take the fine tall ship to sail for her maiden voyage.

The *Lamar* again spun 180° in front of the *Princess Anne* and headed straight back towards the ship she'd just released to the ocean. As the *Lamar* passed on the port side, the captain let out his final orders. "Raise the clear passage flag!" he barked, then turned to Cameron on the top deck. "She's all yours!" Both captains tipped their hats and began with the orders to their ship's crew. "Full steam ahead!" the *Lamar's* captain yelled down to the working decks of his ship.

It was Cameron's turn to yell the orders that were to take the *Princess Anne* to sea. The doors of the stateroom opened under him and out came Joseph Bryan and the fair maiden who accompanied him. Cameron wished they had followed orders and stayed below the deck until the *Princess Anne* was set to sail. He knew his first orders and new rigging would be tested and he didn't want to look a fool to the people, especially the beautiful woman.

The cannon blast from Fort Pulaski sounded with a mighty thunder. The noise was so loud that Cameron, already nervous of his first sail, almost fainted. The startled look in his eyes, as well as those of the crew, was obvious. "That's what we paid for!" Bryan turned and yelled up to Cameron. Still puzzled, Cameron walked to the front of the aft captain's deck and looked down at Bryan, his best captain's look still covering his concern from the blast. "That's the fort notifying the blockade you have safe passage," Bryan said to the captain. "They just saw the safe passage flag on the *Lamar* flying. We are free to go," he said, and then turned to the front of the ship. The young woman was still looking at the stately Cameron; he couldn't help but look back at her beauty.

Cameron regained his courage and at full voice yelled, "Cast the mainsails!" The crew responded, and the long, flowing white sails fell from their perches from high above. The men lined together, tugging the mainsail lines as the riggings snapped taut. "Secure the mainsail lines!" Cameron shouted. He noticed that the young woman was still watching him. "Cast the aft sails!" Cameron yelled out as he tried to look over the beauty of the woman and concentrate on the proudest event of his life. The other beautiful sails fell towards the deck of the ship and were secured into position.

The *Princess Anne* lurched ahead, sails full of the wind that seemed to blow down the Savannah River as they left her mouth. The men on board cheered, and so did the onlookers standing on Tybee Island just off the starboard bow. The new pine masts ached and stretched as the sails became full. The *Princess Anne* was off to sea.

"Starboard rudder at 45°!" Cameron barked out as they turned the *Princess Anne* along the beach of Tybee Island; the wind was full astern. "Take her along the coast, sir," Cameron said to the wheelman as the *Princess Anne* made her way down the gray beaches of Tybee. The once beautiful Fort Pulaski, now badly beaten, began to fade in the distance.

Chris, Cuffie, Jamie, and Tia all walked from below deck and out of the staterooms from their hiding places. Jamie and Tia stood still and stared at the beautiful woman next to Bryan. The lace and the fabrics on her dress blew beautifully in the wind as the *Princess Anne* made her way through the sea. The young woman smiled back at the two young girls. Cuffie ran straight for the bow and grabbed the rails to look alongside of the front spinnaker sail. He had never been on the front or even the decks of a moving ship before in his life; he was truly happy. He looked at the beautiful wooden maiden as she hung under the front sail mast. She seemed to be watching the porpoises dance in front of the ship as she ran at good speed through the shallow, gray waters of the Atlantic. He had never seen anything like this. "They're good luck," Chris said as he looked over the bow next to Cuffie. "The wooden maiden here follows them to lead us out to sea." He laughed as he patted the young man on the back.

"Ship's speed!" Cameron yelled from the aft captain's deck.

"Aye, sir!" Chris responded. "Now you watch me," he said to Cuffie; he then turned towards the bucket and the knotted rope.

"Time!" the first mate said on the aft deck next to Cameron. Chris hurled the bucket overboard and the rope ran through his hands. He counted out loud so Cuffie would know what he was doing. "Time!" the mate yelled as the bucket passed the back of the ship.

Eighteen was the last number Chris had said in the low voice to Cuffie. "Eighteen knots, sir!" Chris yelled to the captain.

The deckhands cheered; the new height of the masts and size of the sails added an enormous amount of speed to the once average ship. Chris began to haul the bucket back towards the ship's bow. Cuffie watched as it skipped along the waves that were formed from the bow splitting the sea. He loved the crisp air and the soft mist that the water made as the ship ran down the Georgia coast. "That's faster than most!" Chris said to Cuffie, then he showed him meticulously how to put the rope into a circle next to the bucket. "It's got to be just like this every time. Okay?" Chris said, and he smiled at the young man. "Now you try." He stood to watch the young man recoil the rope. He looked back at Cameron, and Cameron stared back at the two. Cameron smiled and tried not to break the memory of him and James doing the same thing when he was a young boy, first learning that job on the same boat. His emotions raced while he could picture clearly the old man being watched by the captain doing the same as Chris. Cuffie looked up from the rope lesson and couldn't stop smiling as his eyes met Cameron's.

The beautiful young lady squatted down to the height of the two young girls, Tia and Jamie. Her wide hoop dress gracefully gathered on the deck of the Princess Anne. She reached out to the young girls and motioned for them to come closer. They shyly and, careful of the now moving ship, walked towards the beautiful young Southern belle. Chris patted Cuffie on the shoulder and pointed at the two smiling young girls as they made their way towards the woman in the beautiful dress. Cuffie and Chris watched as the two walked towards her slowly, like they were approaching royalty. "Let's go introduce them," Chris said, and the two started towards the center deck where the girls and Bryan were standing.

When Cuffie and Chris turned from the bow, the hatch from the crew quarters opened and caused them to stop and notice who was coming out of the hold area. It was the two goons who were Bryan's henchmen. "Ahoy, matey!" Chris said in a very pleasant voice to the two.

"Alas, a ship of good speed," the first man said in response.

"Aye, yes, she's not lugging an anchor inside," Chris shot back with a smile.

The second man said, "Aye, a ship of pure wind and void of smoking charcoal is a wave runner to me."

The three men laughed at the comment. Chris grabbed Cuffie on top of the shoulders and continued to walk towards the center of the ship. As they approached the group of Bryan and the small girls, they heard Bryan ask with detest, "What's with the slave children? They will be useless at sea!"

Chris walked up to Bryan's face and stopped just inches short of running into the man. "Useless?" he said. "For your information, sir, there are no slaves aboard this ship." Chris said it loud enough for the whole small group to hear. It was also loud enough for Cameron to hear on the high deck as the wind carried the voices to the captain. Cameron turned and began to descend the steps to the main deck of the ship. "And as for useless, I would have to say that, you, sir, are the only useless person aboard!" Chris said with a laugh.

Chris startled Bryan, and then stood between him and his two men. Bryan looked scared and then darted his head over the shoulders of Chris to signal the men to save him from the insult. The two men pulled their pistols out of their holsters and cocked the hammers. "You should mind your tongue, scallywag, or I will have it removed for you!" Bryan said.

The tension escalated quickly. Cameron could hear the conflict clearly now as he approached the two men. The young woman stood and walked away with the two little ones, Tia and Jamie. She knew Bryan was a dangerous man and trouble was soon to be upon them. She and the two girls went to the corner of the main deck and squatted down together. Chris pushed Bryan with a single shove to the deck of the ship. "Have my tongue removed, huh? Just who do you think is going to be helping you do that, Mr. Bryan?" Chris stood firm, correcting his footing as the ship rocked in the waves.

"Men, take him!" Bryan said, pointing to Chris from where he stayed lying on the deck of the ship. Chris laughed at the comment; the two men behind Chris didn't move. With one smooth action Chris stepped forward, grabbed Bryan by the ear, and snatched him up to his feet.

"Did you know, Bryan," Chris said, "that these two men sailed with me almost around the world? They will be doing nothing but watching me as I cast you off this ship." He yelled this into the ear he was holding, and then forcefully led Bryan to the rail.

Cameron's mouth hung open; he moved slightly out of the way as the two men walked past. Cameron reached out and put his hand on Cuffie's shoulder. With a motion of his head he stopped Cuffie, and the two stood and watched the men walk towards the rail. "You see that beach there in the distance, Bryan?" Chris said as the terrified man's eyes darted in misbelief of the circumstances. "I said! Do you see that beach over there?"

Bryan stuttered a reply. "Ya-Yes!"

"Good," Chris said. "If you try hard, you can swim there. It's Jekyll Island. I'm sure you'll find some friends there. You have none on this ship." He then laughed in his face. "Now off with you!"

With a single motion, Chris threw Joseph Bryan over the ship's railing with the command, "Go."

Cameron and Cuffie could not believe the sight as the man all dressed in black was thrown overboard. The two large men laughed and uncocked their pistols; then they placed them back in their holsters. Chris turned from the railings. "No more of that slave talk, huh?" and joined the laughs of the other two men.

Cameron asked as the three men returned to the center of the ship, "You've known them all along?"

"Aye! They are the best sailors around," Chris said. "They hate that man and were forced to work under him by Cal Lamar as spies on Bryan's operations." He patted both men on the back. "Now you go see about our little passengers over there if you will." Chris turned with the two men and began to introduce them to the other crewmembers on the deck.

Cameron turned to Cuffie and said, "Come on." Cameron and Cuffie gently approached the scared little girls and young woman in the corner of the deck.

"He was a wretched man!" the young woman said as she stood. "He kept me in payment for my father's business failing; we couldn't repay him." The smile left her face. "It's okay, sweethearts," she said as she bowed down to Tia and Jamie's height. "He was a bad man."

"Milady," Cameron said. "My name is Captain Cameron Michael Montgomery. This is my friend Cuffie, and these two little girls are Jamie and Princess Tia." Cuffie, Tia, and Jamie all smiled a very welcome smile at the young woman.

"My name is Lady Stephanie Brooklyn, at your service, sir," she said with a slight curtsy. The two young girls hugged her from both sides. "Princess, huh?" she said as she patted Tia on the head.

"Girls, will you show Lady Stephanie around the ship?" Cameron said as he patted little Jamie on her head. Both girls took one hand each and led their new friend down to the staterooms below. Cameron and Cuffie looked at each other and smiled; without a word they exchanged looks and turned up to the stairs that led to the aft captain's deck.

"Did he say that was Jekyll Island over there?" Cuffie asked as they stood atop the captain's deck, staring at the gray beach in the distance.

"Yes, he did," Cameron answered, and gently placed his arm around Cuffie. "Yes, he did."

The heat of the sun danced on the beach sands of Jekyll Island. Through the mirages of heat rising, Cuffie felt like he could see the souls of the people he'd lost in his life; his eyes started to water. "I don't want to ever return to that place," he said as he looked at Cameron.

"Then we never will!" Cameron responded with a pat on the back and a big smile.

"Navigator, set course to Jamaica," Cameron instructed as he turned from Cuffie. He saw Chris walking up the steps to the aft captain's deck. "We are still going to Jamaica, aren't we?" he said with a smile and a look of uncertainty to Chris.

"Aye, Cap'n, we're off to Jamaica!" Chris said. "When we leave that port, you'll be captain of one of the fastest rumrunners on the high seas." Chris could barely keep in his smile as the cool wind blew in his face with the ship's speed.

"Rumrunners?" Cameron asked.

"Aye, Cap'n, rumrunners we be!" Chris said in his best pirate's voice, and slapped Cameron on the back.

Cameron turned, staring over the bow, the slight salt air misting his face; he thought of the former captain and James, and smiled at the word.

"Rumrunners," he said to himself.

The Last Fire-Eater

April 7, 1865, one week after the Civil War.

THE WAR WAS OVER, OR SO IT WAS READ ALOUD AND WRITten in the papers. General Lee of the Confederate Army had bowed his head in defeat. The president of the Union, Abraham Lincoln, read his Emancipation Proclamation to the waiting ears of the public. The once proud and mighty South had fallen to the outnumbering Union troops. The Union Army pressed forward through Georgia to spread the words of freedom and that the war had ended.

As night fell on the quiet township of Bainbridge, Georgia, the news spread rapidly through its nearly deserted streets. Colonel Cal Lamar sat patiently as his riders gave the news of Butler plantation's fall and the capture of his guns he had privateered up the Savannah River to aid the Confederate Army. Stripped of luxuries in his modest Savannah surroundings, the smoke of Georgia tobacco now surrounded his face when he exhaled from his pipe. "I want to know where the medals I ordered from the French are," he demanded of the officers who were documenting the Confederate positions.

The officers of the dwindling Confederate Army stood in dismay as the colonel paid little regard to the news of the ultimate end of the war and the emancipation of slaves throughout the South. The temperament of the news brewed inside him and the gray Confederate jacket that he wore added to the already hot Southern climate. "Send a rider to the Port of Charleston," he instructed. "Our men—no—our *heroes* of this great campaign shall be decorated accordingly for their gallant effort in this great war," he said as he stood. He walked toward the window that looked down Main Street towards the city market of Bainbridge.

"But, sir," his first officer began. "We—"

Colonel Lamar turned from the window immediately. He ripped the pipe from his sandy beard. The words dressed in pipe's smoke spilled from his mouth. "Our men will be decorated as Confederate heroes." His eyes squinted as he approached the first officer. He pushed the pipe towards the face of the man. A slight trickle of smoke came from the small hole at the end of the pipe just inches away from the now petrified man's face. "I don't care if Lee surrendered; I have no intention of letting our heroes go unnoticed. Now get the rider to Charleston to collect the medals. Have him take them to Savannah to the barns on Broughton Street. I will meet him there with our troops, and surrender our fight only after these men have been recognized with respect in our great city."

He had no intention of surrendering his troops. His men knew any words of surrender from Colonel Cal Lamar would not be anything more than a trick. Colonel Lamar turned back towards the window, placed the pipe firmly between his lips, and drew from its burning ashes of Georgia tobacco. "Do it now, boy!" he said with a slow release of Georgian pride.

The Union's intelligence had led them to Colonel Lamar's ships, his import of weapons and his positions in the South. They had heard from reports of several battles that were led and won by the "Prince of the South," and they knew he would be heading for his shipment of weapons. Not finding him at Butler with them could only mean that he was somewhere between the last battle he was in at Bainbridge and the Butler plantation. That place would most likely be Columbus.

* * *

The Union rider galloped his steed into the Union fortifications in Kentucky. "Sir!" the messenger spoke firmly and with a salute to the commanding officer. The dust from the rider jumped from his dark-blue coat as he snapped his gloved hand to his forehead.

"Colonel Lamar was not at the Butler plantation, sir!" The soldier held himself frozen in his position.

"At ease," the commander replied. The Union commander then pointed at the freshly commissioned rider who had reached to receive the reins of the horse from the messenger. "Make ready for a message to the Butler plantation," he quickly snapped. The commander turned on his heel and proceeded to the office of the fortification. The commanding general stood by the window, watching the riders just outside swap the horse for a fresh steed.

"Well? Did we get him?" the general asked as he turned from the window to the commander. He could tell by the look on the commander's face that the news was not good. "Dammit!" he exclaimed. He sat down in his chair, frustrated, and banged his gloved fist on the desk. The inkbottle jumped from its idle position when the general's fist hit the wooden desk, causing it to land sideways on the map. The blue ink poured like Union blood over the map, slowly covering the Southern states. The general watched the advancement of the ink make its way across the map, almost like the Union Army's advancement over the once mighty Southern empire. It seemed to stop just short of the word *Columbus* on the map.

The fresh rider and steed sped from the darkened Kentucky encampment while night fell. With little regard for sleep, the rider rode through the night, changing horses partway through South Carolina, as the general's words were to be delivered immediately. The exhausted pair of messenger and horse arrived at the Butler plantation, now in Union hands.

The weary rider came off the horse as they stopped in front of the beautiful Butler main house and briefly looked at the return rider, his outstretched arm ready to receive the reins. His look of desperation was clear to the other rider and his shoulders sunken from the long ride in from Kentucky. The commanding officer walked around to the front of the horse as the two riders exchanged looks and immediately their posture corrected; the snap of a dusty salute preceded the message delivered. The Union commander received the message from the horseman and turned to the plantation house, where the general of the Union troops had made temporary residence.

"Sir!" with an attentive snap of his head. "Sir, I have orders just received from Kentucky," the commander said as he entered the formal dining room.

The Union general rose from the silk-covered table. The fine silver and china gave a non-war ambience to the general's many metals and finely pressed uniform. He gently placed his teacup back on the saucer.

"Leave us," he exclaimed to the servants who had just placed his meal on the table. The two servants scattered into the doorway and across the back of the room to the detached kitchen from where they came.

"Sir, we have our orders," the commander spoke as he approached. "We are to organize a militia group of our forty finest men. They are to ride to Columbus, seek out Colonel Cal Lamar, and execute him."

The general's eyes shot up to the commander as the word *execute* came from his lips. The commander continued. "The rest of our troops are to return to Kentucky and be decommissioned." The words from the man were almost shaking with excitement. "We are to take the artillery and what former slaves necessary to move it from this plantation and transport these items back to the North," the commander finished breathlessly.

"The war is over!" the general exclaimed. "And we are to ride to Columbus...with forty of our finest men, and execute a colonel?" He spoke with exasperation.

"But, General, we get to go home!" the commander repeated.

"Yes, I heard the orders. And after the announcement of the president that the war is over, we go now further into this wretched state to assassinate one man?" the general said in disgust. He walked around the table of china and studied the picture on the wall.

"But, sir," the commander said calmly, "It's Cal Lamar."

* * *

The horse stood quietly on the bridge that stretched over the small river in Columbus, Georgia. Colonel Lamar, alone on his horse there, was lost in the memories of the great South and his home and offices there on beautiful River Street in Savannah. The men just under the bridge were loading some pottery onto a small boat at the tiny wharf along the river's bank. He could see the stacked bales of cotton in the warehouses just past them in the broken wooden warehouses just up from the docks.

His mind went back to him being a young boy on his father's steam packet, the *Pulaski*, gently boiling off steam and being loaded with the family's trunks.

"Father, why does the smoke come out of the pipes just there on the ship?"

"Well, Charlie, the men shovel coal into the boilers that are below the decks of the ship, and it boils the water that makes steam," Gazaway explained, squatting down next to his son and pointing at the sooty smoke that came pouring out of the ship.

"The coal they shovel...it makes steam?" young Cal asked.

"No. No, son, the men fill the boilers of the engines with water, and the coal they shovel makes a huge fire to boil the water and make steam to power the engines," he said, smiling. "It's fire that makes the water turn to steam."

"Fire?" Charlie said, looking into his father's eyes.

"Fire!" the Union militia leader shouted.

The explosion of rifles ripped Colonel Lamar from his daydream. The searing lead balls of the Union rifles ripped through his Confederate jacket, knocking him from his saddle and onto the wooden slats of the bridge. Lying face down in a pool of blood, he could see through the gaps in the decking, much like the slaves chained to the decks of the *Wanderer*, only to reveal the eerie African-faced jugs being loaded into the boat's hold below him. Their fading image was his last.

Charles Augustus Lafayette Lamar was the last documented casualty of the Civil War. The medals that were to be issued to the men of the Confederacy, The Stonewall Jackson Medal, were all found in a Savannah barn years after Colonel Lamar's death. It was the only Medal of Honor ever forged during the Civil War. Not one was ever issued.

It seemed the Union had settled the score with the Southern fire-eater who had started the bloodiest war ever fought in history, and put an end to the slavery and persecution manifested in the South.

THE END